CHAPTER I
THE USES OF INTELLIGENCE TESTS

Intelligence tests of retarded school children.

Numerous studies of the age-grade progress of school children have afforded convincing evidence of the magnitude and seriousness of the retardation problem. Statistics collected in hundreds of cities in the United States show that between a third and a half of the school children fail to progress through the grades at the expected rate; that from 10 to 15 per cent are retarded two years or more; and that from 5 to 8 per cent are retarded at least three years. More than 10 per cent of the $400,000,000 annually expended in the United States for school instruction is devoted to re-teaching children what they have already been taught but have failed to learn.

The first efforts at reform which resulted from these findings were based on the supposition that the evils which had been discovered could be remedied by the individualizing of instruction, by improved methods of promotion, by increased attention to children's health, and by other reforms in school administration. Although reforms along these lines have been productive of much good, they have nevertheless been in a measure disappointing. The trouble was, they were too often based upon the assumption that under the right conditions all children would be equally, or almost equally, capable of making satisfactory school progress. Psychological studies of school children by means of standardized intelligence tests have shown that this supposition is not in accord with the facts. It has been found that children do not fall into two well-defined groups, the "feeble-minded" and the "normal." Instead, there are many grades of intelligence, ranging from idiocy on the one hand to genius on the other. Among those classed as normal, vast individual differences have been found to exist in original mental endowment, differences which affect profoundly the capacity to profit from school instruction.

We are beginning to realize that the school must take into account, more seriously than it has yet done, the existence and significance of these differences in endowment. Instead of wasting energy in the vain attempt to hold mentally slow and defective children up to a level of progress which is normal to the average child, it will be wiser to take account of the inequalities of children in original endowment and to differentiate the course of study in such a way that each child will be allowed to progress at the rate which is normal to him, whether that rate be rapid or slow.

While we cannot hold all children to the same standard of school progress, we can at least prevent the kind of retardation which involves failure and the repetition of a school grade. It is well enough recognized that children do not enter with very much zest upon school work in which they have once failed. Failure crushes self-confidence and destroys the spirit of work. It is a sad fact that a large proportion of children in the schools are acquiring the habit of failure. The remedy, of course, is to measure out the work for each child in proportion to his mental ability.

Before an engineer constructs a railroad bridge or trestle, he studies the materials to be used, and learns by means of tests exactly the amount of strain per unit of size his materials will be able to withstand. He does not work empirically, and count upon patching up the mistakes which may later appear under the stress of actual use. The educational engineer should emulate this example. Tests and forethought must take the place of failure and patchwork. Our efforts have been too long directed by "trial and error." It is time to leave off guessing and to acquire a scientific knowledge of the material with which we have to deal. When instruction must be repeated, it means that the school, as well as the pupil, has failed.

Every child who fails in his school work or is in danger of failing should be given a mental examination. The examination takes less than one hour, and the result will contribute more to a real understanding of the case than anything else that could be done. It is necessary to determine whether a given child is unsuccessful in school because of poor native ability, or because of poor instruction, lack of interest, or some other removable cause.

It is not sufficient to establish any number of special classes, if they are to be made the dumping-ground for all kinds of troublesome cases—the feeble-minded, the physically defective, the merely backward, the truants, the incorrigibles, etc. Without scientific diagnosis and classification of these children the educational work of the special class must blunder along in the dark. In such diagnosis and classification our main reliance must always be in mental tests, properly used and properly interpreted.

Intelligence tests of the feeble-minded.

Thus far intelligence tests have found their chief application in the identification and grading of the feeble-minded. Their value for this purpose is twofold. In the first place, it is necessary to ascertain the degree of defect before it is possible to decide intelligently upon either the content or the method of instruction suited to the training of the backward child. In the second place, intelligence tests are rapidly extending our conception of "feeble-mindedness" to include milder degrees of defect than have generally been associated with this term. The earlier methods of diagnosis caused a majority of the higher grade defectives to be overlooked. Previous to the development of psychological methods the low-grade moron was about as high a type of defective as most physicians or even psychologists were able to identify as feeble-minded.

Wherever intelligence tests have been made in any considerable number in the schools, they have shown that not far from 2 per cent of the children enrolled have a grade of intelligence which, however long they live, will never develop beyond the level which is normal to the average child of 11 or 12 years. The large majority of these belong to the moron grade; that is, their mental development will stop somewhere between the 7-year and 12-year level of intelligence, more often between 9 and 12.

The more we learn about such children, the clearer it becomes that they must be looked upon as real defectives. They may be able to drag along to the fourth, fifth, or sixth grades, but even by the age of 16 or 18 years they are never able to cope successfully with the more abstract and difficult parts of the common-school course of study. They may master a certain amount of rote learning, such as that involved in reading and in the manipulation of number combinations but they cannot be taught to meet new conditions effectively or to think, reason, and judge as normal persons do.

It is safe to predict that in the near future intelligence tests will bring tens of thousands of these high-grade defectives under the surveillance and protection of society. This will ultimately result in curtailing the reproduction of feeble-mindedness and in the elimination of an enormous amount of crime, pauperism, and industrial inefficiency. It is hardly necessary to emphasize that the high-grade cases, of the type now so frequently overlooked, are precisely the ones whose guardianship it is most important for the State to assume.

Intelligence tests of delinquents.

One of the most important facts brought to light by the use of intelligence tests is the frequent association of delinquency and mental deficiency. Although it has long been recognized that the proportion of feeble-mindedness among offenders is rather large, the real amount has, until recently, been underestimated even by the most competent students of criminology.

The criminologists have been accustomed to give more attention to the physical than to the mental correlates of crime. Thus, Lombroso and his followers subjected thousands of criminals to observation and measurement with regard to such physical traits as size and shape of the skull, bilateral asymmetries, anomalies of the ear, eye, nose, palate, teeth, hands, fingers, hair, dermal sensitivity, etc. The search was for physical "stigmata" characteristic of the "criminal type."

Although such studies performed an important service in creating a scientific interest in criminology, the theories of Lombroso have been wholly discredited by the results of intelligence tests. Such tests have demonstrated, beyond any possibility of doubt, that the most important trait of at least 25 per cent of our criminals is mental weakness. The physical abnormalities which have been found so common among prisoners are not the stigmata of criminality, but the physical accompaniments of feeble-mindedness. They have no diagnostic significance except in so far as they are indications of mental deficiency. Without exception, every study which has been made of the intelligence level of delinquents has furnished convincing testimony as to the close relation existing between mental weakness and moral abnormality. Some of these findings are as follows:—

Miss Renz tested 100 girls of the Ohio State Reformatory and reported 36 per cent as certainly feeble-minded. In every one of these cases the commitment papers had given the pronouncement "intellect sound."

Under the direction of Dr. Goddard the Binet tests were given to 100 juvenile court cases, chosen at random, in Newark, New Jersey. Nearly half were classified as feeble-minded. One boy 17 years old had 9-year intelligence; another of 15½ had 8-year intelligence.

Of 56 delinquent girls 14 to 20 years of age tested by Hill and Goddard, almost half belonged either to the 9- or the 10-year level of intelligence.

Dr. G. G. Fernald's tests of 100 prisoners at the Massachusetts State Reformatory showed that at least 25 per cent were feeble-minded.

Of 1186 girls tested by Miss Dewson at the State Industrial School for Girls at Lancaster, Pennsylvania, 28 per cent were found to have subnormal intelligence.

Dr. Katherine Bement Davis's report on 1000 cases entered in the Bedford Home for Women, New York, stated that there was no doubt but that at least 157 were feeble-minded. Recently there has been established at this institution one of the most important research laboratories of the kind in the United States, with a trained psychologist, Dr. Mabel Fernald, in charge.

Of 564 prostitutes investigated by Dr. Anna Dwyer in connection with the Municipal Court of Chicago, only 3 per cent had gone beyond the fifth grade in school. Mental tests were not made, but from the data given it is reasonably certain that half or more were feeble-minded.

Tests, by Dr. George Ordahl and Dr. Louise Ellison Ordahl, of cases in the Geneva School for Girls, Geneva, Illinois, showed that, on a conservative basis of classification, at least 18 per cent were feeble-minded. At the Joliet Prison, Illinois, the same authors found 50 per cent of the female prisoners feeble-minded, and 26 per cent of the male prisoners. At the St. Charles School for Boys 26 per cent were feeble-minded.

Tests, by Dr. J. Harold Williams, of 150 delinquents in the Whittier State School for Boys, Whittier, California, gave 28 per cent feeble-minded and 25 per cent at or near the border-line. About 300 other juvenile delinquents tested by Mr. Williams gave approximately the same figures. As a result of these findings a research laboratory has been established at the Whittier School, with Dr. Williams in charge. In the girls' division of the Whittier School, Dr. Grace Fernald collected a large amount of psychological data on more than 100 delinquent girls. The findings of this investigation agree closely with those of Dr. Williams for the boys.

At the State Reformatory, Jeffersonville, Indiana, Dr. von Klein-Schmid, in an unusually thorough psychological study of 1000 young adult prisoners, finds the proportion of feeble-mindedness not far from 50 per cent.

But it is needless to multiply statistics. Those given are but samples. Tests are at present being made in most of the progressive prisons, reform schools, and juvenile courts throughout the country, and while there are minor discrepancies in regard to the actual percentage who are feeble-minded, there is no investigator who denies the fearful rôle played by mental deficiency in the production of vice, crime, and delinquency.[1]

Heredity studies of "degenerate" families have confirmed, in a striking way, the testimony secured by intelligence tests. Among the best known of such families are the "Kallikaks," the "Jukes," the "Hill Folk," the "Nams," the "Zeros," and the "Ishmaelites."

The Kallikak family. Martin Kallikak was a youthful soldier in the Revolutionary War. At a tavern frequented by the militia he met a feeble-minded girl, by whom he became the father of a feeble-minded son. In 1912 there were 480 known direct descendants of this temporary union. It is known that 36 of these were illegitimates, that 33 were sexually immoral, that 24 were confirmed alcoholics, and that 8 kept houses of ill-fame. The explanation of so much immorality will be obvious when it is stated that of the 480 descendants, 143 were known to be feeble-minded, and that many of the others were of questionable mentality.

A few years after returning from the war this same Martin Kallikak married a respectable girl of good family. From this union 496 individuals have been traced in direct descent, and in this branch of the family there were no illegitimate children, no immoral women, and only one man who was sexually loose. There were no criminals, no keepers of houses of ill-fame, and only two confirmed alcoholics. Again the explanation is clear when it is stated that this branch of the family did not contain a single feeble-minded individual. It was made up of doctors, lawyers, judges, educators, traders, and landholders.[2]

The Hill Folk. The Hill Folk are a New England family of which 709 persons have been traced. Of the married women, 24 per cent had given birth to illegitimate offspring, and 10 per cent were prostitutes. Criminal tendencies were clearly shown in 24 members of the family, while alcoholism was still more common. The proportion of feeble-minded was 48 per cent. It was estimated that the Hill Folk have in the last sixty years cost the State of Massachusetts, in charitable relief, care of feeble-minded, epileptic, and insane, conviction and punishment for crime, prostitution pauperism, etc., at least $500,000.[3]

The Nam family and the Jukes give equally dark pictures as regards criminality, licentiousness, and alcoholism, and although feeble-mindedness was not as fully investigated in these families as in the Kallikaks and the Hill Folk, the evidence is strong that it was a leading trait. The 784 Nams who were traced included 187 alcoholics, 232 women and 199 men known to be licentious, and 40 who became prisoners. It is estimated that the Nams have already cost the State nearly $1,500,000.[4]

Of 540 Jukes, practically one fifth were born out of wedlock, 37 were known to be syphilitic, 53 had been in the poorhouse, 76 had been sentenced to prison, and of 229 women of marriageable age 128 were prostitutes. The economic damage inflicted upon the State of New York by the Jukes in seventy-five years was estimated at more than $1,300,000, to say nothing of diseases and other evil influences which they helped to spread.[5]

But why do the feeble-minded tend so strongly to become delinquent? The answer may be stated in simple terms. Morality depends upon two things: (*a*) the ability to foresee and to weigh the possible consequences for self and others of different kinds of behavior; and (*b*) upon the willingness and capacity to exercise self-restraint. That there are many intelligent criminals is due to the fact that (*a*) may exist without (*b*). On the other hand, (*b*) presupposes (*a*). In other words, not all criminals are feeble-minded, but all feeble-minded are at least potential criminals. That every feeble-minded woman is a potential prostitute would hardly be disputed by any one. Moral judgment, like business judgment, social judgment, or any other kind of higher thought process, is a function of intelligence. Morality cannot flower and fruit if intelligence remains infantile.

All of us in early childhood lacked moral responsibility. We were as rank egoists as any criminal. Respect for the feelings, the property rights, or any other kind of rights, of others had to be laboriously acquired under the whip of discipline. But by degrees we learned that only when instincts are curbed, and conduct is made to conform to principles established formally or accepted tacitly by our neighbors, does this become a livable world for any of us. Without the intelligence to generalize the particular, to foresee distant consequences of present acts, to weigh these foreseen consequences in the nice balance of imagination, morality cannot be learned. When the adult body, with its adult instincts, is coupled with the undeveloped intelligence and weak inhibitory powers of a 10-year-old child, the only possible outcome, except in those cases where constant guardianship is exercised by relatives or friends, is some form of delinquency.

Considering the tremendous cost of vice and crime, which in all probability amounts to not less than $500,000,000 per year in the United States alone, it is evident that psychological testing has found here one of its richest applications. Before offenders can be subjected to rational treatment a mental diagnosis is necessary, and while intelligence tests do not constitute a complete psychological diagnosis, they are, nevertheless, its most indispensable part.

Intelligence tests of superior children.

The number of children with very superior ability is approximately as great as the number of feeble-minded. The future welfare of the country hinges, in no small degree, upon the right education of these superior children. Whether civilization moves on and up depends most on the advances made by creative thinkers and leaders in science, politics, art, morality, and religion. Moderate ability can follow, or imitate, but genius must show the way.

Through the leveling influences of the educational lockstep such children at present are often lost in the masses. It is a rare child who is able to break this lockstep by extra promotions. Taking the country over, the ratio of "accelerates" to "retardates" in the school is approximately 1 to 10. Through the handicapping influences of poverty, social neglect, physical defects, or educational maladjustments, many potential leaders in science, art, government, and industry are denied the opportunity of a normal development. The use we have made of exceptional ability reminds one of the primitive methods of surface mining. It is necessary to explore the nation's hidden resources of intelligence. The common saying that "genius will out" is one of those dangerous half-truths with which too many people rest content.

Psychological tests show that children of superior ability are very likely to be misunderstood in school. The writer has tested more than a hundred children who were as much above average intelligence as moron defectives are below. The large majority of these were found located below the school grade warranted by their intellectual level. One third had failed to reap any advantage whatever, in terms of promotion, from their very superior intelligence. Even genius languishes when kept over-long at tasks that are too easy.

Our data show that teachers sometimes fail entirely to recognize exceptional superiority in a pupil, and that the degree of such superiority is rarely estimated with anything like the accuracy which is possible to the psychologist after a one-hour examination. *B. F.*, for example, was a little over 7½ years old when tested. He was in the third grade, and was therefore thought by his teacher to be accelerated in school. This boy's intelligence, however, was found to be above the 12-year level. There is no doubt that his mental ability would have enabled him, with a few months of individual instruction, to carry fifth or even sixth-grade work as easily as third, and without injury to body or mind. Nevertheless, the teacher and both the parents of this child had found nothing remarkable about him. In reality he belongs to a grade of genius not found oftener than once in several thousand cases.

Another illustration is that of a boy of 10½ years who tested at the "average adult" level. He was doing superior work in the sixth grade, but according to the testimony of the teacher had "no unusual ability." It was ascertained from the parents that this boy, at an age when most children are reading fairy stories, had a passion for standard medical literature and textbooks in physical science. Yet, after more than a year of daily contact with this young genius (who is a relative of Meyerbeer, the composer), the teacher had discovered no symptoms of unusual ability.[6]

Teachers should be better trained in detecting the signs of superior ability. Every child who consistently gets high marks in his school work with apparent ease should be given a mental examination, and if his intelligence level warrants it he should either be given extra promotions, or placed in a special class for superior children where faster progress can be made. The latter is the better plan, because it obviates the necessity of skipping grades; it permits rapid but continuous progress.

The usual reluctance of teachers to give extra promotions probably rests upon three factors: (1) mere inertia; (2) a natural unwillingness to part with exceptionally satisfactory pupils; and (3) the traditional belief that precocious children should be held back for fear of dire physical or mental consequences.

In order to throw light on the question whether exceptionally bright children are specially likely to be one-sided, nervous, delicate, morally abnormal, socially unadaptable, or otherwise peculiar, the writer has secured rather extensive information regarding 31 children whose mental age was found by intelligence tests to be 25 per cent above the actual age. This degree of intelligence is possessed by about 2 children out of 100, and is nearly as far above average intelligence as high-grade feeble-mindedness is below. The supplementary information, which was furnished in most cases by the teachers, may be summarized as follows:—

1. *Ability special or general.* In the case of 20 out of 31 the ability is decidedly general, and with 2 it is mainly general. The talents of 5 are described as more or less special, but only in one case is it remarkably so. Doubtful 4.

2. *Health.* 15 are said to be perfectly healthy; 13 have one or more physical defects; 4 of the 13 are described as delicate; 4 have adenoids; 4 have eye-defects; 1 lisps; and 1 stutters. These figures are about the same as one finds in any group of ordinary children.

3. *Studiousness.* "Extremely studious," 15; "usually studious" or "fairly studious," 11; "not particularly studious," 5; "lazy," 0.

4. *Moral traits.* Favorable traits only, 19; one or more unfavorable traits, 8; no answer, 4. The eight with unfavorable moral traits are described as follows: 2 are "very self-willed"; 1 "needs close watching"; 1 is "cruel to animals"; 1 is "untruthful"; 1 is "unreliable"; 1 is "a bluffer"; 1 is "sexually abnormal," "perverted," and "vicious."

   It will be noted that with the exception of the last child, the moral irregularities mentioned can hardly be regarded, from the psychological point of view, as essentially abnormal. It is perhaps a good rather than a bad sign for a child to be self-willed; most children "need close watching"; and a certain amount of untruthfulness in children is the rule and not the exception.

5. *Social adaptability.* Socially adaptable, 25; not adaptable, 2; doubtful, 4.

6. *Attitude of other children.* "Favorable," "friendly," "liked by everybody," "much admired," "popular," etc., 26; "not liked," 1; "inspires repugnance," 1; no answer, 1.

7. *Is child a leader?* "Yes," 14; "no," or "not particularly," 12; doubtful, 5.

8. *Is play life normal?* "Yes," 26; "no," 1; "hardly," 1; doubtful, 3.

9. *Is child spoiled or vain?* "No," 22; "yes," 5; "somewhat," 2; no answer, 2.

According to the above data, exceptionally intelligent children are fully as likely to be healthy as ordinary children; their ability is far more often general than special, they are studious above the average, really serious faults are not common among them, they are nearly always socially adaptable, are sought after as playmates and companions, their play life is usually normal, they are leaders far oftener than other children, and notwithstanding their many really superior qualities they are seldom vain or spoiled.

It would be greatly to the advantage of such children if their superior ability were more promptly and fully recognized, and if (under proper medical supervision, of course) they were promoted as rapidly as their mental development would warrant. Unless they are given the grade of work which calls forth their best efforts, they run the risk of falling into lifelong habits of submaximum efficiency. The danger in the case of such children is not over-pressure, but under-pressure.

Intelligence tests as a basis for grading.

Not only in the case of retarded or exceptionally bright children, but with many others also, intelligence tests can aid in correctly placing the child in school.

The pupil who enters one school system from another is a case in point. Such a pupil nearly always suffers a loss of time. The indefensible custom is to grade the newcomer down a little, because, forsooth, the textbooks he has studied may have differed somewhat from those he is about to take up, or because the school system from which he comes may be looked upon as inferior. Teachers are too often suspicious of all other educational methods besides their own. The present treatment accorded such children, which so often does them injustice and injury, should be replaced by an intelligence test. The hour of time required for the test is a small matter in comparison with the loss of a school term by the pupils.

Indeed, it would be desirable to make all promotions on the basis chiefly of intellectual ability. Hitherto the school has had to rely on tests of information because reliable tests of intelligence have not until recently been available. As trained Binet examiners become more plentiful, the information standard will have to give way to the criterion which asks merely that the child shall be able to do the work of the next higher grade. The brief intelligence test is not only more enlightening than the examination; it is also more hygienic. The school examination is often for the child a source of worry and anxiety; the mental test is an interesting and pleasant experience.

Intelligence tests for vocational fitness.

The time is probably not far distant when intelligence tests will become a recognized and widely used instrument for determining vocational fitness. Of course, it is not claimed that tests are available which will tell us unerringly exactly what one of a thousand or more occupations a given individual is best fitted to pursue. But when thousands of children who have been tested by the Binet scale have been followed out into the industrial world, and their success in various occupations noted, we shall know fairly definitely the vocational significance of any given degree of mental inferiority or superiority. Researches of this kind will ultimately determine the minimum "intelligence quotient" necessary for success in each leading occupation.

Industrial concerns doubtless suffer enormous losses from the employment of persons whose mental ability is not equal to the tasks they are expected to perform. The present methods of trying out new employees, transferring them to simpler and simpler jobs as their inefficiency becomes apparent, is wasteful and to a great extent unnecessary. A cheaper and more satisfactory method would be to employ a psychologist to examine applicants for positions and to weed out the unfit. Any business employing as many as five hundred or a thousand workers, as, for example, a large department store, could save in this way several times the salary of a well-trained psychologist.

That the industrially inefficient are often of subnormal intelligence has already been demonstrated in a number of psychological investigations. Of 150 "hoboes" tested under the direction of the writer by Mr. Knollin, at least 15 per cent belonged to the moron grade of mental deficiency, and almost as many more were border-line cases. To be sure, a large proportion were found perfectly normal, and a few even decidedly superior in mental ability, but the ratio of mental deficiency was ten or fifteen times as high as that holding for the general population. Several had as low as 9- or 10-year intelligence, and one had a mental level of 7 years. The industrial history of such subjects, as given by themselves, was always about what the mental level would lead us to expect—unskilled work, lack of interest in accomplishment, frequent discharge from jobs, discouragement, and finally the "road."

The above findings have been fully paralleled by Mr. Glenn Johnson and Professor Eleanor Rowland, of Reed College, who tested 108 unemployed charity cases in Portland, Oregon. Both of these investigators made use of the Stanford revision of the Binet scale, which is especially serviceable in distinguishing the upper-grade defectives from normals.

It hardly needs to be emphasized that when charity organizations help the feeble-minded to float along in the social and industrial world, and to produce and rear children after their kind, a doubtful service is rendered. A little psychological research would aid the united charities of any city to direct their expenditures into more profitable channels than would otherwise be possible.

Other uses of intelligence tests.

Another important use of intelligence tests is in the study of the factors which influence mental development. It is desirable that we should be able to guard the child against influences which affect mental development unfavorably; but as long as these influences have not been sifted, weighed, and measured, we have nothing but conjecture on which to base our efforts in this direction.

When we search the literature of child hygiene for reliable evidence as to the injurious effects upon mental ability of malnutrition, decayed teeth, obstructed breathing, reduced sleep, bad ventilation, insufficient exercise, etc., we are met by endless assertion painfully unsupported by demonstrated fact. We have, indeed, very little exact knowledge regarding the mental effects of any of the factors just mentioned. When standardized mental tests have come into more general use, such influences will be easy to detect wherever they are really present.

Again, the most important question of heredity is that regarding the inheritance of intelligence; but this is a problem which cannot be attacked at all without some accurate means of identifying the thing which is the object of study. Without the use of scales for measuring intelligence we can give no better answer as to the essential difference between a genius and a fool than is to be found in legend and fiction.

Applying this to school children, it means that without such tests we cannot know to what extent a child's mental performances are determined by environment and to what extent by heredity. Is the place of the so-called lower classes in the social and industrial scale the result of their inferior native endowment, or is their apparent inferiority merely a result of their inferior home and school training? Is genius more common among children of the educated classes than among the children of the ignorant and poor? Are the inferior races really inferior, or are they merely unfortunate in their lack of opportunity to learn?

Only intelligence tests can answer these questions and grade the raw material with which education works. Without them we can never distinguish the results of our educational efforts with a given child from the influence of the child's original endowment. Such tests would have told us, for example, whether the much-discussed "wonder children," such as the Sidis and Wiener boys and the Stoner girl, owe their precocious intellectual prowess to superior training (as their parents believe) or to superior native ability. The supposed effects upon mental development of new methods of mind training, which are exploited so confidently from time to time (e.g., the Montessori method and the various systems of sensory and motor training for the feeble-minded), will have to be checked up by the same kind of scientific measurement.

In all these fields intelligence tests are certain to play an ever-increasing rôle. With the exception of moral character there is nothing as significant for a child's future as his grade of intelligence. Even health itself is likely to have less influence in determining success in life. Although strength and swiftness have always had great survival value among the lower animals, these characteristics have long since lost their supremacy in man's struggle for existence. For us the rule of brawn has been broken, and intelligence has become the decisive factor in success. Schools, railroads, factories, and the largest commercial concerns may be successfully managed by persons who are physically weak or even sickly. One who has intelligence constantly measures opportunities against his own strength or weakness and adjusts himself to conditions by following those leads which promise most toward the realization of his individual possibilities.

All classes of intellects, the weakest as well as the strongest, will profit by the application of their talents to tasks which are consonant with their ability. When we have learned the lessons which intelligence tests have to teach, we shall no longer blame mentally defective workmen for their industrial inefficiency, punish weak-minded children because of their inability to learn, or imprison and hang mentally defective criminals because they lacked the intelligence to appreciate the ordinary codes of social conduct.

FOOTNOTES:

[1] See References at end of volume.

[2] H. H. Goddard: *The Kallikak Family*. (1914.) 141 pp.

[3] Danielson and Davenport: *The Hill Folk*. Eugenics Record Office, Memoir No. 1. 1912. 56 pp.

[4] Estabrook and Davenport: *The Nam Family*. Eugenics Record Office Memoir No. 2. (1912). 85 pp.

[5] R. L. Dugdale: *The Jukes*. (Fourth edition, 1910.) 120 pp. G. P. Putnam's Sons.

[6] See p. <u>26</u> *ff.* for further illustrations of this kind.

CHAPTER II
SOURCES OF ERROR IN JUDGING INTELLIGENCE

Are intelligence tests superfluous?

Binet tells us that he often encountered the criticism that intelligence tests are superfluous, and that in going to so much trouble to devise his measuring scale he was forcing an open door. Those who made this criticism believed that the observant teacher or parent is able to make an offhand estimate of a child's intelligence which is accurate enough. "It is a stupid teacher," said one, "who needs a psychologist to tell her which pupils are not intelligent." Every one who uses intelligence tests meets this attitude from time to time.

This should not be surprising or discouraging. It is only natural that those who are unfamiliar with the methods of psychology should occasionally question their validity or worth, just as there are many excellent people who do not "believe in" vaccination against typhoid and small pox, operations for appendicitis, etc.

There is an additional reason why the applications of psychology have to overcome a good deal of conservatism and skepticism; namely, the fact that every one, whether psychologically trained or not, acquires in the ordinary experiences of life a certain degree of expertness in the observation and interpretation of mental traits. The possession of this little fund of practical working knowledge makes most people slow to admit any one's claim to greater expertness. When the astronomer tells us the distance to Jupiter, we accept his statement, because we recognize that our ordinary experience affords no basis for judgment about such matters. But every one acquires more or less facility in distinguishing the coarser differences among people in intelligence, and this half-knowledge naturally generates a certain amount of resistance to the more refined method of tests.

It should be evident, however, that we need more than the ability merely to distinguish a genius from a simpleton, just as a physician needs something more than the ability to distinguish an athlete from a man dying of consumption. It is necessary to have a definite and accurate diagnosis, one which will differentiate more finely the many degrees and qualities of intelligence. Just as in the case of physical illness, we need to know not merely that the patient is sick, but also why he is sick, what organs are involved, what course the illness will run, and what physical work the patient can safely undertake, so in the case of a retarded child, we need to know the exact degree of intellectual deficiency, what mental functions are chiefly concerned in the defect, whether the deficiency is due to innate endowment, to physical illness, or to faults of education, and what lines of mental activity the child will be able to pursue with reasonable hope of success. In the diagnosis of a case of malnutrition, the up-to-date physician does not depend upon general symptoms, but instead makes a blood test to determine the exact number of red corpuscles per cubic millimeter of blood and the exact percentage of hæmoglobin. He has learned that external appearances are often misleading. Similarly, every psychologist who is experienced in the mental examination of school children knows that his own or the teacher's estimate of a child's intelligence is subject to grave and frequent error.

The necessity of standards.

In the first place, in order to judge an individual's intelligence it is necessary to have in mind some standard as to what constitutes normal intelligence. This the ordinary parent or teacher does not have. In the case of school children, for example, each pupil is judged with reference to the average intelligence of the class. But the teacher has no means of knowing whether the average for her class is above, equal to, or below that for children in general. Her standard may be too high, too low, vague, mechanical, or fragmentary. The same, of course, holds in the case of parents or any one else attempting to estimate intelligence on the basis of common observation.

The intelligence of retarded children usually overestimated.

One of the most common errors made by the teacher is to overestimate the intelligence of the over-age pupil. This is because she fails to take account of age differences and estimates intelligence on the basis of the child's school performance in the grade where he happens to be located. She tends to overlook the fact that quality of school work is no index of intelligence unless age is taken into account. The question should be, not, "Is this child doing his school work well?" but rather, "In what school grade should a child of this age be able to do satisfactory work?" A high-grade imbecile may do average work in the first grade, and a high-grade moron average work in the third or fourth grade, provided only they are sufficiently over-age for the grade in question.

Our experience in testing children for segregation in special classes has time and again brought this fallacy of teachers to our attention. We have often found one or more feeble-minded children in a class after the teacher had confidently asserted that there was not a single exceptionally dull child present. In every case where there has been opportunity to follow the later school progress of such a child the validity of the intelligence test has been fully confirmed.

The following are typical examples of the neglect of teachers to take the age factor into account when estimating the intelligence of the over-age child:—

A. R. Girl, age 11; in low second grade. She was able to do the work of this grade, not well, but passably. The teacher's judgment as to this child's intelligence was "dull but not defective." What the teacher overlooked was the fact that she had judged the child by a 7-year standard, and that, instead of only being able to do the work of the second grade indifferently, a child of this age should have been equal to the work of the fifth grade. In reality, A. R. is definitely feeble-minded. Although she is from a home of average culture, is 11 years old, and has attended school five years, she has barely the intelligence of the average child of six years.

D. C. Boy, age 17; in fifth grade. His teacher knew that he was dull, but had not thought of him as belonging to the class of feeble-minded. She had judged this boy by the 11-year standard and had perhaps been further misled by his normal appearance and exceptionally satisfactory behavior. The Binet test quickly showed that he had a mental level of approximately 9 years. There is little probability that his comprehension will ever surpass that of the average 10-year-old.

R. A. Boy, age 17; mental age 11; sixth grade; school work "nearly average"; teacher's estimate of intelligence "average." Test plainly shows this child to be a high-grade moron, or border-liner at best. Had attended school regularly 11 years and had made 6 grades. Teacher had compared child with his 12-year-old classmates.

H. A. Boy, age 14; mental age 9-6; low fourth grade; school work "inferior"; teacher's estimate of intelligence "average." The teacher blamed the inferior quality of school work to "bad home environment." As a matter of fact, the boy's father is feeble-minded and the normality of the mother is questionable. An older brother is in a reform school. We are perfectly safe in predicting that this boy will not complete the eighth grade even if he attends school till he is 21 years of age.

F. I. Boy, age 12-11; mental age 9-4; third grade; school work "average"; teacher's estimate of intelligence "average"; social environment "average"; health good and attendance regular. Intelligence and school success are what we should expect of an average 9-year-old.

D. A. Boy, age 12; mental age 9-2; third grade; school work "inferior"; teacher's estimate of intelligence "average." Teacher imputes inferior school work to "absence from school and lack of interest in books"; we have yet to find a child with a mental age 25 per cent below chronological age who *was* particularly interested in books or enthusiastic about school.

C. U. Girl, age 10; mental age 7-8; second grade; school work "average"; teacher's estimate of intelligence "average." Teacher blames adenoids and bad teeth for retardation. No doubt of child's mental deficiency.

P. I. Girl, age 8-10; mental age 6-7; has been in first grade 2½ years; school work "average"; teacher's estimate of intelligence "average." The mother and one brother of this girl are both feeble-minded.

H. O. Girl, age 7-10; mental age 5-2; first grade for 2 years; school work "inferior"; teacher's estimate of intelligence "average." The teacher nevertheless adds, "This child is not normal, but her ability to respond to drill shows that she has intelligence." It is of course true that even feeble-minded children of 5-year intelligence are able to profit a little from drill. Their weakness comes to light in their inability to perform higher types of mental activity.

The intelligence of superior children usually underestimated.

We have already mentioned the frequent failure of teachers and parents to recognize superior ability.[7] The fallacy here is again largely due to the neglect of the age factor, but the resulting error is in the opposite direction from that set forth above. The superior child is likely to be a year or two younger than the average child of his grade, and is accordingly judged by a standard which is too high. The following are illustrations:—

M. L. Girl, age 11-2; mental age "average adult" (16); sixth grade; school work "superior"; teacher's estimate of intelligence "average." Teacher credits superior school work to "unusual home advantages." Father a college professor. The teacher considers the child accelerated in school. In reality she ought to be in the second year of high school instead of in the sixth grade.

H. A. Boy, age 11; mental age 14; sixth grade; school work "average"; teacher's estimate of intelligence "average." According to the supplementary information the boy is "wonderfully attentive," "studious," and possessed of "all-round ability." The estimate of "average intelligence" was probably the result of comparing him with classmates who averaged about a year older.

K. R. Girl, age 6-1; mental age 8-5; second grade; school work "average"; teacher's estimate of intelligence "superior"; social environment "average." Is it not evident that a child from ordinary social environment, who does work of average quality in the second grade when barely 6 years of age, should be judged "very superior" rather than merely "superior" in intelligence? The intelligence quotient of this girl is 140, which is not reached by more than one child in two hundred.

S. A. Boy, age 8-10; mental age 10-9; fourth grade; school work "average"; teacher's estimate of intelligence "average." Teacher attributed school acceleration to "studiousness" and "delight in school work." It would be more reasonable to infer that these traits are indications of unusually superior intelligence.

Other fallacies in the estimation of intelligence.

Another source of error in the teacher's judgment comes from the difficulty in distinguishing genuine dullness from the mental condition which results sometimes from unfavorable social environment or lack of training.

V. P. Boy, age 7. Had attended school one year and had profited very little from the instruction. He had learned to read very little, spoke chiefly in monosyllables, and seemed "queer." The teacher suspected his intelligence and asked for a mental examination. The Binet test showed that except for vocabulary, which was unusually low, there was practically no mental retardation. Inquiry disclosed the fact that the boy's parents were uneducated deaf-mutes, and that the boy had associated little with other children. Four years later this boy was doing fairly well in school, though a year retarded because of his unfavorable home environment.

X. Y. Boy, age 10. Son of a successful business man, he was barely able to read in the second reader. The Binet test revealed an intelligence level which was absolutely normal. The boy was removed to a special class where he could receive individual attention, and two years later was found doing good work in a regular class of the fifth grade. His bad beginning seemed to have been due to an unfavorable attitude toward school work, due in turn to lack of discipline in the home, and to the fact that because of the father's frequent change of business headquarters the boy had never attended one school longer than three months.

Another source of error in judging intelligence from common observation is the tendency to overestimate the intelligence of the sprightly, talkative, sanguine child, and to underestimate the intelligence of the child who is less emotional, reacts slowly, and talks little. One occasionally finds a feeble-minded adult, perhaps of only 9- or 10-year intelligence, whose verbal fluency, mental liveliness, and self-confidence would mislead the offhand judgment of even the psychologist. One individual of this type, a border-line case at best, was accustomed to harangue street audiences and had served as "major" in "Kelly's Army," a horde of several hundred unemployed men who a few years ago organized and started to march from San Francisco to Washington.

Binet's questionnaire on teachers' methods of judging intelligence.[8]

Aroused by the skepticism so often shown toward his test method, Binet decided to make a little study of the methods by which teachers are accustomed to arrive at a judgment as to a child's intelligence. Accordingly, through the coöperation of the director of elementary education in Paris, he secured answers from a number of teachers to the following questions:—

1. *By what means do you judge the intelligence of your pupils?*
2. *How often have you been deceived in your judgments?*

About 40 replies were received. Most of the answers to the first question were vague, one-sided, "verbal," or bookish. Only a few showed much psychological discrimination as to what intelligence is and what its symptoms are. There was a very general tendency to judge intelligence by success in one or more of the school studies. Some thought that ability to master arithmetic was a sure criterion. Others were influenced almost entirely by the pupil's ability to read. One teacher said that the child who can "read so expressively as to make you feel the punctuation" is certainly intelligent, an observation which is rather good, as far as it goes. A few judged intelligence by the pupil's knowledge of such subjects as history and geography, which, as Binet points out, is to confound intelligence with the ability to memorize. "Memory," says Binet, is a "great simulator of intelligence." It is a wise teacher who is not deceived by it. Only a small minority mentioned resourcefulness in play, capacity to adjust to practical situations, or any other out-of-school criteria.

Some suggested asking the pupil such questions as the following:—

"Why do you love your parents?" "If it takes three persons seven hours to do a piece of work, would it take seven persons any longer?" "Which would you rather have, a fourth of a pie, or a half of a half?" "Which is heavier, a pound of feathers or a pound of lead?" "If you had twenty cents what would you do with it?"

A great many based their judgment mainly on the general appearance of the face and eyes. An "active" or "passive" expression of the eyes was looked upon as especially significant. One teacher thought that a mere "glance of the eye" was sufficient to display the grade of intelligence. If the eyes are penetrating, reflective, or show curiosity, the child must be intelligent; if they are heavy and expressionless, he must be dull. The mobility of countenance came in for frequent mention, also the shape of the head.

No one will deny that intelligence displays itself to a greater or less extent in the features; but how, asks Binet, are we going to *standardize* a "glance of the eye" or an "expression of curiosity" so that it will serve as an exact measure of intelligence?

The fact is, the more one sees of feeble-minded children, the less reliance one comes to place upon facial expression as a sign of intelligence. Some children who are only slightly backward have the general appearance of low-grade imbeciles. On the other hand, not a few who are distinctly feeble-minded are pretty and attractive. With many such children a ready smile takes the place of comprehension. If the smile is rather sweet and sympathetic, as is often the case, the observer is almost sure to be deceived.

As regards the shape of the head, peculiar conformation of the ears, and other "stigmata," science long ago demonstrated that these are ordinarily of little or no significance.

In reply to the second question, some teachers stated that they never made a mistake, while others admitted failure in one case out of three. Still others said, "Once in ten years," "once in twenty years," "once in a thousand times," etc.

As Binet remarks, the answers to this question are not very enlightening. In the first place, the teacher as a rule loses sight of the pupil when he has passed from her care, and seldom has opportunity of finding out whether his later success belies her judgment or confirms it. Errors go undiscovered for the simple reason that there is no opportunity to check them up. In the second place, her estimate is so rough that an error must be very great in order to have any meaning. If I say that a man is six feet and two inches tall, it is easy enough to apply a measuring stick and prove the correctness or incorrectness of my assertion. But if I say simply that the man is "rather tall," or "very tall," the error must be very extreme before we can expose it, particularly since the estimate can itself be checked up only by observation and not by controlled experiment.

The teachers' answers seem to justify three conclusions:—

1. Teachers do not have a very definite idea of what constitutes intelligence. They tend to confuse it variously with capacity for memorizing, facility in reading, ability to master arithmetic, etc. On the whole, their standard is too academic. They fail to appreciate the one-sidedness of the school's demands upon intelligence.

In a quaintly humorous passage discussing this tendency, Binet characterizes the child in a class as *dénaturé*, a French word which we may translate (though rather too literally) as "denatured." Too often this "denatured" child of the classroom is the only child the teacher knows.

2. In judging intelligence teachers are too easily deceived by a sprightly attitude, a sympathetic expression, a glance of the eye, or a chance "bump" on the head.

3. Although a few teachers seem to realize the many possibilities of error, the majority show rather undue confidence in the accuracy of their judgment.

Binet's experiment on how teachers test intelligence.[9]

Finally, Binet had three teachers come to his laboratory to judge the intelligence of children whom they had never seen before. Each spent an afternoon in the laboratory and examined five pupils. In each case the teacher was left free to arrive at a conclusion in her own way. Binet, who remained in the room and took notes, recounts with playful humor how the teachers were unavoidably compelled to resort to the much-abused test method, although their attempts at using it were sometimes, from the psychologist's point of view, amusingly clumsy.

One teacher, for example, questioned the children about some canals and sluices which were in the vicinity, asking what their purpose was and how they worked. Another showed the children some pretty pictures, which she had brought with her for the purpose, and asked questions about them. Showing the picture of a garret, she asked how a garret differs from an ordinary room. One teacher asked whether in building a factory it was best to have the walls thick or thin. As King Edward had just died, another teacher questioned the children about the details of this event, in order to find out whether they were in the habit of reading the newspapers, or understood the things they heard others read. Other questions related to the names of the streets in the neighborhood, the road one should take to reach a certain point in the vicinity, etc. Binet notes that many of the questions were special, and were only applicable with the children of this particular school.

The method of proposing the questions and judging the responses was also at fault. The teachers did not adhere consistently to any definite formula in giving a particular test to the different children. Instead, the questions were materially altered from time to time. One teacher scored the identical response differently for two children, giving one child more credit than the other because she had already judged his intelligence to be superior. In several cases the examination was needlessly delayed in order to instruct the child in what he did not know.

The examination ended, quite properly for a teacher's examination, with questions about history, literature, the metric system, etc., and with the recitation of a fable.

A comparison of the results showed hardly any agreement among the estimates of the three teachers. When questioned about the standard that had been taken in arriving at their conclusions, one teacher said she had taken the answers of the first pupil as a point of departure, and that she had judged the other pupils by this one. Another judged all the children by a child of her acquaintance whom she knew to be intelligent. This was, of course, an unsafe method, because no one could say how the child taken as an ideal would have responded to the tests used with the five children.

In summarizing the result of his little experiment, Binet points out that the teachers employed, as if by instinct, the very method which he himself recommends. In using it, however, they made numerous errors. Their questions were often needlessly long. Several were "dilemma questions," that is, answerable by *yes* or *no*. In such cases chance alone will cause fifty per cent of the answers to be correct. Some of the questions were merely tests of school knowledge. Others were entirely special, usable only with the children of this particular school on this particular day. Not all of the questions were put in the same terms, and a given response did not always receive the same score. When the children responded incorrectly or incompletely, they were often given help, but not always to the same extent. In other words, says Binet, it was evident that "the teachers employed very awkwardly a very excellent method."

The above remark is as pertinent as it is expressive. As the statement implies, the test method is but a refinement and standardization of the common-sense approach. Binet remarks that most people who inquire into his method of measuring intelligence do so expecting to find something very surprising and mysterious; and on seeing how much it resembles the methods which common sense employs in ordinary life, they heave a sigh of disappointment and say, "Is that all?" Binet reminds us that the difference between the scientific and unscientific way of doing a thing is not necessarily a difference in the *nature* of the method; it is often merely a difference in *exactness*. Science does the thing better, because it does it more accurately.

It was of course not the purpose of Binet to cast a slur upon the good sense and judgment of teachers. The teachers who took part in the little experiment described above were Binet's personal friends. The errors he points out in his entertaining and good-humored account of the experiment are inherent in the situation. They are the kind of errors which any person, however discriminating and observant, is likely to make in estimating the intelligence of a subject without the use of standardized tests.

It is the writer's experience that the teacher's estimate of a child's intelligence is much more reliable than that of the average parent; more accurate even than that of the physician who has not had psychological training.

Indeed, it is an exceptional school physician who is able to give any very valuable assistance to teachers in the classification of mentally exceptional children for special pedagogical treatment.

This is only to be expected, for the physician has ordinarily had much less instruction in psychology than the teacher, and of course infinitely less experience in judging the mental performances of children. Even if graduated from a first-rank medical school, the instruction he has received in the important subject of mental deficiency has probably been less adequate than that given to the students of a standard normal school. As a rule, the doctor has no equipment or special fitness which gives him any advantage over the teacher in acquiring facility in the use of intelligence tests.

As for parents, it would of course be unreasonable to expect from them a very accurate judgment regarding the mental peculiarities of their children. The difficulty is not simply that which comes from lack of special training. The presence of parental affection renders impartial judgment impossible. Still more serious are the effects of habituation to the child's mental traits. As a result of such habituation the most intelligent parent tends to develop an unfortunate blindness to all sorts of abnormalities which exist in his own children.

The only way of escape from the fallacies we have mentioned lies in the use of some kind of refined psychological procedure. Binet testing is destined to become universally known and practiced in schools, prisons, reformatories, charity stations, orphan asylums, and even ordinary homes, for the same reason that Babcock testing has become universal in dairying. Each is indispensable to its purpose.

FOOTNOTES:

[7] See p. 13 *ff.*

[8] See p. 169 *ff.* of reference 2, at end of this book

[9] See p. 182 *ff.* of reference 2 at end of this book.

CHAPTER III
DESCRIPTION OF THE BINET-SIMON METHOD

Essential nature of the scale.

The Binet scale is made up of an extended series of tests in the nature of "stunts," or problems, success in which demands the exercise of intelligence. As left by Binet, the scale consists of 54 tests, so graded in difficulty that the easiest lie well within the range of normal 3-year-old children, while the hardest tax the intelligence of the average adult. The problems are designed primarily to test native intelligence, not school knowledge or home training. They try to answer the question "How intelligent is this child?" How much the child has learned is of significance only in so far as it throws light on his ability to learn more.

Binet fully appreciated the fact that intelligence is not homogeneous, that it has many aspects, and that no one kind of test will display it adequately. He therefore assembled for his intelligence scale tests of many different types, some of them designed to display differences of memory, others differences in power to reason, ability to compare, power of comprehension, time orientation, facility in the use of number concepts, power to combine ideas into a meaningful whole, the maturity of apperception, wealth of ideas, knowledge of common objects, etc.

How the scale was derived.

The tests were arranged in order of difficulty, as found by trying them upon some 200 normal children of different ages from 3 to 15 years. It was found, for illustration, that a certain test was passed by only a very small proportion of the younger children, say the 5-year-olds, and that the number passing this test increased rapidly in the succeeding years until by the age of 7 or 8 years, let us say, practically all the children were successful. If, in our supposed case, the test was passed by about two thirds to three fourths of the normal children aged 7 years, it was considered by Binet a test of 7-year intelligence. In like manner, a test passed by 65 to 75 per cent of the normal 9-year-olds was considered a test of 9-year intelligence, and so on. By trying out many different tests in this way it was possible to secure five tests to represent each age from 3 to 10 years (excepting age 4, which has only four tests), five for age 12, five for 15, and five for adults, making 54 tests in all.

List of tests.

The following is the list of tests as arranged by Binet in 1911, shortly before his untimely death:—

Age 3:
  1. Points to nose, eyes, and mouth.
  2. Repeats two digits.
  3. Enumerates objects in a picture.
  4. Gives family name.
  5. Repeats a sentence of six syllables.

Age 4:
  1. Gives his sex.
  2. Names key, knife, and penny.
  3. Repeats three digits.
  4. Compares two lines.

Age 5:
  1. Compares two weights.
  2. Copies a square.
  3. Repeats a sentence of ten syllables.
  4. Counts four pennies.
  5. Unites the halves of a divided rectangle.

Age 6:
  1. Distinguishes between morning and afternoon.
  2. Defines familiar words in terms of use.
  3. Copies a diamond.
  4. Counts thirteen pennies.

5. Distinguishes pictures of ugly and pretty faces.

Age 7:
1. Shows right hand and left ear.
2. Describes a picture.
3. Executes three commissions, given simultaneously.
4. Counts the value of six sous, three of which are double.
5. Names four cardinal colors.

Age 8:
1. Compares two objects from memory.
2. Counts from 20 to 0.
3. Notes omissions from pictures.
4. Gives day and date.
5. Repeats five digits.

Age 9:
1. Gives change from twenty sous.
2. Defines familiar words in terms superior to use.
3. Recognizes all the pieces of money.
4. Names the months of the year, in order.
5. Answers easy "comprehension questions."

Age 10:
1. Arranges five blocks in order of weight.
2. Copies drawings from memory.
3. Criticizes absurd statements.
4. Answers difficult "comprehension questions."
5. Uses three given words in not more than two sentences.

Age 12:
1. Resists suggestion.
2. Composes one sentence containing three given words.
3. Names sixty words in three minutes.
4. Defines certain abstract words.
5. Discovers the sense of a disarranged sentence.

Age 15:
1. Repeats seven digits.
2. Finds three rhymes for a given word.
3. Repeats a sentence of twenty-six syllables.
4. Interprets pictures.

5. Interprets given facts.

Adult:

1. Solves the paper-cutting test.
2. Rearranges a triangle in imagination.
3. Gives differences between pairs of abstract terms.
4. Gives three differences between a president and a king.
5. Gives the main thought of a selection which he has heard read.

It should be emphasized that merely to name the tests in this way gives little idea of their nature and meaning, and tells nothing about Binet's method of conducting the 54 experiments. In order to use the tests intelligently it is necessary to acquaint one's self thoroughly with the purpose of each test, its correct procedure, and the psychological interpretation of different types of response.[10]

In fairness to Binet, it should also be borne in mind that the scale of tests was only a rough approximation to the ideal which the author had set himself to realize. Had his life been spared a few years longer, he would doubtless have carried the method much nearer perfection.

How the scale is used.

By means of the Binet tests we can judge the intelligence of a given individual by comparison with standards of intellectual performance for normal children of different ages. In order to make the comparison it is only necessary to begin the examination of the subject at a point in the scale where all the tests are passed successfully, and to continue up the scale until no more successes are possible. Then we compare our subject's performances with the standard for normal children of the same age, and note the amount of acceleration or retardation.

Let us suppose the subject being tested is 9 years of age. If he goes as far in the tests as normal 9-year-old children ordinarily go, we can say that the child has a "mental age" of 9 years, which in this case is normal (our child being 9 years of age). If he goes only as far as normal 8-year-old children ordinarily go, we say that his "mental age" is 8 years. In like manner, a mentally defective child of 9 years may have a "mental age" of only 4 years, or a young genius of 9 years may have a mental age of 12 or 13 years.

Special characteristics of the Binet-Simon method.

Psychologists had experimented with intelligence tests for at least twenty years before the Binet scale made its appearance. The question naturally suggests itself why Binet should have been successful in a field where previous efforts had been for the most part futile. The answer to this question is found in three essential differences between Binet's method and those formerly employed.

1. *The use of age standards.*

Binet was the first to utilize the idea of age standards, or norms, in the measurement of intelligence. It will be understood, of course, that Binet did not set out to invent tests of 10-year intelligence, 6-year intelligence, etc. Instead, as already explained, he began with a series of tests ranging from very easy to very difficult, and by trying these tests on children of different ages and noting the percentages of successes in the various years, he was able to locate them (approximately) in the years where they belonged.

This plan has the great advantage of giving us standards which are easily grasped. To say, for illustration, that a given subject has a grade of intelligence equal to that of the average child of 8 years is a statement whose general import does not need to be explained. Previous investigators had worked with subjects the degree of whose intelligence was unknown, and with tests the difficulty of which was equally unknown. An immense amount of ingenuity was spent in devising tests which were used in such a way as to preclude any very meaningful interpretation of the responses.

The Binet method enables us to characterize the intelligence of a child in a far more definite way than had hitherto been possible. Current descriptive terms like "bright," "moderately bright," "dull," "very dull," "feeble-minded," etc., have had no universally accepted meaning. A child who is designated by one person as "moderately bright" may be called "very bright" by another person. The degree of intelligence which one calls "moderate dullness," another may call "extreme dullness," etc. But every one knows what is meant by the term 8-year mentality, 4-year mentality, etc., even if he is not able to define these grades of intelligence in psychological terms; and by ascertaining experimentally what intellectual tasks children of different ages can perform, we are, of course, able to make our age standards as definite as we please.

Why should a device so simple have waited so long for a discoverer? We do not know. It is of a class with many other unaccountable mysteries in the development of scientific method. Apparently the idea of an age-grade method, as this is called, did not come to Binet himself until he had experimented with intelligence tests for some fifteen years. At least his first provisional scale, published in 1905, was not made up according to the age-grade plan. It consisted merely of 30 tests, arranged roughly in order of difficulty. Although Binet nowhere gives any account of the steps by which this crude and ungraded scale was transformed into the relatively complete age-grade scale of 1908, we can infer that the original and ingenious idea of utilizing age norms was suggested by the data collected with the 1905 scale. However the discovery was made, it ranks, perhaps, from the practical point of view, as the most important in all the history of psychology.

2. *The kind of mental functions brought into play.*

In the second place, the Binet tests differ from most of the earlier attempts in that they are designed to test the higher and more complex mental processes, instead of the simpler and more elementary ones. Hence they set problems for the reasoning powers and ingenuity, provoke judgments about abstract matters, etc., instead of attempting to measure sensory discrimination, mere retentiveness, rapidity of reaction, and the like. Psychologists had generally considered the higher processes too complex to be measured directly, and accordingly sought to get at them indirectly by correlating supposed intelligence with simpler processes which could readily be measured, such as reaction time, rapidity of tapping, discrimination of tones and colors, etc. While they were disputing over their contradictory findings in this line of exploration, Binet went directly to the point and succeeded where they had failed.

It is now generally admitted by psychologists that higher intelligence is little concerned in such elementary processes as those mentioned above. Many of the animals have keen sensory discrimination. Feeble-minded children, unless of very low grade, do not differ very markedly from normal children in sensitivity of the skin, visual acuity, simple reaction time, type of imagery, etc. But in power of comprehension, abstraction, and ability to direct thought, in the nature of the associative processes, in amount of information possessed, and in spontaneity of attention, they differ enormously.

3. Binet would test "general intelligence."

Finally, Binet's success was largely due to his abandonment of the older "faculty psychology" which, far from being defunct, had really given direction to most of the earlier work with mental tests. Where others had attempted to measure memory attention, sense discrimination, etc., as separate faculties or functions, Binet undertook to ascertain the *general level* of intelligence. Others had thought the task easier of accomplishment by measuring each division or aspect of intelligence separately, and summating the results. Binet, too, began in this way, and it was only after years of experimentation by the usual methods that he finally broke away from them and undertook, so to speak, to triangulate the height of his tower without first getting the dimensions of the individual stones which made it up.

The assumption that it is easier to measure a part, or one aspect, of intelligence than all of it, is fallacious in that the parts are not separate parts and cannot be separated by any refinement of experiment. They are interwoven and intertwined. Each ramifies everywhere and appears in all other functions. The analogy of the stones of the tower does not really apply. Memory, for example, cannot be tested separately from attention, or sense-discrimination separately from the associative processes. After many vain attempts to disentangle the various intellective functions, Binet decided to test their combined functional capacity without any pretense of measuring the exact contribution of each to the total product. It is hardly too much to say that intelligence tests have been successful just to the extent to which they have been guided by this aim.

Memory, attention, imagination, etc., are terms of "structural psychology." Binet's psychology is dynamic. He conceives intelligence as the sum total of those thought processes which consist in mental adaptation. This adaptation is not explicable in terms of the old mental "faculties." No one of these can explain a single thought process, for such process always involves the participation of many functions whose separate rôles are impossible to distinguish accurately. Instead of measuring the intensity of various mental states (psycho-physics), it is more enlightening to measure their combined effect on adaptation. Using a biological comparison, Binet says the old "faculties" correspond to the separate tissues of an animal or plant, while his own "scheme of thought" corresponds to the functioning organ itself. For Binet, psychology is the science of behavior.

Binet's conception of general intelligence.

In devising tests of intelligence it is, of course, necessary to be guided by some assumption, or assumptions, regarding the nature of intelligence. To adopt any other course is to depend for success upon happy chance.

However, it is impossible to arrive at a final definition of intelligence on the basis of *a-priori* considerations alone. To demand, as critics of the Binet method have sometimes done, that one who would measure intelligence should first present a complete definition of it, is quite unreasonable. As Stern points out, electrical currents were measured long before their nature was well understood. Similar illustrations could be drawn from the processes involved in chemistry physiology, and other sciences. In the case of intelligence it may be truthfully said that no adequate definition can possibly be framed which is not based primarily on the symptoms empirically brought to light by the test method. The best that can be done in advance of such data is to make tentative assumptions as to the probable nature of intelligence, and then to subject these assumptions to tests which will show their correctness or incorrectness. New hypotheses can then be framed for further trial, and thus gradually we shall be led to a conception of intelligence which will be meaningful and in harmony with all the ascertainable facts.

Such was the method of Binet. Only those unacquainted with Binet's more than fifteen years of labor preceding the publication of his intelligence scale would think of accusing him of making no effort to analyze the mental processes which his tests bring into play. It is true that many of Binet's earlier assumptions proved untenable, and in this event he was always ready, with exceptional candor and intellectual plasticity, to acknowledge his error and to plan a new line of attack.

Binet's conception of intelligence emphasizes three characteristics of the thought process: (1) Its tendency to take and maintain a definite direction; (2) the capacity to make adaptations for the purpose of attaining a desired end; and (3) the power of auto-criticism.[11]

How these three aspects of intelligence enter into the performances with various tests of the scale is set forth from time to time in our directions for giving and interpreting the individual tests.[12] An illustration which may be given here is that of the "patience test," or uniting the disarranged parts of a divided rectangle. As described by Binet, this operation has the following elements: "(1) to keep in mind the end to be attained, that is to say, the figure to be formed; (2) to try different combinations under the influence of this directing idea, which guides the efforts of the subject even though he may not be conscious of the fact; and (3) to judge the combination which has been made, to compare it with the model, and to decide whether it is the correct one."

Much the same processes are called for in many other of the Binet tests, particularly those of arranging weights, rearranging dissected sentences, drawing a diamond or square from copy, finding a sentence containing three given words, counting backwards, etc.

However, an examination of the scale will show that the choice of tests was not guided entirely by any single formula as to the nature of intelligence. Binet's approach was a many-sided one. The scale includes tests of time orientation, of three or four kinds of memory, of apperception, of language comprehension, of knowledge about common objects, of free association, of number mastery, of constructive imagination, and of ability to compare concepts, to see contradictions, to combine fragments into a unitary whole, to comprehend abstract terms, and to meet novel situations.

Other conceptions of intelligence.

It is interesting to compare Binet's conception of intelligence with the definitions which have been offered by other psychologists. According to Ebbinghaus, for example, the essence of intelligence lies in comprehending together in a unitary, meaningful whole, impressions and associations which are more or less independent, heterogeneous, or even partly contradictory. "Intellectual ability consists in the elaboration of a whole into its worth and meaning by means of many-sided combination, correction, and completion of numerous kindred associations.... It is a *combination activity*."

Meumann offers a twofold definition. From the psychological point of view, intelligence is the power of independent and creative elaboration of new products out of the material given by memory and the senses. From the practical point of view, it involves the ability to avoid errors, to surmount difficulties, and to adjust to environment.

Stern defines intelligence as "the general capacity of an individual consciously to adjust his thinking to new requirements: it is general adaptability to new problems and conditions of life."

Spearman, Hart, and others of the English school define intelligence as a "common central factor" which participates in all sorts of special mental activities. This factor is explained in terms of a psycho-physiological hypothesis of "cortex energy," "cerebral plasticity," etc.

The above definitions are only to a slight extent contradictory or inharmonious. They differ mainly in point of view or in the location of the emphasis. Each expresses a part of the truth, and none all of it. It will be evident that the conception of Binet is broad enough to include the most important elements in each of the other definitions quoted.

Guiding principles in choice and arrangement of tests.

In choosing his tests Binet was guided by the conception of intelligence which we have set forth above. Tests were devised which would presumably bring into play the various mental processes thought to be concerned in intelligence, and then these tests were tried out on normal children of different ages. If the percentage of passes for a given test increased but little or not at all in going from younger to older children this test was discarded. On the other hand, if the proportion of passes increased rapidly with age, and if children of a given age, who on other grounds were known to be bright, passed more frequently than children of the same age who were known to be dull, then the test was judged a satisfactory test of intelligence. As we have shown elsewhere,[13] practically all of Binet's tests fulfill these requirements reasonably well, a fact which bears eloquent testimony to the keen psychological insight of their author.

In arranging the tests into a system Binet's guiding principle was to find an arrangement of the tests which would cause an average child of any given age to test "at age"; that is, the average 5-year-old must show a mental age of 5 years, the average 8-year-old a mental age of 8 years, etc. In order to secure this result Binet found that his data seemed to require the location of an individual test in that year where it was passed by about two thirds to three fourths of unselected children.

It was in the assembling of the tests that the most serious faults of the scale had their origin. Further investigation has shown that a great many of the tests were misplaced as much as one year, and several of them two years. On the whole, the scale as Binet left it was decidedly too easy in the lower ranges, and too difficult in the upper. As a result, the average child of 5 years was caused to test at not far from 6 years, the average child of 12 years not far from 11. In the Stanford revision an effort has been made to correct this fault, along with certain other generally recognized imperfections.

Some avowed limitations of the Binet tests.

The Binet tests have often been criticized for their unfitness to perform certain services which in reality they were never meant to render. This is unfair. We cannot make a just evaluation of the scale without bearing in mind its avowed limitations.

For example, the scale does not pretend to measure the entire mentality of the subject, but only *general intelligence.* There is no pretense of testing the emotions or the will beyond the extent to which these naturally display themselves in the tests of intelligence. The scale was not designed as a tool for the analysis of those emotional or volitional aberrations which are concerned in such mental disorders as hysteria, insanity, etc. These conditions do not present a progressive reduction of intelligence to the infantile level, and in most of them other factors besides intelligence play an important rôle. Moreover, even in the normal individual the fruitfulness of intelligence, the direction in which it shall be applied, and its methods of work are to a certain extent determined by the extraneous factors of emotion and volition.

It should, nevertheless, be pointed out that defects of intelligence, in a large majority of cases, also involve disturbances of the emotional and volitional functions. We do not expect to find perfectly normal emotions or will power of average strength coupled with marked intellectual deficiency, and as a matter of fact such a combination is rare indeed. In the course of an examination with the Binet tests, the experienced clinical psychologist is able to gain considerable insight into the subject's emotional and volitional equipment, even though the method was designed primarily for another purpose.

A second misunderstanding can be avoided by remembering that the Binet scale does not pretend to bring to light the idiosyncrasies of special talent, but only to measure the general level of intelligence. It cannot be used for the discovery of exceptional ability in drawing, painting, music, mathematics, oratory, salesmanship, etc., because no effort is made to explore the processes underlying these abilities. It can, therefore, never serve as a *detailed chart* for the vocational guidance of children, telling us which will succeed in business, which in art, which in medicine, etc. It is not a new kind of phrenology. At the same time, as we have already pointed out, *it is capable of bounding roughly the vocational territory in which an individual's intelligence will probably permit success, nothing else preventing.*[14]

In the third place, it must not be supposed that the scale can be used as a complete pedagogical guide. Although intelligence tests furnish data of the greatest significance for pedagogical procedure, they do not suggest the appropriate educational methods in detail. These will have to be worked out in a practical way for the various grades of intelligence, and at great cost of labor and patience.

Finally, in arriving at an estimate of a subject's grade of intelligence and his susceptibility to training, it would be a mistake to ignore the data obtainable from other sources. No competent psychologist, however ardent a supporter of the Binet method he might be, would recommend such a policy. Those who accept the method as all-sufficient are as much in error as those who consider it as no more important than any one of a dozen other approaches. Standardized tests have already become and will remain by far the most reliable single method for grading intelligence, but the results they furnish will always need to be interpreted in the light of supplementary information regarding the subject's personal history, including medical record, accidents, play habits, industrial efficiency, social and moral traits, school success, home environment, etc. Without question, however, the improved Binet tests will contribute more than all other data combined to the end of enabling us to forecast a child's possibilities of future improvement, and this is the information which will aid most in the proper direction of his education.

FOOTNOTES:

[10] See Part II of this volume, and References 1 and 29, for discussion and interpretation of the individual tests.

[11] See Binet and Simon: "L'intelligence des imbeciles," in *L'Année Psychologique* (1909), pp. 1–147. The last division of this article is devoted to a discussion of the essential nature of the higher thought processes, and is a wonderful example of that keen psychological analysis in which Binet was so gifted.

[12] See especially pages 162 and 238.

[13] See p. 55.

[14] See p. 17.

CHAPTER IV
NATURE OF THE STANFORD REVISION AND EXTENSION

Although the Binet scale quickly demonstrated its value as an instrument for the classification of mentally-retarded and otherwise exceptional children, it had, nevertheless, several imperfections which greatly limited its usefulness. There was a dearth of tests at the higher mental levels, the procedure was so inadequately defined that needless disagreement came about in the interpretation of data, and so many of the tests were misplaced as to make the results of an examination more or less misleading, particularly in the case of very young subjects and those near the adult level. It was for the purpose of correcting these and certain other faults that the Stanford investigation was planned.[15]

Sources of data.

Our revision is the result of several years of work, and involved the examination of approximately 2300 subjects, including 1700 normal children, 200 defective and superior children, and more than 400 adults.

Tests of 400 of the 1700 normal children had been made by Childs and Terman in 1910–11, and of 300 children by Trost, Waddle, and Terman in 1911–12. For various reasons, however, the results of these tests did not furnish satisfactory data for a thoroughgoing revision of the scale. Accordingly a new investigation was undertaken, somewhat more extensive than the others, and more carefully planned. Its main features may be described as follows:—

1. The first step was to assemble as nearly as possible all the results which had been secured for each test of the scale by all the workers of all countries. The result was a large sheet of tabulated data for each individual test, including percentages passing the test at various ages, conditions under

which the results were secured, method of procedure, etc. After a comparative study of these data, and in the light of results we had ourselves secured, a provisional arrangement of the tests was prepared for try-out.

2. In addition to the tests of the original Binet scale, 40 additional tests were included for try-out. This, it was expected, would make possible the elimination of some of the least satisfactory tests, and at the same time permit the addition of enough new ones to give at least six tests, instead of five, for each age group.

3. A plan was then devised for securing subjects who should be as nearly as possible representative of the several ages. The method was to select a school in a community of average social status, a school attended by all or practically all the children in the district where it was located. In order to get clear pictures of age differences the tests were confined to children who were within two months of a birthday. To avoid accidental selection, *all* the children within two months of a birthday were tested, in whatever grade enrolled. Tests of foreign-born children, however, were eliminated in the treatment of results. There remained tests of approximately 1000 children, of whom 905 were between 5 and 14 years of age.

4. The children's responses were, for the most part, recorded *verbatim*. This made it possible to re-score the records according to any desired standard, and thus to fit a test more perfectly to the age level assigned it.

5. Much attention was given to securing uniformity of procedure. A half-year was devoted to training the examiners and another half-year to the supervision of the testing. In the further interests of uniformity all the records were scored by one person (the writer).

Method of arriving at a revision.

The revision of the scale below the 14-year level was based almost entirely on the tests of the above-mentioned 1,000 unselected children. The guiding principle was to secure an arrangement of the tests and a standard of scoring which would cause the median mental age of the unselected children of each age group to coincide with the median chronological age. That is, a correct scale must cause the *average* child of 5 years to test exactly at 5, the *average* child at 6 to test exactly at 6, etc. Or, to express the same fact in terms of intelligence quotient,[16] a correct scale must give a median intelligence quotient of unity, or 100 per cent, for unselected children of each age.

If the median mental age resulting at any point from the provisional arrangement of tests was too high or too low, it was only necessary to change the location of certain of the tests, or to change the standard of scoring, until an order of arrangement and a standard of passing were found which would throw the median mental age where it belonged. We had already become convinced, for reasons too involved for presentation here, that no satisfactory revision of the Binet scale was possible on any theoretical considerations as to the percentage of passes which an individual test ought to show in a given year in order to be considered standard for that year.

As was to be expected, the first draft of the revision did not prove satisfactory. The scale was still too hard at some points, and too easy at others. In fact, three successive revisions were necessary, involving three separate scorings of the data and as many tabulations of the mental ages, before the desired degree of accuracy was secured. As finally revised, the scale gives a median intelligence quotient closely approximating 100 for the unselected children of each age from 4 to 14.

Since our school children who were above 14 years and still in the grades were retarded left-overs, it was necessary to base the revision above this level on the tests of adults. These included 30 business men and 150 "migrating" unemployed men tested by Mr. H. E. Knollin, 150 adolescent delinquents tested by Mr. J. Harold Williams, and 50 high-school students tested by the writer.

The extension of the scale in the upper range is such that ordinarily intelligent adults, little educated, test up to what is called the "average adult" level. Adults whose intelligence is known from other sources to be superior are found to test well up toward the "superior adult" level, and this holds whether the subjects in question are well educated or practically unschooled. The almost entirely unschooled business men, in fact, tested fully as well as high-school juniors and seniors.

Figure 1 shows the distribution of mental ages for 62 adults, including the 30 business men and the 32 high-school pupils who were over 16 years of age. It will be noted that the middle section of the graph represents the "mental ages" falling between 15 and 17. This is the range which we have designated as the "average adult" level. Those above 17 are called "superior adults," those between 13 and 15, "inferior adults." Subjects much over 15 years of age who test in the neighborhood of 12 years may ordinarily be considered border-line cases.

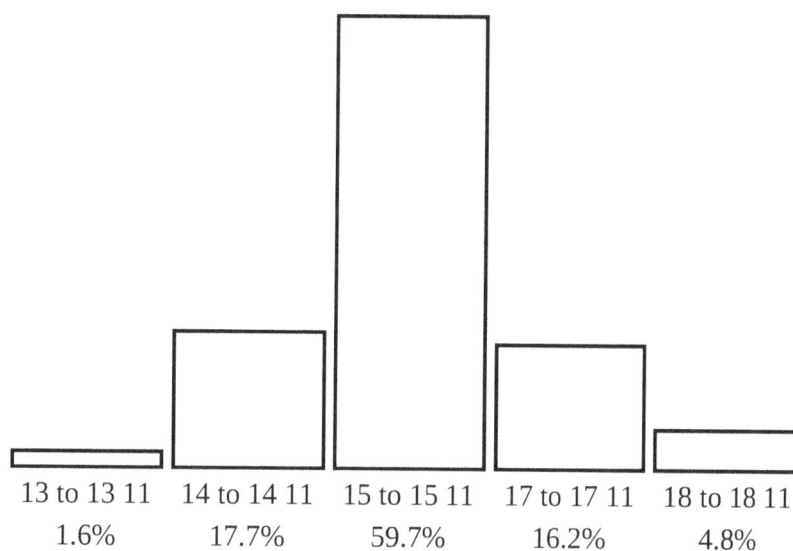

| 13 to 13 11 | 14 to 14 11 | 15 to 15 11 | 17 to 17 11 | 18 to 18 11 |
| 1.6% | 17.7% | 59.7% | 16.2% | 4.8% |

FIG. 1. DISTRIBUTION OF MENTAL AGES OF 62 NORMAL ADULTS

The following method was employed for determining the validity of a test. The children of each age level were divided into three groups according to intelligence quotient, those testing below 90, those between 90 and 109, and those with an intelligence quotient of 110 or above. The percentages of passes on each individual test at or near that age level were then ascertained separately for these three groups. If a test fails to show a decidedly higher proportion of passes in the superior I Q group than in the inferior I Q group, it cannot be regarded as a satisfactory test of intelligence. On the other hand, a test which satisfies this criterion must be accepted as valid or the entire scale must be rejected. Henceforth it stands or falls with the scale as a whole.

When tried out by this method, some of the tests which have been most criticized showed a high degree of reliability; certain others which have been considered excellent proved to be so little correlated with intelligence that they had to be discarded.

After making a few necessary eliminations, 90 tests remained, or 36 more than the number included in the Binet 1911 scale. There are 6 at each age level from 3 to 10, 8 at 12, 6 at 14, 6 at "average adult," 6 at "superior adult," and 16 alternative tests. The alternative tests, which are distributed among the different groups, are intended to be used only as substitutes when one or more of the regular tests have been rendered, by coaching or otherwise, undesirable.[17]

Of the 36 new tests, 27 were added and standardized in the various Stanford investigations. Two tests were borrowed from the Healy-Fernald series, one from Kuhlmann, one was adapted from Bonser, and the remaining five were amplifications or adaptations of some of the earlier Binet tests.

Following is a complete list of the tests of the Stanford revision. Those designated *al.* are alternative tests. The guide for giving and scoring the tests is presented at length in Part II of this volume.

The Stanford revision and extension

Year III. (*6 tests, 2 months each.*)
1. Points to parts of body. (3 to 4.)
    Nose; eyes; mouth; hair.
2. Names familiar objects. (3 to 5.)
    Key, penny, closed knife, watch, pencil.
3. Pictures, enumeration or better. (At least 3 objects enumerated in one picture.)
    (*a*) Dutch Home; (*b*) River Scene; (*c*) Post-Office.
4. Gives sex.
5. Gives last name.
6. Repeats 6 to 7 syllables. (1 to 3.)
    Al. Repeats 3 digits. (1 success in 3 trials. Order correct.)

Year IV. (*6 tests, 2 months each.*)

    1. Compares lines. (3 trials, no error.)

    2. Discrimination of forms. (Kuhlmann.) (Not over 3 errors.)

    3. Counts 4 pennies. (No error.)

    4. Copies square. (Pencil. 1 to 3.)

    5. Comprehension, 1st degree. (2 to 3.) (Stanford addition.)
          "What must you do": "When you are sleepy?" "Cold?" "Hungry?"

    6. Repeats 4 digits. (1 to 3. Order correct.) (Stanford addition.)

    Al. Repeats 12 to 13 syllables. (1 to 3 absolutely correct, or 2 with 1 error each.)

Year V. (*6 tests, 2 months each.*)

    1. Comparison of weights. (2 to 3.)
          3–15;   15–3;   3–15.

    2. Colors. (No error.)
          Red; yellow; blue; green.

    3. Æsthetic comparison. (No error.)

    4. Definitions, use or better. (4 to 6.)
          Chair; horse; fork; doll; pencil; table.

    5. Patience, or divided rectangle. (2 to 3 trials. 1 minute each.)

    6. Three commissions. (No error. Order correct.)

    Al. Age.

Year VI. (*6 tests, 2 months each.*)

    1. Right and left. (No error.)
          Right hand; left ear; right eye.

    2. Mutilated pictures. (3 to 4 correct.)

    3. Counts 13 pennies. (1 to 2 trials, without error.)

    4. Comprehension, 2d degree. (2 to 3.) "What's the thing for you to do":
        a. "If it is raining when you start to school?"
        b. "If you find that your house is on fire?"
        c. "If you are going some place and miss your car?"

    5. Coins. (3 to 4.)
          Nickel; penny; quarter; dime.

    6. Repeats 16 to 18 syllables. (1 to 3 absolutely correct, or 2 with 1 error each.)

    Al. Morning or afternoon.

Year VII. (*6 tests, 2 months each.*)

    1. Fingers. (No error.) Right; left; both.

    2. Pictures, description or better. (Over half of performance description:) Dutch Home; River Scene; Post-Office.

    3. Repeats 5 digits. (1 to 3. Order correct.)

4. Ties bow-knot. (Model shown. 1 minute.) (Stanford addition.)

5. Gives differences. (2 to 3.)
    Fly and butterfly; stone and egg; wood and glass.

6. Copies diamond. (Pen. 2 to 3.)

    Al. 1. Names days of week. (Order correct. 2 to 3 checks correct.)

    Al. 2. Repeats 3 digits backwards. (1 to 3.)

Year VIII. (*6 tests, 2 months each.*)

1. Ball and field. (Inferior plan or better.) (Stanford addition.)

2. Counts 20 to 1. (40 seconds. 1 error allowed.)

3. Comprehension, 3d degree. (2 to 3.) "What's the thing for you to do":

    a. "When you have broken something which belongs to some one else?"

    b. "When you are on your way to school and notice that you are in danger of being tardy?"

    c. "If a playmate hits you without meaning to do it?"

4. Gives similarities, two things. (2 to 4.) (Stanford addition.)
    Wood and coal; apple and peach; iron and silver; ship and automobile.

5. Definitions superior to use. (2 to 4.)
    Balloon; tiger; football; soldier.

6. Vocabulary, 20 words. (Stanford addition. For list of words used, see record booklet.)

    Al. 1. First six coins. (No error.)

    Al. 2. Dictation. ("See the little boy." Easily legible. Pen. 1 minute.)

Year IX. (*6 tests, 2 months each.*)

1. Date. (Allow error of 3 days in *c*, no error in *a*, *b*, or *d*.)

    a. day of week;

    b. month;

    c. day of month;

    d. year.

2. Weights. (3, 6, 9, 12, 15. Procedure not illustrated. 2 to 3.)

3. Makes change. (2 to 3. No coins, paper, or pencil.)
    10 – 4; 15 – 12; 25 – 4.

4. Repeats 4 digits backwards. (1 to 3.) (Stanford addition.)

5. Three words. (2 to 3. Oral. 1 sentence or not over 2 coördinate clauses.)
    Boy, river, ball; work, money, men; desert, rivers, lakes.

6. Rhymes. (3 rhymes for two of three words. 1 minute for each part.)
    Day; mill; spring.

    Al. 1. Months. (15 seconds and 1 error in naming. 2 checks of 3 correct.)

    Al. 2. Stamps, gives total value. (Second trial if individual values are known.)

Year X. (*6 tests, 2 months each.*)

1. Vocabulary, 30 words. (Stanford addition.)
2. Absurdities. (4 to 5. Warn. Spontaneous correction allowed.) (Four of Binet's, one Stanford.)
3. Designs. (1 correct, 1 half correct. Expose 10 seconds.)
4. Reading and report. (8 memories. 35 seconds and 2 mistakes in reading.) (Binet's selection.)
5. Comprehension, 4th degree. (2 to 3. Question may be repeated.)

   a. "What ought you to say when some one asks your opinion about a person you don't know very well?"

   b. "What ought you to do before undertaking (beginning) something very important?"

   c. "Why should we judge a person more by his actions than by his words?"

6. Names 60 words. (Illustrate with clouds, dog, chair, happy.)

   Al. 1. Repeats 6 digits. (1 to 2. Order correct.) (Stanford addition.)

   Al. 2. Repeats 20 to 22 syllables. (1 to 3 correct, or 2 with 1 error each.)

   Al. 3. Form board. (Healy-Fernald Puzzle A. 3 times in 5 minutes.)

Year XII. (*8 tests, 3 months each.*)
1. Vocabulary, 40 words. (Stanford addition.)
2. Abstract words. (3 to 5.)
   Pity; revenge; charity; envy; justice.
3. Ball and field. (Superior plan.) (Stanford addition.)
4. Dissected sentences. (2 to 3. 1 minute each.)
5. Fables. (Score 4; i.e., two correct or the equivalent in half credits.) (Stanford addition.)
   Hercules and Wagoner; Maid and Eggs; Fox and Crow; Farmer and Stork; Miller, Son, and Donkey.
6. Repeats 5 digits backwards. (1 to 3.) (Stanford addition.)
7. Pictures, interpretation. (3 to 4. "Explain this picture.")
   Dutch Home; River Scene; Post-Office; Colonial Home.
8. Gives similarities, three things. (3 to 5.) (Stanford addition.)
   Snake, cow, sparrow; book, teacher, newspaper; wool, cotton, leather; knife-blade, penny, piece of wire; rose, potato, tree.

Year XIV. (*6 tests, 4 months each.*)
1. Vocabulary, 50 words. (Stanford addition.)
2. Induction test. (Gets rule by 6th folding.) (Stanford addition.)
3. President and king. (Power; accession; tenure. 2 to 3.)
4. Problems of fact. (2 to 3.) (Binet's two and one Stanford addition.)
5. Arithmetical reasoning. (1 minute each. 2 to 3.) (Adapted from Bonser.)
6. Clock. (2 to 3. Error must not exceed 3 or 4 minutes.)
   6.22.   8.10.   2.46.

   Al. Repeats 7 digits. (1 to 2. Order correct.)

"AVERAGE ADULT." (*6 tests, 5 months each.*)

1. Vocabulary, 65 words. (Stanford addition.)
2. Interpretation of fables. (Score 8.) (Stanford addition.)
3. Difference between abstract words. (3 real contrasts out of 4.)
    Laziness and idleness; evolution and revolution; poverty and misery; character and reputation.
4. Problem of the enclosed boxes. (3 to 4.) (Stanford addition.)
5. Repeats 6 digits backwards. (1 to 3.) (Stanford addition.)
6. Code, writes "Come quickly." (2 errors. Omission of dot counts half error. Illustrate with "war" and "spy.") (From Healy and Fernald.)
    Al. 1. Repeats 28 syllables. (1 to 2 absolutely correct.)
    Al. 2. Comprehension of physical relations. (2 to 3.) (Stanford addition.)
        Path of cannon ball; weight of fish in water; hitting distant mark.

"SUPERIOR ADULT." (*6 tests, 6 months each.*)

1. Vocabulary, 75 words. (Stanford addition.)
2. Binet's paper-cutting test. (Draws, folds, and locates holes.)
3. Repeats 8 digits. (1 to 3. Order correct.) (Stanford addition.)
4. Repeats thought of passage heard. (1 to 2.) (Binet's and Wissler's selections adapted.)
5. Repeats 7 digits backwards. (1 to 3.) (Stanford addition.)
6. Ingenuity test. (2 to 3. 5 minutes each.) (Stanford addition.)

Summary of changes.

A comparison of the above list with either the Binet 1908 or 1911 series will reveal many changes. On the whole, it differs somewhat more from the Binet 1911 scale than from that of 1908. Thus, of the 49 tests below the "adult" group in the 1911 scale, 2 are eliminated and 29 are relocated. Of these, 25 are moved downward and 4 upward. The shifts are as follows:—

```
Down 1 year,   18
Down 2 years,   4
Down 3 years,   2
Down 6 years,   1
Up    1 year,   3
Up    2 years,   1
```

Of the adult group in Binet's 1911 series 1 is eliminated, 2 are moved up to "superior adult," and 1 is moved up to 14. Accordingly, of Binet's entire 54 tests, we have eliminated 3 and relocated 32, leaving only 19 in the positions assigned them by Binet. The 3 eliminated are: repeating 2 digits, resisting suggestion, and "reversed triangle."

The revision is really more extensive than the above figures would suggest, since minor changes have been made in the scoring of a great many tests in order to make them fit better the locations assigned them. Throughout the scale the procedure and scoring have been worked over and made more definite with the idea of promoting uniformity. This phase of the revision is perhaps more important than the mere relocation of tests. Also, the addition of numerous tests in the upper ranges of the scale affects very considerably the mental ages above the level of 10 or 11 years.

Effects of the revision on the mental ages secured.

The most important effect of the revision is to reduce the mental ages secured in the lower ranges of the scale, and to raise considerably the mental ages above 10 or 11 years. This difference also obtains, though to a somewhat smaller extent, between the Stanford revision and those of Goddard and Kuhlmann.

For example, of 104 adult individuals testing by the Stanford revision between 12 and 14 years, and who were therefore somewhat above the level of feeble-mindedness as that term is usually defined, 50 per cent tested below 12 years by the Goddard revision. That the dull and border-line adults are so much more readily distinguished from the feeble-minded by the Stanford revision than by other Binet series is due as much to the addition of tests in the upper groups as to the relocation of existing tests.

On the other hand, the Stanford revision causes young subjects to test lower than any other version of the Binet scale. At 5 or 6 years the mental ages secured by the Stanford revision average from 6 to 10 months lower than other revisions yield.

The above differences are more significant than would at first appear. An error of 10 months in the mental age of a 5-year-old is as serious as an error of 20 months in the case of a 10-year-old. Stating the error in terms of the intelligence quotient makes it more evident. Thus, an error of 10 months in the mental age of a 5-year-old means an error of almost 15 per cent in the intelligence quotient. A scale which tests this much too low would cause the child with a true intelligence quotient of 75 (which ordinarily means feeble-mindedness or border-line intelligence) to test at 90, or only slightly below normal.

Three serious consequences came from the too great ease of the original Binet scale at the lower end, and its too great difficulty at the upper end:—

1. In young subjects the higher grades of mental deficiency were overlooked, because the scale caused such subjects to test only a little below normal.

2. The proportion of feeble-mindedness among adult subjects was greatly overestimated, because subjects who were really of the 12- or 13-year mental level could only earn a mental age of about 11 years.

3. Confusion resulted in efforts to trace the mental growth of either feeble-minded or normal children. For example, by other versions of the Binet scale an average 5-year-old will show an intelligence quotient probably not far from 110 or 115; at 9, an intelligence quotient of about 100; and at 14, an intelligence quotient of about 85 or 90.

By such a scale the true border-line case would test approximately as follows:—

> At age 5, 90 I Q (apparently not far below normal).
> At age 9, 75 I Q (border-line).
> At age 14, 65 I Q (moron deficiency).

On the other hand, re-tests of children by the Stanford revision have been found to yield intelligence quotients almost identical with those secured from two to four years earlier by the same tests. Those who graded feeble-minded in the first test graded feeble-minded in the second test: the dull remained dull, the average remained average, the superior remained superior, and always in approximately the same degree.[18]

It is unnecessary to emphasize further the importance of having an intelligence scale which is equally accurate at all points. Absolute perfection in this respect is not claimed for the Stanford revision, but it is believed to be at least free from the more serious errors of other Binet arrangements.

FOOTNOTES:

[15] The writer wishes to acknowledge his very great indebtedness to Miss Grace Lyman, Dr. George Ordahl, Dr. Louise Ellison Ordahl, Miss Neva Galbreath, Mr. Wilford Talbert, Dr. J. Harold Williams, Mr. Herbert E. Knollin, and Miss Irene Cuneo for their coöperation in making the tests on which the Stanford revision is chiefly based. Without their loyal assistance the investigation could not have been carried through.

Grateful acknowledgment is also made to the many public school teachers and principals for their generous and invaluable coöperation in furnishing subjects for the tests, and in supplying, sometimes at considerable cost of labor, the supplementary information which was called for regarding the pupils tested. Their contribution was made in the interest of educational science, and without expectation of personal benefits of any kind. Their professional spirit cannot be too highly commended.

[16] The intelligence quotient (often designated as I Q) is the ratio of mental age to chronological age. (See pp. 65 *ff.* and 78 *ff.*)

[17] See p. 137 *ff.* for explanations regarding the calculation of mental age and the use of alternative tests.

[18] See "Some Problems relating to the Detection of Border-line Cases of Mental Deficiency," by Lewis M. Terman and H. E. Knollin, in *Journal of Psycho-Asthemes*, June, 1916.

CHAPTER V
ANALYSIS OF 1000 INTELLIGENCE QUOTIENTS

An extended account of the 1000 tests on which the Stanford revision is chiefly based has been presented in a separate monograph. This chapter will include only the briefest summary of some of those results of the investigation which contribute to the intelligent use of the revision.

The distribution of intelligence.

The question as to the manner in which intelligence is distributed is one of great practical as well as theoretical importance. One of the most vital questions which can be asked by any nation of any age is the following: "How high is the average level of intelligence among our people, and how frequent are the various grades of ability above and below the average?" With the development of standardized tests we are approaching, for the first time in history, a possible answer to this question.

Most of the earlier Binet studies, however, have thrown little light on the distribution of intelligence because of their failure to avoid the influence of accidental selection in choosing subjects for testing. The method of securing subjects for the Stanford revision makes our results on this point especially interesting.[19] It is believed that the subjects used for this investigation were as nearly representative of average American-born children as it is possible to secure.

The intelligence quotients for these 1000 unselected children were calculated, and their distribution was plotted for the ages separately. The distribution was found fairly symmetrical at each age from 5 to 14. At 15 the range is on either side of 90 as a median, and at 16 on either side of 80 as a median. That the 15- and 16-year-olds test low is due to the fact that these children are left-over retardates and are below average in intelligence.

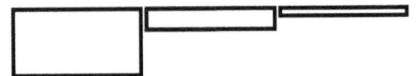

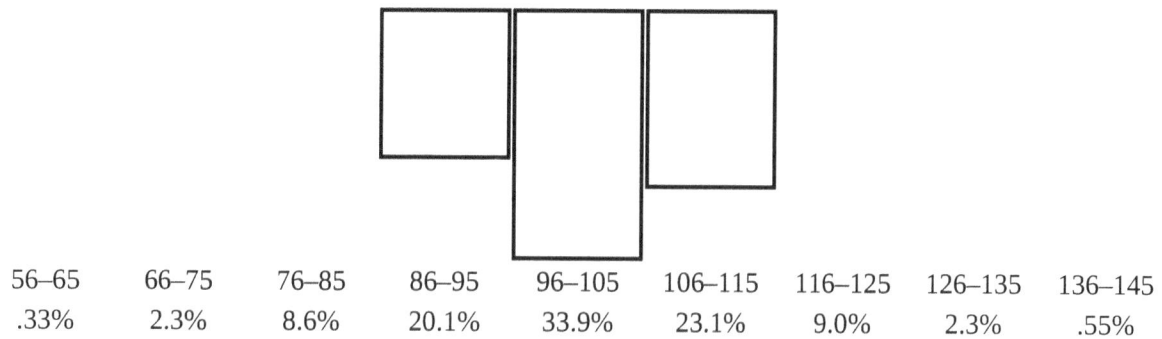

56–65	66–75	76–85	86–95	96–105	106–115	116–125	126–135	136–145
.33%	2.3%	8.6%	20.1%	33.9%	23.1%	9.0%	2.3%	.55%

FIG. 2. DISTRIBUTION OF I Q'S OF 905 UNSELECTED CHILDREN. 5–14 YEARS OF AGE

The I Q's were then grouped in ranges of ten. In the middle group were thrown those from 96 to 105; the ascending groups including in order the I Q's from 106 to 115, 116 to 125, etc.; correspondingly with the descending groups. Figure 2 shows the distribution found by this grouping for the 905 children of ages 5 to 14 combined. The subjects above 14 are not included in this curve because they are left-overs and not representative of their ages.

The distribution for the ages combined is seen to be remarkably symmetrical. The symmetry for the separate ages was hardly less marked, considering that only 80 to 120 children were tested at each age. In fact, the range, including the middle 50 per cent of I Q's, was found practically constant from 5 to 14 years. The tendency is for the middle 50 per cent to fall (approximately) between 93 and 108.

Three important conclusions are justified by the above facts:—

1. Since the frequency of the various grades of intelligence decreases *gradually* and at no point abruptly on each side of the median, it is evident that there is no definite dividing line between normality and feeble-mindedness, or between normality and genius. Psychologically, the mentally defective child does not belong to a distinct type, nor does the genius. There is no line of demarcation between either of these extremes and the so-called "normal" child. The number of mentally defective individuals in a population will depend upon the standard arbitrarily set up as to what constitutes mental deficiency. Similarly for genius. It is exactly as we should undertake to classify all people into the three groups: abnormally tall, normally tall, and abnormally short.[20]

2. The common opinion that extreme deviations below the median are more frequent than extreme deviations above the median seems to have no

foundation in fact. Among unselected school children, at least, for every child of any given degree of deficiency there is another child as far above the average I Q as the former is below. We have shown elsewhere the serious consequences of neglect of this fact.[21]

3. The traditional view that variability in mental traits becomes more marked during adolescence is here contradicted, as far as intelligence is concerned, for the distribution of I Q's is practically the same at each age from 5 to 14. For example, 6-year-olds differ from one another fully as much as do 14-year-olds.

The validity of the intelligence quotient.

The facts presented above argue strongly for the validity of the I Q as an expression of a child's intelligence status. This follows necessarily from the similar nature of the distributions at the various ages. The inference is that a child's I Q, as measured by this scale, remains relatively constant. Re-tests of the same children at intervals of two to five years support the inference. Children of superior intelligence do not seem to deteriorate as they get older, nor dull children to develop average intelligence. Knowing a child's I Q, we can predict with a fair degree of accuracy the course of his later development.

The mental age of a subject is meaningless if considered apart from chronological age. It is only the ratio of retardation or acceleration to chronological age (that is, the I Q) which has significance.

It follows also that if the I Q is a valid expression of intelligence, as it seems to be, then the Binet-Simon "age-grade method" becomes transformed automatically into a "point-scale method," if one wants to use it that way. As such it is superior to any other point scale that has been proposed, because it includes a larger number of tests and its points have definite meaning.[22]

Sex differences.

The question as to the relative intelligence of the sexes is one of perennial interest and great social importance. The ancient hypothesis, the one which dates from the time when only men concerned themselves with scientific hypotheses, took for granted the superiority of the male. With the development of individual psychology, however, it was soon found that as far as the evidence of mental tests can be trusted the *average* intelligence of women and girls is as high as that of men and boys.

If we accept this result we are then confronted with the difficult problem of finding an explanation for the fact that so few of those who have acquired eminence in the various intellectual fields have been women. Two explanations have been proposed: (1) That women become eminent less often than men simply for lack of opportunity and stimulus; and (2) that while the average intelligence of the sexes is the same, extreme variations may be more common in males. It is pointed out that not only are there more eminent men than eminent women, but that statistics also show a preponderance of males in institutions for the mentally defective. Accordingly it is often said that women are grouped closely about the average, while men show a wider range of distribution.

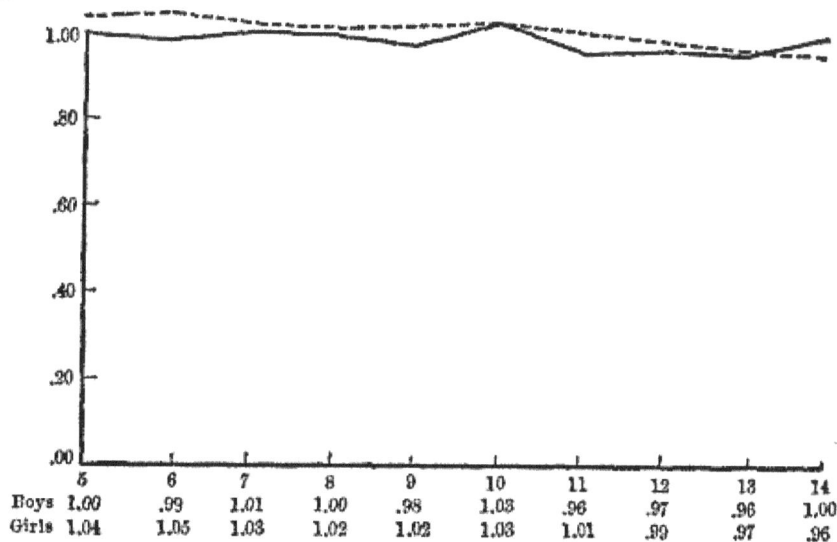

	5	6	7	8	9	10	11	12	13	14
Boys	1.00	.99	1.01	1.00	.98	1.03	.96	.97	.96	1.00
Girls	1.04	1.05	1.03	1.02	1.02	1.03	1.01	.99	.97	.96

FIG. 3. MEDIAN I Q OF 457 BOYS (UNBROKEN LINE) AND 448 GIRLS (DOTTED LINE) FOR THE AGES 5–14 YEARS

Many hundreds of articles and books of popular or quasi-scientific nature have been written on one aspect or another of this question of sex difference in intelligence; but all such theoretical discussions taken together are worth less than the results of one good experiment. Let us see what our 1000 I Q's have to offer toward a solution of the problem.

1. When the I Q's of the boys and girls were treated separately there was found a small but fairly constant superiority of the girls up to the age of

13 years. At 14, however, the curve for the girls dropped below that for boys. This is shown in Figure 3.

The supplementary data, including the teachers' estimates of intelligence on a scale of five, the teachers' judgments in regard to the quality of the school work, and records showing the age-grade distribution of the sexes, were all sifted for evidence as to the genuineness of the apparent superiority of the girls age for age. The results of all these lines of inquiry support the tests in suggesting that the superiority of the girls is probably real even up to and including age 14, the apparent superiority of the boys at this age being fully accounted for by the more frequent elimination of 14-year-old girls from the grades by promotion to the high school.[23]

2. However, the superiority of girls over boys is so slight (amounting at most ages to only 2 to 3 points in terms of I Q) that for practical purposes it would seem negligible. This offers no support to the opinion expressed by Yerkes and Bridges that "at certain ages serious injustice will be done individuals by evaluating their scores in the light of norms which do not take account of sex differences."

3. Apart from the small superiority of girls, the distribution of intelligence in the two sexes is not different. The supposed wider variation of boys is not found. Girls do not group themselves about the median more closely than do boys. The range of I Q including the middle fifty per cent is approximately the same for the two sexes.[24]

4. When the results for the individual tests were examined, it was found that not many showed very extreme differences as to the per cent of boys and girls passing. In a few cases, however, the difference was rather marked.

The boys were decidedly better in arithmetical reasoning, giving differences between a president and a king, solving the form board, making change, reversing hands of clock, finding similarities, and solving the "induction test." The girls were superior in drawing designs from memory, æsthetic comparison, comparing objects from memory, answering the "comprehension questions," repeating digits and sentences, tying a bow-knot, and finding rhymes.

Accordingly, our data, which for the most part agree with the results of others, justify the conclusion that the intelligence of girls, at least up to

14 years, does not differ materially from that of boys either as regards the average level or the range of distribution. It may still be argued that the mental development of boys beyond the age of 14 years lasts longer and extends farther than in the case of girls, but as a matter of fact this opinion receives little support from such tests as have been made on men and women college students.

The fact that so few women have attained eminence may be due to wholly extraneous factors, the most important of which are the following: (1) The occupations in which it is possible to achieve eminence are for the most part only now beginning to open their doors to women. Women's career has been largely that of home-making, an occupation in which eminence, in the strict sense of the word, is impossible. (2) Even of the small number of women who embark upon a professional career, a majority marry and thereafter devote a fairly large proportion of their energy to bearing and rearing children. (3) Both the training given to girls and the general atmosphere in which they grow up are unfavorable to the inculcation of the professional point of view, and as a result women are not spurred on by deep-seated motives to constant and strenuous intellectual endeavor as men are. (4) It is also possible that the emotional traits of women are such as to favor the development of the sentiments at the expense of innate intellectual endowment.

Intelligence of the different social classes.

Of the 1000 children, 492 were classified by their teachers according to social class into the following five groups: *very inferior, inferior, average, superior,* and *very superior*. A comparative study was then made of the distribution of I Q's for these different groups.[25]

The data may be summarized as follows:—

1. The median I Q for children of the superior social class is about 7 points above, and that of the inferior social class about 7 points below, the median I Q of the average social group. This means that by the age of 14 inferior class children are about one year below, and superior class children one year above, the median mental age for all classes taken together.

2. That the children of the superior social classes make a better showing in the tests is probably due, for the most part, to a superiority in original endowment. This conclusion is supported by five supplementary lines of evidence: (*a*) the teachers' rankings of the children according to intelligence; (*b*) the age-grade progress of the children; (*c*) the quality of the school work; (*d*) the comparison of older and younger

children as regards the influence of social environment; and (*e*) the study of individual cases of bright and dull children in the same family.

3. In order to facilitate comparison, it is advisable to express the intelligence of children of all social classes in terms of the same objective scale of intelligence. This scale should be based on the median for all classes taken together.

4. As regards their responses to individual tests, our children of a given social class were not distinguishable from children of the same intelligence in any other social class.

The relation of the I Q to the quality of the child's school work.

The school work of 504 children was graded by the teachers on a scale of five grades: *very inferior, inferior, average, superior,* and *very superior*. When this grouping was compared with that made on the basis of I Q, fairly close agreement was found. However, in about one case out of ten there was rather serious disagreement; a child, for example, would be rated as doing *average* school work when his I Q would place him in the *very inferior* intelligence group.

When the data were searched for explanations of such disagreements it was found that most of them were plainly due to the failure of teachers to take into account the age of the child when grading the quality of his school work. [26] When allowance was made for this tendency there were no disagreements which justified any serious suspicion as to the accuracy of the intelligence scale. Minor disagreements may, of course, be disregarded, since the quality of school work depends in part on other factors than intelligence, such as industry, health, regularity of attendance, quality of instruction, etc.

The relation between I Q and grade progress.

This comparison, which was made for the entire 1000 children, showed a fairly high correlation, but also some astonishing disagreements. Nine-year intelligence was found all the way from grade 1 to grade 7, inclusive; 10-year intelligence all the way from grade 2 to grade 7; and 12-year intelligence all the way from grade 3 to grade 8. Plainly the school's efforts at grading fail to give homogeneous groups of children as regards mental ability. On the whole, the grade location of the children did not fit their mental ages much better than it did their chronological ages.

When the data were examined, it was found that practically every child whose grade failed to correspond fairly closely with his mental age was either exceptionally bright or exceptionally dull. Those who tested between 96 and 105 I Q were never seriously misplaced in school. The very dull children, however, were usually located from one to three grades above where they belonged by mental age, and the duller the child the more serious, as a rule, was the misplacement. On the other hand, the very bright children were nearly always located from one to three grades below where they belonged by mental age, and the brighter the child the more serious the school's mistake. The child of 10-year mental age in the second grade, for example, is almost certain to be about 7 or 8 years old; the child of 10-year intelligence in the sixth grade is almost certain to be 13 to 15 years of age.

All this is due to one fact, and one alone: *the school tends to promote children by age rather than ability*. The bright children are held back, while the dull children are promoted beyond their mental ability. The retardation problem is exactly the reverse of what we have thought it to be. It is the bright children who are retarded, and the dull children who are accelerated.

The remedy is to be sought in differentiated courses (special classes) for both kinds of mentally exceptional children. Just as many special classes are needed for superior children as for the inferior. The social consequences of suitable educational advantages for children of superior ability would no doubt greatly exceed anything that could possibly result from the special instruction of dullards and border-line cases.[27]

Special study of the I Q's between 70 and 79 revealed the fact that a child of this grade of intelligence *never* does satisfactory work in the grade where he belongs by chronological age. By the time he has attended school four or five years, such a child is usually found doing "very inferior" to "average" work in a grade from two to four years below his age.

On the other hand, the child with an I Q of 120 or above is almost never found below the grade for his chronological age, and occasionally he is one or two grades above. Wherever located, his work is always "superior" or "very superior," and the evidence suggests strongly that it would probably remain so even if extra promotions were granted.

Correlation between I Q and the teachers' estimates of the children's intelligence.

By the Pearson formula the correlation found between the I Q's and the teachers' rankings on a scale of five was .48. This is about what others have found, and is both high enough and low enough to be significant. That it is moderately high in so far corroborates the tests. That it is not higher means that either the teachers or the tests have made a good many mistakes.

When the data were searched for evidence on this point, it was found, as we have shown in Chapter II, that the fault was plainly on the part of the teachers. The serious mistakes were nearly all made with children who were either over age or under age for their grade, mostly the former. In estimating children's intelligence, just as in grading their school success, the teachers often failed to take account of the age factor. For example, the child whose mental age was, say, two years below normal, and who was enrolled in a class with children about two years younger than himself, was often graded "average" in intelligence.

The tendency of teachers is to estimate a child's intelligence according to the quality of his school work *in the grade where he happens to be located*. This results in overestimating the intelligence of older, retarded children, and underestimating the intelligence of the younger, advanced children. The disagreements between the tests and the teachers' estimates are thus found, when analyzed, to confirm the validity of the test method rather than to bring it under suspicion.

The validity of the individual tests.

The validity of each test was checked up by measuring it against the scale as a whole in the manner described on p. 55. For example, if 10-year-old children having 11-year intelligence succeed with a given test decidedly better than 10-year-old children who have 9-year intelligence, then either this test must be accepted as valid or the scale as a whole must be rejected. Since we know, however, that the scale as a whole has at least a reasonably high degree of reliability, this method becomes a sure and ready means of judging the worth of a test.

When the tests were tried out in this way it was found that some of those which have been most criticized have in reality a high correlation with intelligence. Among these are naming the days of the week, giving the value of stamps, counting thirteen pennies, giving differences between president and king, finding rhymes, giving age, distinguishing right and left, and interpretation of pictures. Others having a high reliability are the vocabulary tests, arithmetical reasoning, giving differences, copying a diamond, giving date, repeating digits in reverse order, interpretation of fables, the dissected sentence test, naming sixty words, finding omissions in pictures, and recognizing absurdities.

Among the somewhat less satisfactory tests are the following: repeating digits (direct order), naming coins, distinguishing forenoon and afternoon, defining in terms of use, drawing designs from memory, and æsthetic comparison. Binet's "line suggestion" test correlated so little with intelligence that it had to be thrown out. The same was also true of two of the new tests which we had added to the series for try-out.

Tests showing a medium correlation with the scale as a whole include arranging weights, executing three commissions, naming colors, giving number of fingers, describing pictures, naming the months, making change, giving superior definitions, finding similarities, reading for memories, reversing hands of clock, defining abstract words, problems of fact, bow-knot, induction test, and comprehension questions.

A test which makes a good showing on this criterion of agreement with the scale as a whole becomes immune to theoretical criticisms. Whatever it appears to be from mere inspection, it is a real measure of intelligence. Henceforth it stands or falls with the scale as a whole.

The reader will understand, of course, that no single test used alone will determine accurately the general level of intelligence. A great many tests are required; and for two reasons: (1) because intelligence has many aspects; and (2) in order to overcome the accidental influences of training or environment. If many tests are used no one of them need show more than a moderately high correlation with the scale as a whole. As stated by Binet, "Let the tests be rough, if there are only enough of them."

FOOTNOTES:

[19] See p. 52 *ff.* for method used to avoid accidental selection of subjects for the Stanford investigation.

[20] See Chapter VI for discussion of the significance of various I Q's.

[21] See p. 12 *ff.*

[22] For discussion of the supposed advantages of the "point-scale method," see Yerkes and Bridges: *A New Point Scale for Measuring Mental Ability.* (Warwick and York, 1915.)

[23] It will be remembered that this series of tests did not follow up and test those who had been promoted to high school.

[24] For an extensive summary of other data on the variability of the sexes see the article by Leta S. Hollingworth, in *The American Journal of Sociology* (January, 1914), pp. 510–30. It is shown that the findings of others support the conclusions set forth above.

[25] The results of this comparison have been set forth in detail in the monograph of source material and some of the conclusions have been set forth on p. 115 *ff.* of the present volume.

[26] See p. 24 *ff.*

[27] See Chapter VI for further discussion of the school progress possible to children of various I Q's.

CHAPTER VI
THE SIGNIFICANCE OF VARIOUS INTELLIGENCE QUOTIENTS

Frequency of different degrees of intelligence.

Before we can interpret the results of an examination it is necessary to know how frequently an I Q of the size found occurs among unselected children. Our tests of 1000 unselected children enable us to answer this question with some degree of definiteness. A study of these 1000 I Q's shows the following significant facts:—

The lowest	1%	go to	70	or below,	the highest			1%	reach	130	or above	
"	"	2%	" "	73	"	"	"	"	2%	"	128	"	"
"	"	3%	" "	76	"	"	"	"	3%	"	125	"	"
"	"	5%	" "	78	"	"	"	"	5%	"	122	"	"
"	"	10%	" "	85	"	"	"	"	10%	"	116	"	"
"	"	15%	" "	88	"	"	"	"	15%	"	113	"	"
"	"	20%	" "	91	"	"	"	"	20%	"	110	"	"
"	"	25%	" "	92	"	"	"	"	25%	"	108	"	"
"	"	33⅓%	" "	95	"	"	"	"	33⅓%	"	106	"	"

Or, to put some of the above facts in another form:—

The child reaching	110	is equalled or excelled by	20	out of 100
"	" "	(about)	115	"	"	"	"	"	10	" " "
"	"	"	"	125	"	"	"	"	"	3	" " "
"	"	"	"	130	"	"	"	"	"	1	" " "

Conversely, we may say regarding the subnormals that:—

The child testing at (about)	90	is equalled or excelled by	80	out of 100
"	"	"	"	"	85	"	"	"	"	"	90	" " "
"	"	"	"	"	75	"	"	"	"	"	97	" " "
"	"	"	"	"	70	"	"	"	"	"	99	" " "

Classification of intelligence quotients.

What do the above I Q's imply in such terms as feeble-mindedness, border-line intelligence, dullness, normality, superior intelligence genius, etc.? When we use these terms two facts must be borne in mind: (1) That the boundary lines between such groups are absolutely arbitrary, a matter of definition only; and (2) that the individuals comprising one of the groups do not make up a homogeneous type.

Nevertheless, since terms like the above are convenient and will probably continue to be used, it is desirable to give them as much definiteness as possible. On the basis of the tests we have made, including many cases of all grades of intelligence, the following suggestions are offered for the classification of intelligence quotients:—

I Q	Classification
Above 140	"Near" genius or genius.
120–140	Very superior intelligence.
110–120	Superior intelligence.
90–110	Normal, or average, intelligence.
80– 90	Dullness, rarely classifiable as feeble-mindedness.
70– 80	Border-line deficiency, sometimes classifiable as dullness, often as feeble-mindedness.
Below 70	Definite feeble-mindedness.

Of the feeble-minded, those between 50 and 70 I Q include most of the morons (high, middle, and low), those between 20 or 25 and 50 are ordinarily to be classed as imbeciles, and those below 20 or 25 as idiots. According to this classification the adult idiot would range up to about 3-year intelligence as the limit, the adult imbecile would have a mental level between 3 and 7 years, and the adult moron would range from about 7-year to 11-year intelligence.

It should be added, however, that the classification of I Q's for the various sub-grades of feeble-mindedness is not very secure, for the reason that the exact curves of mental growth have not been worked out for such grades. As far as the public schools are concerned this does not greatly matter, as they never enroll idiots and very rarely even the high-grade imbecile. School defectives are practically all of the moron and border-line grades, and these it is important teachers should be able to recognize. The following discussions and illustrative cases will perhaps give a fairly definite idea of the significance of various grades of intelligence.[28]

Feeble-mindedness (rarely above 75 I Q.)

There are innumerable grades of mental deficiency ranging from somewhat below average intelligence to profound idiocy. In the literal sense every individual below the average is more or less mentally weak or feeble. Only a relatively small proportion of these, however, are technically known as feeble-minded. It is therefore necessary to set forth the criterion as to what constitutes feeble-mindedness in the commonly accepted sense of that word.

The definition in most general use is the one framed by the Royal College of Physicians and Surgeons of London, and adopted by the English Royal Commission on Mental Deficiency. It is substantially as follows:—

A feeble-minded person is one who is incapable, because of mental defect existing from birth or from an early age, (a) of competing on equal terms with his normal fellows; or (b) of managing himself or his affairs with ordinary prudence.

Two things are to be noted in regard to this definition: In the first place, it is stated in terms of social and industrial efficiency. Such efficiency, however, depends not merely on the degree of intelligence, but also on emotional, moral, physical, and social traits as well. This explains why some individuals with I Q somewhat below 75 can hardly be classed as feeble-minded in the ordinary sense of the term, while others with I Q a little above 75 could hardly be classified in any other group.

In the second place, the criterion set up by the definition is not very definite because of the vague meaning of the expression "ordinary prudence." Even the expression "competing on equal terms" cannot be taken literally, else it would include also those who are merely dull. It is the second part of the definition that more nearly expresses the popular criterion, for as long as an individual manages his affairs in such a way as to be self-supporting, and in such a way as to avoid becoming a nuisance or burden to his fellowmen, he escapes the institutions for defectives and may pass for normal.

The most serious defect of the definition comes from the lax interpretation of the term "ordinary prudence," etc. The popular standard is so low that hundreds of thousands of high grade defectives escape identification as such. Moreover, there are many grades of severity in social and industrial competition. For example, most of the members of such families as the Jukes, the Nams, the Hill Folk, and the Kallikaks are able to pass as normal in their own crude environment, but when compelled to compete with average American stock their deficiency becomes evident. It is therefore necessary to supplement the social criterion with a more strictly psychological one.

For this purpose there is nothing else as significant as the I Q. All who test below 70 I Q by the Stanford revision of the Binet-Simon scale should be considered feeble-minded, and it is an open question whether it would not be justifiable to consider 75 I Q as the lower limit of "normal" intelligence. Certainly a large proportion falling between 70 and 75 can hardly be classed as other than feeble-minded, even according to the social criterion.

Examples of feeble-minded school children

F. C. Boy, age 8-6; mental age 4-2; I Q approximately 50. From a very superior home. Has had the best medical care and other attention. Attended a private kindergarten until rejected because he required so much of the teacher's time and appeared uneducable. Will probably develop to about the 6- or 7-year mental level. High grade imbecile. Has since been committed to a state institution. Cases as low as F. C. very rarely get into the public schools.

R. W. Boy, age 13-10; mental age 7-6; I Q approximately 55. Home excellent. Is pubescent. Because of age and maturity has been promoted to the third grade, though he can hardly do the work of the second. Has attended school more than six years. Will probably never develop much if any beyond 8 years, and will never be self-supporting. Low-grade moron.

FIG. 4. DIAMOND DRAWN BY R. W., AGE 13-10; MENTAL AGE 7-6

M. S. Girl, age 7-6; mental age 4-6; I Q 60. Father a gardener, home conditions and medical attention fair. Has twice attempted first grade, but without learning to read more than a few words. In each case teacher requested parents to withdraw her. "Takes" things. Is considered "foolish" by the other children. Will probably never develop beyond a mental level of 8 years.

R. M. Boy, age 15; mental age 9; I Q 60. Decidedly superior home environment and care. After attending school eight years is in fifth grade, though he cannot do the work of the fourth grade. Parents unable to teach him to respect property. Boys torment him and make his life miserable. At middle-moron level and has probably about reached the limit of his development. Has since been committed to a state institution.

FIG. 5. WRITING FROM DICTATION. R. M., AGE 15; MENTAL AGE 9

S. M. Girl, age 19-2; mental age 10; I Q approximately 65 (not counting age beyond 16). From very superior family. Has attended public and private schools twelve years and has been promoted to seventh grade, where she cannot do the work. Appears docile and childlike, but is subject to spells of disobedience and stubbornness. Did not walk until 4 years old. Plays with young children. Susceptible to attention from men and has to be constantly guarded. Writing excellent, knows the number combinations, but missed all the absurdities and has the vocabulary of an average 10-year-old. The type from which prostitutes often come.

R. H. Boy, age 14; mental age 8-4; I Q 65. Father Irish, mother Spanish. Family comfortable and home care average. Has attended school eight years and is unable to do fourth-grade work satisfactorily. Health excellent and attendance regular. Reads in fourth reader without expression and with little comprehension of what is read. Fair skill in number combinations. Writing and drawing very poor. Cannot use a ruler. Has no conception of an inch.

R. H. is described as high-tempered, irritable, lacking in physical activity, clumsy, and unsteady. Plays little. Just "stands around." Indifferent to praise or blame, has little sense of duty, plays underhand tricks. Is slow, absent-minded, easily confused, in thought, never shows appreciation or interest. So apathetic that he does not hear commands. Voice droning. Speech poor in colloquial expressions.

Three years later, at age of 17, was in a special class attempting sixth-grade work. Reported as doing "absolutely nothing" in that grade. Still sullen, indifferent, and slow in grasping directions, and lacking in play interests. "No apperception of anything, but has mastered such mechanical things as reading (calling the words) and the fundamentals in arithmetic."

In school work, moral traits, and out-of-school behavior R. H. shows himself to be a typical case of moron deficiency.

I. M. Girl, age 14-2; mental age 9; I Q approximately 65. Father a laborer. Does unsatisfactory work in fourth grade. Plays with little girls. A menace to the morals of the school because of her sex interests and lack of self-restraint. Rather good-looking if one does not hunt for appearances of intelligence. Mental reactions intolerably slow. Will develop but little further and will always pass as feeble-minded in any but the very lowest social environment.

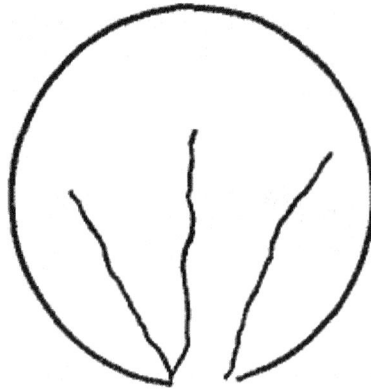

FIG. 6. BALL AND FIELD TEST. I. M., AGE 14-2; MENTAL AGE 9

G. V. Boy, age 10; mental age 6-4; I Q 65. Father Spanish, mother English. Family poor but fairly respectable. Brothers and sisters all retarded. In high first grade. Work all very poor except writing, drawing, and hand work, in all of which he excels. Is quiet and inactive, lacks self-confidence, and plays little. Mentally slow, inert, "thick," and inattentive. Health fair.

Three years later G. V. was in the low third grade and still doing extremely poor work in everything except manual training, drawing, and writing. Is not likely ever to go beyond the fourth or fifth grade however long he remains in school.

V. J. Girl, age 11-6; mental age 8; I Q 70. Has been tested three times in the last five years, always with approximately the same result in terms of I Q. Home fair to inferior. Has been in a special class two years and in school altogether nearly six years. Is barely able to do third-grade work. Her feeble-mindedness is recognized by teachers and by other pupils. Belongs at about middle-moron to high-moron level.

A. W. Boy, age 9-4; mental age 7; I Q 75. A year and a half ago he tested at 6-2. From superior family, brothers of very superior intelligence. In school three years and has made about a grade and a half. Has higher I Q than V. J. described above, but his deficiency is fully as evident. Is generally recognized as mentally defective. Slyly abstracted one of the pennies used in the test and slipped it into his pocket. Has caused much trouble at school by puncturing bicycle tires. High-grade moron.

FIG. 7. DIAMOND DRAWN BY A. W.

A. C. Boy, age 12; mental age 8-5; I Q 70. From Portuguese family of ten children. Has a feeble-minded brother. Parents in comfortable circumstances and respectable. A. C. has attended school regularly since he was 6 years old. Trying unsuccessfully to do the work of the fourth grade. Reads poorly in the third reader. Hesitates, repeats, miscalls words, and never gets the thought. Writes about like a first-grade pupil. Cannot solve such simple problems as "How many marbles can you buy for ten cents if one marble costs five cents?" even when he has marbles and money in his hands. Described by teacher as "mentally slow and inert, inattentive, easily distracted, memory poor, ideas vague and often absurd, does not appreciate stories, slow at comprehending commands." Is also described as "unruly, boisterous, disobedient, stubborn, and lacking sense of propriety. Tattles."

Three years later, at age of 15, was in a special class and was little if any improved. He had, however, learned the mechanics of reading and had mastered the number combinations. Deficiencies described as "of wide range." Conduct, however, had improved. Was "working hard to get on."

A. C. must be considered definitely feeble-minded.

H. S. Boy, age 11; mental age 8-3; I Q approximately 75. At 8 years tested at 6. Parents highly educated, father a scholar. Brother and sister of very superior intelligence. Started to school at 7, but was withdrawn because of lack of progress. Started again at 8 and is now doing poor work in the second grade. Weakly and nervous. Painfully aware of his inability to learn. During the test keeps saying, "I tried anyway," "It's all I can do if I try my best, ain't it?" etc. Regarded defective by other children. Will probably never be able to do work beyond the fourth or fifth grade and is not likely to develop above the 11-year level, if as high.

FIG. 8. DRAWING DESIGNS FROM MEMORY. H. S., AGE 11; MENTAL AGE 8-3

I. S. Boy, age 9-6; mental age 7; I Q 75. German parentage. Started to school at 6. Now in low second grade and unable to do the work. Health good. Inattentive, mentally slow and inert, easily distracted, speech is monotone. Equally poor in reading, writing, and numbers. I. S. is described as quiet, sullen, indifferent, lazy, and stubborn. Plays little.

Three years later had advanced from low second to low fourth grade, but was as poor as ever in his school work. "Miscalls the simplest words." Moral traits unsatisfactory. May reach sixth or seventh grade if he remains in school long enough.

I. S. learned to walk at 2 years and to talk at 3.

The above are cases of such marked deficiency that there could be no disagreement among competent judges in classifying them in the group of "feeble-minded." All are definitely institutional cases. It is a matter of record, however, that one of the cases, H. S., was diagnosed by a physician (without test) as "backward but not a defective." and with the added encouragement that "the backwardness will be outgrown." Of course the reverse is the case; the deficiency is becoming more and more apparent as the boy approaches the age where more is expected of him.

In at least three of the above cases (S. M., I. S., and I. M.) the teachers had not identified the backwardness as feeble-mindedness. Not far from 2 children out of 100, or 2 out of 1000, in the average public school are as defective as some of those just described. Teachers get so accustomed to seeing a few of them in every group of 200 or 300 pupils that they are likely to regard them as merely dull,—"dreadfully dull," of course,—but not defective.

Children like these, for their own good and that of other pupils, should be kept out of the regular classes. They will rarely be equal to the work of the fifth grade, however long they attend school. They will make a little progress in a well-managed special class, but with the approach of adolescence, at latest, the State should take them into custodial care for its own protection.

Border-line cases (usually between 70 and 80 I Q).

The border-line cases are those which fall near the boundary generally recognized as such and the higher group usually classed as normal but dull. They are the doubtful cases, the ones we are always trying (rarely with success) to restore to normality.

It must be emphasized, however, that this doubtful group is not marked off by definite I Q limits. Some children with I Q as high as 75 or even 80 will have to be classified as feeble-minded; some as low as 70 I Q may be so well endowed in other mental traits that they may manage as adults to get along fairly well in a simple environment. The ability to compete with one's fellows in the social and industrial world does not depend upon intelligence alone. Such factors as moral traits, industry, environment to be encountered, personal appearance, and influential relatives are also involved. Two children classified above as feeble-minded had an I Q as high as 75. In these cases the emotional, moral, or physical qualities were so defective as to render a normal social life out of the question. This is occasionally true even with an I Q as high as 80. Some of the border-line cases, with even less intelligence, may be so well endowed in other mental traits that they are capable of becoming dependable unskilled laborers, and of supporting a family after a fashion.

Examples of border-line deficiency

S. F. Girl, age 17; mental age 11-6; I Q approximately 72 (disregarding age above 16 years). Father intelligent; mother probably high-grade defective. Lives in a good home with aunt, who is a woman of good sense and skillful in her management of the girl. S. F. has attended excellent schools for eleven years and has recently been promoted to the seventh grade. The teacher admits, however, that she cannot do the work of that grade, but says, "I haven't the heart to let her fail in the sixth grade for the third time." She studies very hard and says she wants to become a teacher! At the time the test was made she was actually studying her books from two to three hours daily at home. The aunt, who is very intelligent, had never thought of this girl as feeble-minded, and had suffered much concern and humiliation because of her inability to teach her to conduct herself properly toward men and not to appropriate other people's property.

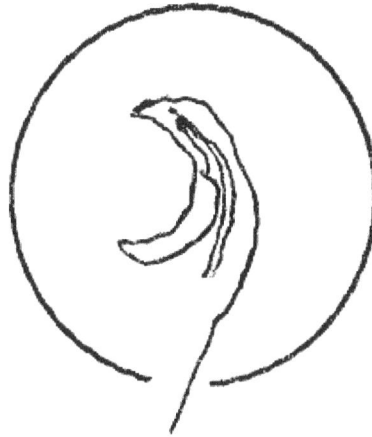

FIG. 9. BALL AND FIELD TEST S. F., AGE 17; MENTAL AGE 11-6

S. F. is ordinarily docile, but is subject to fits of anger and obstinacy. She finally determined to leave her home, threatening to take up with a man unless allowed to work elsewhere. Since then she has been tried out in several families, but after a little while in a place she flies into a rage and leaves. She is a fairly capable houseworker when she tries.

This young woman is feeble-minded and should be classed as such. She is listed here with the border-line cases simply for the reason that she belongs to a group whose mental deficiency is almost never recognized without the aid of a psychological test. Probably no physician could be found who would diagnose the case, on the basis of a medical examination alone, as one of feeble-mindedness.

F. H. Boy, age 16-6; mental age 11-5; I Q approximately 72 (disregarding age above 16 years). Tested for three successive years without change of more than four points in I Q. Father a laborer, dull, subject to fits of rage, and beats the boy. Mother not far from border-line. F. H. has always had the best of school advantages and has been promoted to the seventh grade. Is really about equal to fifth-grade work. Fairly rapid and accurate in number combinations, but cannot solve arithmetical problems which require any reasoning. Reads with reasonable fluency, but with little understanding. Appears exceedingly good-natured, but was once suspended from school for hurling bricks at a fellow pupil. Played a "joke" on another pupil by fastening a dangerous, sharp-pointed, steel paper-file in the pupil's seat for him to sit down on. He is cruel, stubborn, and plays truant, but is fairly industrious when he gets a job as errand or delivery boy. Discharged once for taking money.

F. H. is generally called "queer," but is not ordinarily thought of as feeble-minded. His deficiency is real, however, and it is altogether doubtful whether he will be able to make a living and to keep out of trouble, though he is now (at age 20) employed as messenger boy for the Western Union at $30 per month. This is considerably less than pick-and-shovel men get in the community where he lives. Delinquents and criminals often belong to this level of intelligence.

W. C. Boy, age 16-8; mental age 12; I Q 75 (disregarding age above 16 years). Father a college professor. All the other children in the family of unusually superior intelligence. When tested (four years ago) was trying to do seventh-grade work, but with little success. Wanted to leave school and learn farming, but father insisted on his getting the usual grammar-school and high-school education. Made $25 one summer by raising vegetables on a vacant lot. In the four years since the test was made he has managed to get into high school. Teachers say that in spite of his best efforts he learns next to nothing, and they regard him as hopelessly dull. Is docile, lacks all aggressiveness, looks stupid, and has head circumference an inch below normal.

Here is a most pitiful case of the overstimulated backward child in a superior family. Instead of nagging at the boy and urging him on to attempt things which are impossible to his inferior intelligence, his parents should take him out of school and put him at some kind of work which he could do. If the boy had been the son of a common laborer he would probably have left school early and have become a dependable and contented laborer. In a very simple environment he would probably not be considered defective.

C. P. Boy, age 10-2; mental age 7-11; I Q 78. Portuguese boy, son of a skilled laborer. One of eleven children, most of whom have about this same grade of intelligence. Has attended school regularly for four years. Is in the third grade, but cannot do the work. Except for extreme stubbornness his social development is fairly normal. Capable in plays and games, but is regarded as impossible in his school work. Like his brother, M. P., the next case to be described, he will doubtless become a fairly reliable laborer at unskilled work and will not be regarded, in his rather simple environment, as a defective. From the psychological point of view, however, his deficiency is real. He will probably never develop beyond the 11- or 12-year level or be able to do satisfactory school work beyond the fifth or sixth grade.

FIG. 10. WRITING FROM DICTATION. C. P., AGE 10-2; MENTAL AGE 7-11

M. P. Boy, age 14; mental age 10-8; I Q 77. Has been tested four successive years, I Q being always between 75 and 80. Brother to C. P. above. In school nearly eight years and has been promoted to the fifth grade. At 16 was doing poor work in the sixth grade. Good school advantages, as the father has tried conscientiously to give his children "a good education." Perfectly normal in appearance and in play activities and is liked by other children. Seems to be thoroughly dependable both in school and in his outside work. Will probably become an excellent laborer and will pass as perfectly normal, notwithstanding a grade of intelligence which will not develop above 11 or 12 years.

FIG. 11. BALL AND FIELD TEST. M. P., AGE 14; MENTAL AGE 10-8

What shall we say of cases like the last two which test at high-grade moronity or at border-line, but are well enough endowed in moral and personal traits to pass as normal in an uncomplicated social environment? According to the classical definition of feeble-mindedness such individuals cannot be considered defectives. Hardly any one would think of them as institutional cases. Among laboring men and servant girls there are thousands like them. They are the world's "hewers of wood and drawers of water." And yet, as far as intelligence is concerned, the tests have told the truth. These boys are uneducable beyond the merest rudiments of training. No amount of school instruction will ever make them intelligent voters or capable citizens in the true sense of the word. Judged psychologically they cannot be considered normal.

It is interesting to note that M. P. and C. P. represent the level of intelligence which is very, very common among Spanish-Indian and Mexican families of the Southwest and also among negroes. Their dullness seems to be racial, or at least inherent in the family stocks from which they come. The fact that one meets this type with such extraordinary frequency among Indians, Mexicans, and negroes suggests quite forcibly that the whole question of racial differences in mental traits will have to be taken up anew and by experimental methods. The writer predicts that when this is done there will be discovered enormously significant racial differences in general intelligence, differences which cannot be wiped out by any scheme of mental culture.

Children of this group should be segregated in special classes and be given instruction which is concrete and practical. They cannot master abstractions, but they can often be made efficient workers, able to look out for themselves.

There is no possibility at present of convincing society that they should not be allowed to reproduce, although from a eugenic point of view they constitute a grave problem because of their unusually prolific breeding.

Dull normals (I Q usually 80 to 90).

In this group are included those children who would not, according to any of the commonly accepted social standards, be considered feeble-minded, but who are nevertheless far enough below the actual average of intelligence among races of western European descent that they cannot make ordinary school progress or master other intellectual difficulties which average children are equal to. A few of this class test as low as 75 to 80 I Q, but the majority are not far from 85. The unmistakably normal children who go much below this (in California, at least) are usually Mexicans, Indians, or negroes.

R. G. Negro boy, age 13-5; mental age 10-6; I Q approximately 80. Normal in appearance and conduct, but very dull. Is attempting fifth-grade work in a special class, but is failing. From a fairly good home and has had ordinary school advantages. In the examination his intelligence is very even as far as it goes, but stops rather abruptly after the 10-year tests. Will unquestionably pass as normal among unskilled laborers, but his intelligence will never exceed the 12-year level and he is not likely to advance beyond the seventh grade, if as far.

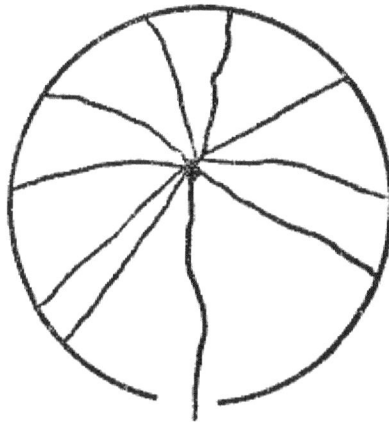

FIG. 12. BALL AND FIELD. R. G., AGE 13-5, MENTAL AGE 10-6

F. D. Boy, tested at age 10-2; I Q 83, and again at 14-1; I Q 79. Mental age in the first test was 8-6 and in the second test 11. Son of a barber. Father dead; mother capable; makes a good home, and cares for her children well. At 10 was doing unsatisfactory work in the fourth grade, and at 12 unsatisfactory work in low sixth. Good-looking, normal in appearance and social development, and though occasionally obstinate is usually steady. Any one unacquainted with his poor school work and low I Q would consider him perfectly normal. No physical or moral handicaps of any kind that could possibly account for his retardation. Is simply dull. Needs purely a vocational training, but may be able to complete the eighth grade with low marks by the age of 16 or 17.

G. G. Girl, age 12-4; mental age 10-10; I Q 82. From average home. Excellent educational advantages and no physical handicaps. At 12 years was doing very poor work in fifth grade. Appearance, play life, and attitude toward other children normal. Simply dull. Will probably never go beyond the 12- or 13-year level and is not likely to get as far as the high school.

Those testing 80 and 90 will usually be able to reach the eighth grade, but ordinarily only after from one to three or four failures. They are so very numerous (about 15 per cent of the school enrollment) that it is doubtful whether we can expect soon to have special classes enough to accommodate all. The most feasible solution is a differentiated course of study with parallel classes in which every child will be allowed to make the best progress of which he is capable, without incurring the risk of failure and non-promotion. The so-called Mannheim system, or something similar to it, is what we need.

Average intelligence (I Q 90 to 110).

It is often said that the schools are made for the average child, but that "the average child does not exist." He does exist, and in very large numbers. About 60 per cent of all school children test between 90 and 110 I Q, and about 40 per cent between 95 and 105. That these children are average is attested by their school records as well as by their I Q's. Our records show that, of more than 200 children below 14 years of age and with I Q between 95 and 105, not one was making much more nor much less than average school progress. Four were two years retarded, but in each case this was due to late start, illness, or irregular attendance. Children who test close to 90, however, often fail to get along satisfactorily, while those testing near 110 are occasionally able to win an extra promotion.

The children of this average group are seldom school problems, as far as ability to learn is concerned. Nor are they as likely to cause trouble in discipline as the dull and border-line cases. It is therefore hardly necessary to give illustrative cases here.

The high school, however, does not fit their grade of intelligence as well as the elementary and grammar schools. High schools probably enroll a disproportionate number of pupils in the I Q range above 100. That is, the average intelligence among high-school pupils is above the average for the population in general. It is probably not far from 110. College students are, of course, a still more selected group, perhaps coming chiefly from the range above 115. The child whose school marks are barely average in the elementary grades, when measured against children in general, will ordinarily earn something less than average marks in high school, and perhaps excessively poor marks in college.

Superior intelligence (I Q 110 to 120).

Children of this group ordinarily make higher marks and are capable of making somewhat more rapid progress than the strictly average child. Perhaps most of them could complete the eight grades in seven years as easily as the average child does in eight years. They are not usually the best scholars, but on a scale of excellent, good, fair, poor, and failure they will usually rank as good, though of course the degree of application is a factor. It is rare, however, to find a child of this level who is positively indolent in his school work or who dislikes school. In high school they are likely to win about the average mark.

Intelligence of 110 to 120 I Q is approximately five times as common among children of superior social status as among children of inferior social status; the proportion among the former being about 24 per cent of all, and among the latter only 5 per cent of all. The group is made up largely of children of the fairly successful mercantile or professional classes.

The total number of children between 110 and 120 is almost exactly the same as the number between 80 and 90; namely, about 15 per cent. The distance between these two groups (say between 85 and 115) is as great as the distance between average intelligence and border-line deficiency, and it would be absurd to suppose that they could be taught to best advantage in the same classes. As a matter of fact, pupils between 110 and 120 are usually held back to the rate of progress which the average child can make. They are little encouraged to do their best.

Very superior intelligence (I Q 120 to 140).

Children of this group are better than somewhat above average. They are unusually superior. Not more than 3 out of 100 go as high as 125 I Q, and only about 1 out of 100 as high as 130. In the schools of a city of average population only about 1 child in 250 or 300 tests as high as 140 I Q.

In a series of 476 unselected children there was not a single one reaching 120 whose social class was described as "below average."[29] Of the children of superior social status, about 10 per cent reached 120 or better. The 120–140 group is made up almost entirely of children whose parents belong to the professional or very successful business classes. The child of a skilled laborer belongs here occasionally, the child of a common laborer very rarely indeed. At least this is true in the smaller cities of California among populations made up of native-born Americans. In all probability it would not have been true in the earlier history of the country when ordinary labor was more often than now performed by men of average intelligence, and it would probably not hold true now among certain immigrant populations of good stock, but limited social and educational advantages.

What can children of this grade of ability do in school? The question cannot be answered as satisfactorily as one could wish, for the simple reason that such children are rarely permitted to do what they can. What they do accomplish is as follows: Of 54 children (of the 1000 unselected cases) falling in this group, 12½ per cent were advanced in the grades two years, approximately 54 per cent were advanced one year, 28 per cent were in the grade where they belonged by chronological age, and three children, or 5½ per cent, were actually retarded one year. But wherever located, such children rarely get anything but the highest marks, and the evidence goes to show that most of them could easily be prepared for high school by the age of 12 years. Serious injury is done them by schools which believe in "putting on the brakes."

The following are illustrations of children testing between 130 and 145. Not all are taken from the 1000 unselected tests. The writer has discovered several children of this grade as a result of lectures before teachers' institutes. It is his custom, in such lectures, to ask the teachers to bring in for a demonstration test the "brightest child in the city" (or county, etc.). The I Q resulting from such a test is usually between 130 and 140, occasionally a little higher.

Examples of very superior intelligence

Margaret P. Age 8-10; mental age 11-1; I Q 130. Father only a skilled laborer (house painter), but a man of unusual intelligence and character for his social class. Home care above average. M. P. has attended school a little less than three years and is completing fourth grade. Marks all "excellent." Health perfect. Social and moral traits of the very best. Is obedient, conscientious, and unusually reliable for her age. Quiet and confident bearing, but no touch of vanity.

M. P. is known to be related on her father's side to John Wesley, and her maternal grandfather was a highly skilled mechanic and the inventor of an important train-coupling device used on all railroads.

Although she is not yet 9 years old and is completing the fourth grade, she is still about a grade below where she belongs by mental age. She could no doubt easily be made ready for high school by the age of 12.

J. R. Girl, age 12-9; mental age 16 (average adult); I Q approximately 130. Daughter of a university professor. In first year of high school. From first grade up her marks have been nearly all of the A rank. For first semester of high school four of six grades were A, the others B. A wonderfully charming, delightful girl in every respect. Play life perfectly normal.

J. R.'s parents have moved about a great deal and she has attended eight different schools. She is two years above grade in school, but of this gain only one-half grade was made in school; *the other grade and a half she gained in a little over a year by staying out of school and working a little each day under the instruction of her mother.* But for this she would doubtless now be in the seventh grade instead of in high school. As it is she is at least a grade below where she belongs by mental age. Something better than an average college record may be safely predicted for J. R.

E. B. Girl, age 7-9; mental age 10-2; I Q 130. E. B. was selected by the teachers of a small California city as the brightest school child in that city (school population about 500). Her parents are said to be unusually intelligent. E. B. is in the third grade, a year advanced, but her mental level shows that she belongs in the fourth. The test was made as a demonstration test in the presence of about 150 teachers, all of whom were charmed by her delightful personality and keen responses. No trace of vanity or queerness of any kind. Health excellent. E. B. ought to be ready for high school at 12; she will really have the intelligence to do high-school work by 11.

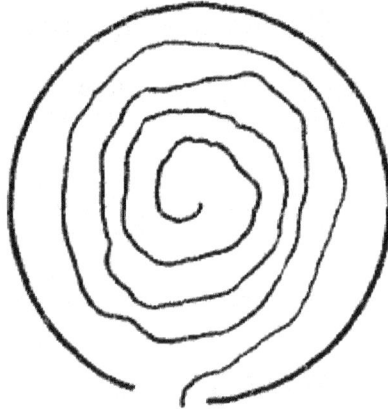

FIG. 13. BALL AND FIELD TEST. E. B., AGE 7-9; I Q 130

L. B. Girl, age 8-6; mental age 11-6; I Q 135. Tested nearly three years earlier, age 5-11; mental age 7-6; I Q 127. Daughter of a university professor. At age of 8-6 was doing very superior work in the fifth grade. Later, at age of 10-6, is in the seventh grade with all her marks excellent. Has two sisters who test almost as high, both completing the eighth grade at barely 12 years of age. L. B. looks rather delicate, and though a little nervous is ordinarily strong. We have known her since her early childhood. Like both her sisters, she is a favorite with young and old, as nearly perfection as the most charming little girl could be.

R. S. Boy, age 6-5; mental age 9-6; I Q 148. When tested at age 5-2 he had a mental age of 7-6, I Q 142. Father a university professor. R. S. entered school at exactly 6 years of age, and at the present writing is 7½ years old and is entering the third grade. Leads his class in school and takes delight in the work. Is normal in play life and social traits and is dependable and thoughtful beyond his years. Should enter high school not later than 12; could probably be made ready a year earlier, but as he is somewhat nervous this might not be wise.

T. F. Boy, age 10-6; mental age 14; I Q 133. At 13-6 tested at "superior adult," and had vocabulary of 13,000 (also "superior adult"). Son of a college professor. Did not go to school till age of 9 years and was not taught to read till 8½. At this writing he is 15½ years old and is a senior in high school. He will complete the high-school course in three and one-half years with A to B marks, mostly A. Gets his hardest mathematics lessons in five to ten minutes. Science is his play. When he discovered Hodge's *Nature Study and Life* at age of 11 years he literally slept with the book till he almost knew it by heart. Since age 12 he has given much time to magazines on mechanics and electricity. At 13 he installed a wireless apparatus without other aid than his electrical magazines. He has, for a boy of his age, a rather remarkable understanding of the principles underlying electrical applications. He is known by his playmates as "the boy with a hobby." Stamp collections, butterfly and moth collections (over 70 different varieties), seashore collections, and wireless apparatus all show that the appellation is fully merited. He chooses his hobbies and "rides" them entirely on his own initiative.

J. S. Boy, age 8-2; mental age 11-4; I Q 138. Father was a lawyer, parents now dead. Is in high fourth grade. Leads his class. Attractive, healthy, normal-appearing lad. Full of good humor. Is loving and obedient, strongly attached to his foster mother (an aunt). Composes verses and fables for pastime. Here are a couple of verses composed before his eighth birthday. They are reproduced without change of spelling or punctuation:—

Christmas

Hurrah for Christmas
And all it's joy's
That come that day
For girls and boy's.

Flowers

Flowers in the garden.
That is all you see
Who likes them best?
That's the honey bee.

J. S. ought to be in the fifth grade, instead of the fourth. He will easily be able to enter college by the age of 15 if he is allowed to make the progress which would be normal to a child of his intelligence. But it is too much to expect that the school will permit this.

F. McA. Boy, age 10-3; mental age 14-6; I Q 142. Father a school principal. F. is leading his class of 24 pupils in the high seventh grade. Has received so many extra promotions only because his father insisted that the teachers allow him to try the next grade. The dire consequences which they predicted have never followed. F. is perfectly healthy and one of the most attractive lads the writer has ever seen. He has the normal play instincts, but when not at play he has the dignified bearing of a young prince, although without vanity. His vocabulary is 9000 (14 years), and his ability is remarkably even in all directions. F. should easily enter college by the age of 15.

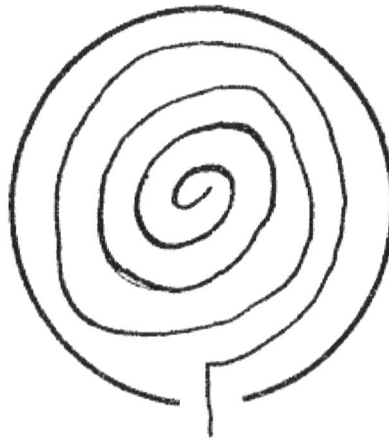

FIG. 14. BALL AND FIELD F. McA., AGE 10-3, MENTAL AGE 14-6

E. M. Boy, age 6-11; mental age 10; I Q 145. Learned to read at age of 5 without instruction and shortly afterward had learned from geography maps the capitals of all the States of the Union. Started to school at 7½. Entered the first grade at 9 A.M. and had been promoted to the fourth grade by 3 P.M. of the same day! Has now attended school a half-year and is in the fifth grade, age 7 years, 8 months. Father is on the faculty of a university.

E. M. is as superior in personal and moral traits as in intelligence. Responsible, sturdy, playful, full of humor, loving, obedient. Health is excellent. Has had no home instruction in school work. His progress has been perfectly natural.

The above list of "very superior" children includes only a few of those we have tested who belong to this grade of intelligence. Every child in the list is so interesting that it is hard to omit any. We have found all such children (with one or two exceptions not included here) so superior to average children in all sorts of mental and moral traits that one is at a loss to understand how the popular superstitions about the "queerness" of bright children could have originated or survived. Nearly every child we have found with I Q above 140 is the kind one feels, before the test is over, one would like to adopt. If the crime of kidnaping could ever be forgiven it would be in the case of a child like one of these.

FIG. 15. DRAWING DESIGNS FROM MEMORY. E. M., AGE 6-11; MENTAL AGE 10, I Q 145
(This performance is satisfactory for year 10)

Genius and "near" genius.

Intelligence tests have not been in use long enough to enable us to define genius definitely in terms of I Q. The following two cases are offered as among the highest test records of which the writer has personal knowledge. It is doubtful whether more than one child in 10,000 goes as high as either. One case has been reported, however, in which the I Q was not far from 200. Such a record, if reliable, is certainly phenomenal.

E. F. Russian boy, age 8-5; mental age 13; I Q approximately 155. Mother is a university student apparently of very superior intelligence. E. F. has a sister almost as remarkable as himself. E. F. is in the sixth grade and at the head of his class. Although about four grades advanced beyond his chronological age he is still one grade retarded! He could easily carry seventh-grade work. In all probability E. F. could be made ready for college by the age of 12 years without injury to body or mind. His mother has taken the only sensible course; she has encouraged him without subjecting him to overstimulation.

E. F. was selected for the test as probably one of the brightest children in a city of a third of a million population. He may not be the brightest in that city, but he is one of the three or four most intelligent the writer has found after a good deal of searching. He is probably equaled by not more than one in several thousand unselected children. How impatiently one waits to see the fruit of such a budding genius!

B. F. Son of a minister, age 7-8; mental age 12-4; I Q 160. Vocabulary 7000 (12 years). This test was not made by the writer, but by one of his graduate students. The record included the *verbatim* responses, so that it was easy to verify the scoring. There can be no doubt as to the substantial accuracy of the test. This I Q of 160 is the highest one in the Stanford University records. B. F. has excellent health, normal play interests, and is a favorite among his playfellows. Parents had not thought of him as especially remarkable. He is only in the third grade, and is therefore about three grades below his mental age.

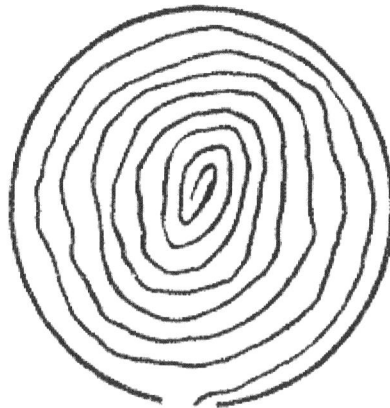

FIG. 16. BALL AND FIELD. B. F., AGE 7-8; MENTAL AGE 12-4; I Q 160 (This is a 12-year performance)

It is especially noteworthy that not one of the children we have described with I Q above 130 has ever had any unusual amount or kind of home instruction. In most cases the parents were not aware of their very great superiority. Nor can we give the credit to the school or its methods. The school has in most cases been a deterrent to their progress, rather than a help. These children have been taught in classes with average and inferior children, like those described in the first part of this chapter. Their high I Q is only an index of their extraordinary cerebral endowment. This endowment is for life. There is not the remotest probability that any of these children will deteriorate to the average level of intelligence with the onset of maturity. Such an event would be no less a miracle (barring insanity) than the development of an imbecile into a successful lawyer or physician.

Is the I Q often misleading?

Do the cases described in this chapter give a reliable picture as to what one may expect of the various I Q levels? Does the I Q furnish anything like a reliable index of an individual's general educational possibilities and of his social worth? Are there not "feeble-minded geniuses," and are there not children of exceptionally high I Q who are nevertheless fools?

We have no hesitation in saying that there is not one case in fifty in which there is any serious contradiction between the I Q and the child's performances in and out of school. We cannot deny the existence of "feeble-minded geniuses," but after a good deal of search we have not found one. Occasionally, of course, one finds a feeble-minded person who is an expert penman, who draws skillfully, who plays a musical instrument tolerably well, or who handles number combinations with unusual rapidity; but these are not geniuses; they are not authors, artists, musicians, or mathematicians.

As for exceptionally intelligent children who appear feeble-minded, we have found but one case, a boy of 10 years with an I Q of about 125. This boy, whom we have tested several times and whose development we have followed for five years, was once diagnosed by a physician as feeble-minded. His behavior among other persons than his familiar associates is such as to give this impression. Nothing less than an entire chapter would be adequate for a description of this case, which is in reality one of disturbed emotional and social development with superior intelligence.

It should be emphasized, however, that what we have said about the significance of various I Q's holds only for the I Q's secured by the use of the Stanford revision. As we have shown elsewhere (p. 62 *ff.*) the I Q yielded by other versions of the Binet tests are often so inaccurate as to be misleading.

We have not found a single child who tested between 70 and 80 I Q by the Stanford revision who was able to do satisfactory school work in the grade where he belonged by chronological age. Such children are usually from two to three grades retarded by the age of 12 years. On the other hand, the child with an I Q of 120 or above is almost never found below the grade for his chronological age, and occasionally he is one or two grades above. Wherever located, his school work is so superior as to suggest strongly the desirability of extra promotions. Those who test between 96 and 105 are almost never more than one grade above or below where they belong by chronological age, and even the small displacement of one year is usually determined by illness, age of beginning school, etc.

FOOTNOTES:

[28] The clinical descriptions to be given are not complete and are designed merely to aid the examiner in understanding the significance of intelligence quotients found.

[29] In other investigations, however, we have found even brighter children from very inferior homes. See p. 117 for an example.

CHAPTER VII
RELIABILITY OF THE BINET-SIMON METHOD

General value of the method.

In a former chapter we have noted certain imperfections of the scale devised by Binet and Simon; namely, that many of the tests were not correctly located, that the choice of tests was in a few cases unsatisfactory, that the directions for giving and scoring the tests were sometimes too indefinite, and that the upper and lower ranges of the scale especially stood in need of extensions and corrections. All of these faults have been quite generally admitted. The method itself, however, after being put to the test by psychologists of all countries and of all faiths, by the skeptical as well as the friendly, has amply demonstrated its value. The agreement on this point is as complete as it is regarding the scale's imperfections.

The following quotations from prominent psychologists who have studied the method will serve to show how it is regarded by those most entitled to an opinion:—

There can be no question about the fact that the Binet-Simon tests do not make half as frequent or half as great errors in the mental ages (of feeble-minded children) as are included in gradings based on careful, prolonged general observation by experienced observers.[30]

All of the different authors who have made these researches (with Binet's method) are in a general way unanimous in recognizing that the principle of the scale is extremely fortunate, and all believe that it offers the basis of a most useful method for the examination of intelligence.[31]

It serves as a relatively simple and speedy method of securing, by means accessible to every one, a true insight into the average level of ability of a child between 3 and 15 years of age.[32]

That, despite the differences in race and language, despite the divergences in school organization and in methods of instruction, there should be so decided agreement in the reactions of the children—is, in my opinion, the best vindication of the *principle* of the tests that one could imagine, because this agreement demonstrates that *the tests do actually reach and discover the general developmental conditions of intelligence* (so far as these are operative in public-school children of the present cultural epoch), and not mere fragments of knowledge and attainments acquired by chance.[33]

It is without doubt the most satisfactory and accurate method of determining a child's intelligence that we have, and so far superior to everything else which has been proposed that as yet there is nothing else to be considered.[34]

The value of the method lies both in the swiftness and the accuracy with which it works. One who knows how to apply the tests correctly and who is experienced in the psychological interpretation of responses can in forty minutes arrive at a more accurate judgment as to a subject's intelligence than would be possible without the tests after months or even years of close observation. The reasons for this have already been set forth. [35] The difference is something like that between measuring a person's height with a yardstick and estimating it by guess. That this is not an unfair statement of the case is well shown by the following candid confession by a psychologist who tested 200 juvenile delinquents brought before Judge Lindsey's court:—

As a matter of interest I estimated the mental ages of 150 of my subjects before testing them. In 54 of the estimates the error was not more than one year in either direction; 70 of the subjects were estimated too high, the average error being 2 years and 7 months; 26 of the subjects were estimated too low, the average error being 2 years and 2 months. *These figures would seem to imply that an estimate with nothing to support it is wholly unreliable, more especially as many of the estimates were four or five years wide of the mark.*[36]

Criticisms of the Binet method have also been frequently voiced, but chiefly by persons who have had little experience with it or by those whose scientific training hardly justifies an opinion. It cannot be too strongly emphasized that eminence in law, medicine, education, or any other profession does not of itself enable any one to pass judgment on the validity of a psychological method.

Dependence of the scale's reliability on the training of the examiner.

On this point two radically different opinions have been urged. On the one hand, some have insisted that the results of a test made by other than a thoroughly trained psychologist are absolutely worthless. At the opposite extreme are a few who seem to think that any teacher or physician can secure perfectly valid results after a few hours' acquaintance with the tests.

The dispute is one which cannot be settled by the assertion of opinion, and, unfortunately, thoroughgoing investigations have not yet been made as to the frequency and extent of errors made by untrained or partially trained examiners. The only study of this kind which has so far been reported is the following:—[37]

Dr. Kohs gives the results of tests made by 58 inexperienced teachers who were taking a summer course in the Training School at Vineland. The class met three times a week for instruction in the use of the Binet scale. During the first week the students listened to three lectures by Dr. Goddard. The second week was given over to demonstration testing. Each student saw four children tested, and attended two discussion periods of an hour each. During the third, fourth, and fifth weeks each student tested one child per week, and observed the testing of two others. The student was allowed to carry the test through in his own way, but received criticism after it was finished. Twice a week Dr. Goddard spent an hour with the class, discussing experimental procedure. The subjects tested were feeble-minded children whose exact mental ages were already known, and for this reason it was possible to check up the accuracy of each student's work.

Kohs's table of results for the trial testing of the 174 children showed:
—

1. That 50 per cent of the work was as exact as any one in the laboratory could make it;

2. That in an additional 38 per cent the results were within three fifths of a year of being exact;

3. That nearly 90 per cent of the work of the summer students was sufficiently accurate for all practical purposes;

4. That the records improved during the brief training so that during the third week only one test missed the real mental age by as much as a year.

Since hardly any of these students had had any previous experience with the Binet tests, Dr. Kohs seems to be entirely justified in his conclusion that it is possible, in the brief period of six weeks, to teach people to use the tests with a reasonable degree of accuracy.

What shall we say of the teacher or of the physician who has not even had this amount of instruction? The writer's experience forces him to agree with Binet and with Dr. Goddard, that any one with intelligence enough to be a teacher, and who is willing to devote conscientious study to the mastery of the technique, can use the scale accurately enough to get a better idea of a child's mental endowment than he could possibly get in any other way. It is necessary, however, for the untrained person to recognize his own lack of experience, and in no case would it be justifiable to base important action or scientific conclusions upon the results of the inexpert examiner. As Binet himself repeatedly insisted, the method is not absolutely mechanical, and cannot be made so by elaboration of instructions.

It is sometimes held that the examination and classification of backward children for special instruction should be carried out by the school physicians. The fact is, however, that there is nothing in the physician's training to give him any advantage over the ordinary teacher in the use of the Binet tests. Because of her more intimate knowledge of children and because of her superior tact and adaptability, the average teacher is perhaps better equipped than the average physician to give intelligence tests.

Finally, it should be emphasized that whatever the previous training or experience of the examiner may have been, his ability to adjust to the child's personality and his willingness to follow conscientiously the directions for giving the tests are important factors in his equipment.

Influence of the subject's attitude.

One continually meets such queries as, "How do you know the subject did his best?" "Possibly the child was nervous or frightened," or, "Perhaps incorrect answers were purposely given." All such objections may be disposed of by saying that the competent examiner can easily control the experiment in such a way that embarrassment is soon replaced by self-confidence, and in such a way that effort is kept at its maximum. As for mischievous deception, it would be a poor clinicist who could not recognize and deal with the little that is likely to arise.

Cautions regarding embarrassment, fatigue, fright, illness, etc. are given in <u>Chapter IX</u>. Most of the errors which have been reported along this line are such as can nearly always be avoided by ordinary prudence, coupled with a little power of observation.[38] We must not charge the mistakes of untrained and indiscreet examiners against the validity of the method itself.

It is possibly true that even if the examiner is tactful and prudent an unfavorable attitude on the part of the subject may occasionally affect the results of a test to some extent, but it ought not seriously to invalidate one examination out of five hundred. The greatest danger is in the case of a young subject who has been recently arrested and brought before a court. Even here a little common sense and scientific insight should enable one to guard against a mistaken diagnosis.

The influence of coaching.

It might be supposed that after the intelligence scale had been used with a few pupils in a given school all of their fellows would soon be apprised of the nature of the tests, and so learn the correct responses. Experience shows, however, that there is little likelihood of such influence except in the case of a small minority of the tests. Experiments in the psychology of testimony have demonstrated that children's ability to report upon a complex set of experiences is astonishingly weak. In testing with the Stanford revision a child is ordinarily given from twenty-four to thirty different tests, many of which are made up of three or more items. Of the total forty to fifty items the child is ordinarily able to report but few, and these not always correctly.

Such tests as memory for sentences and digits, drawing the square and diamond, reproducing the designs from memory, comparing weights and lines, describing and interpreting pictures, æsthetic comparison, vocabulary, dissected sentences, fables, reading for memories, finding differences and similarities, arithmetical reasoning, and the form-board test, are hardly subject to report at all. While almost any of the other tests might, theoretically, be communicated, there is little danger that many of them will be. It is assumed, of course, that the examiner will take proper precautions to prevent any of his blanks or other materials from falling into the hands of those who are to be examined.

The following tests are the ones most subject to the influence of coaching: Ball and field, giving date, naming sixty words, finding rhymes, changing hands of clock, comprehension of physical relations, "induction test," and "ingenuity test."

In several instances we have interviewed children an hour or two after they had taken the examination, in order to find out how many of the tests they could recall. A boy of 4 years, after repeated questioning, could only say: "He showed me some pictures. He had a knife and a penny. He told me to shut the door." A girl of 3 years could recall nothing whatever that was intelligible.

An 8-year-old boy said: "He made me tie a knot. He asked me about a ship and an auto. He wanted me to count backwards. He made me say over some things, numbers and things."

A boy of 12 years said: "He told me to say all the words I could think of. He said some foolish things and asked what was foolish [he could not repeat a single absurdity]. I had to put some blocks together. I had to do some problems in arithmetic [he could not repeat a single problem]. He read some fables to me. [Asked about the fables he was able to recall only part of one, that of the fox and the crow.] He showed me the picture of a field and wanted to know how to find a ball."

It is evident from the above samples of report that the danger of coaching increases considerably with the age of the children concerned. With young subjects the danger is hardly present at all; with children of the upper-grammar grades, in the high school, and most of all in prisons and reformatories, it must be taken into account. Alternative tests may sometimes be used to advantage when there is evidence of coaching on any of the regular tests. It would be desirable to have two or three additional scales which could be used interchangeably with the Binet-Simon.

Reliability of repeated tests.

Will the same tests give consistent results when used repeatedly with the same subject? In general we may say that they do. Something depends, however, on the age and intelligence of the subject and on the time interval between the examinations.

Goddard proves that feeble-minded individuals whose intelligence has reached its full development continue to test at exactly the same mental age by the Binet scale, year after year. In their case, familiarity with the tests does not in the least improve the responses. At each retesting the responses given at previous examinations are repeated with only the most trivial variations. Of 352 feeble-minded children tested at Vineland, three years in succession, 109 gave absolutely no variation, 232 showed a variation of not more than two fifths of a year, while 22 gained as much as one year in the three tests. The latter, presumably, were younger children whose intelligence was still developing.

Goddard has also tested 464 public-school children for three successive years. Approximately half of these showed normal progress or more in mental age, while most of the remainder showed somewhat less than normal progress.

Bobertag's retesting of 83 normal children after an interval of a year gave results entirely in harmony with those of Goddard. The reapplication of the tests showed absolutely no influence of familiarity, the correlation of the two tests being almost perfect (.95). Those who tested "at age" in the first test had advanced, on the average, exactly one year. Those who tested *plus* in the first test advanced in the twelve months about a year and a quarter, as we should expect those to do whose mental development is accelerated. Correspondingly, those who tested *minus* at the first test advanced only about three fourths of a year in mental age during the interval.[39]

Our own results with a mixed group of normal, superior, dull and feeble-minded children agree fully with the above findings. In this case the two tests were separated by an interval of two to four years, and the correlation between their results was practically perfect. The average difference between the I Q obtained in the second test and that obtained in the first was only 4 per cent, and the greatest difference found was only 8 per cent.[40]

The repetition of the test at shorter intervals will perhaps affect the result somewhat more, but the influence is much less than one might expect. The writer has tested, at intervals of only a few days to a few weeks, 14 backward children of 12 to 18 years, and 8 normal children of 5 to 13 years. The backward children showed an average improvement in the second test of about two months in mental age, the normal children an average improvement of little more than three months. No child varied in the second test more than half a year from the mental age first secured. On the whole, normal children profit more from the experience of a previous test than do the backward and feeble-minded.

Berry tested 45 normal children and 50 defectives with the Binet 1908 and 1911 scales at brief intervals. The author does not state which scale was applied first, but the mental ages secured by the two scales were practically the same when allowance was made for the slightly greater difficulty of the 1911 series of tests.[41]

We may conclude, therefore, that while it would probably be desirable to have one or more additional scales for alternative use in testing the same children at very brief intervals, the same scale may be used for repeated tests at intervals of a year or more with little danger of serious inaccuracy. Moreover, results like those set forth above are important evidence as to the validity of the test method.

Influence of social and educational advantages.

The criticism has often been made that the responses to many of the tests are so much subject to the influence of school and home environment as seriously to invalidate the scale as a whole. Some of the tests most often named in this connection are the following: Giving age and sex; naming common objects, colors, and coins; giving the value of stamps; giving date; naming the months of the year and the days of the week; distinguishing forenoon and afternoon; counting; making change; reading for memories; naming sixty words; giving definitions; finding rhymes; and constructing a sentence containing three given words.

It has in fact been found wherever comparisons have been made that children of superior social status yield a higher average mental age than children of the laboring classes. The results of Decroly and Degand and of Meumann, Stern, and Binet himself may be referred to in this connection. In the case of the Stanford investigation, also, it was found that when the unselected school children were grouped in three classes according to social status (superior, average, and inferior), the average I Q for the superior social group was 107, and that of the inferior social group 93. This is equivalent to a difference of one year in mental age with 7-year-olds, and to a difference of two years with 14-year-olds.

However, the common opinion that the child from a cultured home does better in tests solely by reason of his superior home advantages is an entirely gratuitous assumption. Practically all of the investigations which have been made of the influence of nature and nurture on mental performance agree in attributing far more to original endowment than to environments. Common observation would itself suggest that the social class to which the family belongs depends less on chance than on the parents' native qualities of intellect and character.

The results of five separate and distinct lines of inquiry based on the Stanford data agree in supporting the conclusion that the children of successful and cultured parents test higher than children from wretched and ignorant homes for the simple reason that their heredity is better. The results of this investigation are set forth in full elsewhere.[42]

It would, of course, be going too far to deny all possibility of environmental conditions affecting the result of an intelligence test. Certainly no one would expect that a child reared in a cage and denied all intercourse with other human beings could by any system of mental measurement test up to the level of normal children. There is, however, no reason to believe that *ordinary* differences in social environment (apart from heredity), differences such as those obtaining among unselected children attending approximately the same general type of school in a civilized community, affects to any great extent the validity of the scale.

A crucial experiment would be to take a large number of very young children of the lower classes and, after placing them in the most favorable environment obtainable, to compare their later mental development with that of children born into the best homes. No extensive study of this kind has been made, but the writer has tested twenty orphanage children who, for the most part, had come from very inferior homes. They had been in a well-conducted orphanage for from two to several years, and had enjoyed during that time the advantages of an excellent village school. Nevertheless, all but three tested below average, ranging from 75 to 90 I Q.

The impotence of school instruction to neutralize individual differences in native endowment will be evident to any one who follows the school career of backward children. The children who are seriously retarded in school are not normal, and cannot be made normal by any refinement of educational method. As a rule, the longer the inferior child attends school, the more evident his inferiority becomes. It would hardly be reasonable, therefore, to expect that a little incidental instruction in the home would weigh very heavily against these same native differences in endowment. Cases like the following show conclusively that it does not:—

X is the son of unusually intelligent and well-educated parents. The home is everything one would expect of people of scholarly pursuits and cultivated tastes. But X has always been irresponsible, troublesome, childish, and queer. He learned to walk at 2 years, to talk at 3, and has always been delicate and nervous. When brought for examination he was 8 years old. He had twice attempted school work, but could accomplish nothing and was withdrawn. His play-life was not normal, and other children, younger than himself, abused and tormented him. The Binet tests gave an I Q of approximately 75; that is, the retardation amounted to about two years. The child was examined again three years later. At that time, after attending school two years, he had recently completed the first grade. This time the I Q was 73. Strange to say, the mother is encouraged and hopeful because she sees that her boy is learning to read. She does not seem to realize that at his age he ought to be within three years of entering high school.

The forty-minute test had told more about the mental ability of this boy than the intelligent mother had been able to learn in eleven years of daily and hourly observation. For X is feeble-minded; he will never complete the grammar school; he will never be an efficient worker or a responsible citizen.

Let us change the picture. Z is a bright-eyed, dark-skinned girl of 9 years. She is dark-skinned because her father is a mixture of Indian and Spanish. The mother is of Irish descent. With her strangely mated parents and two brothers she lives in a dirty, cramped, and poorly furnished house in the country. The parents are illiterate, and the brothers are retarded and dull, though not feeble-minded.

It is Z's turn to be tested. I inquire the name. It is familiar, for I have already tested the two stupid brothers. I also know her ignorant parents and the miserable cabin in which she lives. The examination begins with the 8-year tests. The responses are quick and accurate. We proceed to the 9-year group. There is no failure, and there is but one minor error. Successes and failures alternate for a while until the latter prevail. Z has tested at 11 years. In spite of her wretched home, she is mentally advanced nearly 25 per cent. By the vocabulary test she is credited with a knowledge of nearly 6000 words, or nearly four times as many as X, the boy of cultured home and scholarly parents, had learned by the age of 8 years.

Five years have passed. When given the test, Z was in the fourth grade and, as we have already stated, 9 years of age. As a result of the test she was transferred to the fifth grade. Later she skipped again and at the age of 14 is a successful student in the second year of high school. To assay her intelligence and determine its quality was a task of forty-five minutes.

The above cases, each of which could be paralleled by many others which we have found, will serve to illustrate the fact that exceptionally superior endowment is discoverable by the tests, however unfavorable the home from which it comes, and that inferior endowment cannot be normalized by all the advantages of the most cultured home. Quoting again from Stern, "The tests actually reach and discover the general developmental conditions of intelligence, and not mere fragments of knowledge and attainments acquired by chance."

FOOTNOTES:

[30] Dr. F. Kuhlmann: "The Binet-Simon Tests of Intelligence in Grading Feeble-Minded Children," in *Journal of Psycho-Asthenics* (1912), p. 189.

[31] Dr. Otto Bobertag: "L'échelle métrique de l'intelligence," in *L'Année Psychologique* (1912), p. 272.

[32] Dr. Ernest Meumann: *Experimentelle Pädagogik* (1913), vol. II, p. 277.

[33] Dr. W. Stern: *The Psychological Methods of Testing Intelligence.* Translated by Whipple (1913), p. 49.

[34] Dr. H. H. Goddard: "The Binet Measuring Scale of Intelligence; What it is and How it is to be Used," in *The Training School Bulletin* (1912).

[35] See this volume, p. 24 *ff.*

[36] C. S. Bluemel: "Binet Tests on 200 Delinquents," in *The Training School Bulletin* (1915), p. 192. (Italics inserted.)

[37] Samuel C. Kohs: "The Binet Test and the Training of Teachers," in *The Training School Bulletin* (1914), pp. 113–17.

[38] See, for example, the rather ludicrous "errors" of the Binet method reported in *The Psychological Clinic* for 1915, pp. 140 *ff.* and 167 *ff.*

[39] Otto Bobertag: "Ueber Intelligenz Prüfungen," in *Zeitsch. f. Angew. Psychol.* (1912), p. 521 *ff.*

[40] See *The Stanford Revision and Extension of the Binet-Simon Scale for Measuring Intelligence.* (Warwick and York, 1916.)

[41] Charles Scott Berry: "A Comparison of the Binet Tests of 1908 and 1911," in *Journal of Educational Psychology* (1912), pp. 444–51.

[42] See *The Stanford Revision and Extension of the Binet-Simon Measuring Scale of Intelligence.* (Warwick and York, 1916)

PART II
GUIDE FOR THE USE OF THE STANFORD REVISION
AND EXTENSION

CHAPTER VIII
GENERAL INSTRUCTIONS

Necessity of securing attention and effort.

The child's intelligence is to be judged by his success in the performance of certain tasks. These tasks may appear to the examiner to be very easy, indeed; but we must bear in mind that they are often anything but easy for the child. Real effort and attention are necessary for his success, and occasionally even his best efforts fall short of the desired result. If the tests are to display the child's real intellectual ability it will be necessary, therefore, to avoid as nearly as possible every disturbing factor which would divide his attention or in any other way injure the quality of his responses. To insure this it will be necessary to consider somewhat in detail a number of factors which influence effort, such as degree of quiet, the nature of surroundings, presence or absence of others, means of gaining the child's confidence, the avoidance of embarrassment, fatigue, etc.

One should not expect, however, to secure an absolutely equal degree of attention from all subjects. The power to give sustained attention to a difficult task is characteristically weak in dull and feeble-minded children. What we should labor to secure is the maximum attention of which the child is capable, and if this is unsatisfactory without external cause, we are to regard the fact as symptomatic of inferior mental ability, not as an extenuating factor or an excuse for lack of success in the tests.

Attention, of course, cannot be normal if any acute physical or mental disturbance is present. Toothache, headache, earache, nausea, fever, cold, etc., all render the test inadvisable. The same is true of mental anxiety or fear, as in the case of the child who has just been arrested and brought before the court.

Quiet and seclusion.

The tests should be conducted in a quiet room, located where the noises of the street and other outside distractions cannot enter. A reasonably small room is better than a very large one, because it is more homelike. The furnishings of the room should be simple. A table and two chairs are sufficient. If the room contains a number of unfamiliar objects, such as psychological apparatus, pictures on the walls, etc., the attention of the child is likely to be drawn away from the tasks which he is given to do. The halls and corridors which it is sometimes necessary to use in testing school children are usually noisy, cold, or otherwise objectionable.

Presence of others.

A still more disturbing influence is the presence of other persons. Generally speaking, if accurate results are to be secured it is not permissible to have any auditor, besides possibly an assistant to record the responses. Even the assistant, however quiet and unobtrusive, is sometimes a disturbing element. Though something of a convenience, the assistant is by no means necessary, after the examiner has thoroughly mastered the procedure of the tests and has acquired some skill in the use of abbreviations in recording the answers. If an assistant or any other person is present, he should be seated somewhat behind the child, not too close, and should take no notice of the child either when he enters the room or at any time during the examination.

At all events, the presence of parent, teacher, school principal, or governess is to be avoided. Contrary to what one might expect, these distract the child much more than a strange personality would do. Their critical attitude toward the child's performance is very likely to cause embarrassment. If the child is alone with the examiner, he is more at ease from the mere fact that he does not feel that there is a reputation to sustain. The praise so lavishly bestowed upon him by the friendly and sympathetic examiner lends to the same effect.

As Binet emphasizes, if the presence of others cannot be avoided, it is at least necessary to require of them absolute silence. Parents, and sometimes teachers, have an almost irrepressible tendency to interrupt the examination with excuses for the child's failures and with disturbing explanations which are likely to aid the child in comprehending the required task. Without the least intention of doing so, they sometimes practically tell the child how to respond. Parents, especially, cannot refrain from scolding the child or showing impatience when his answers do not come up to expectation. This, of course, endangers the child's success still further.

The psychologist is not surprised at such conduct. It would be foolish to expect average parents, even apart from their bias in the particular case at hand, to adopt the scientific attitude of the trained examiner. Since we cannot in a few moments at our disposal make them over into psychologists, our only recourse is to deal with them by exclusion.

This is not to say that it is impossible to test a child satisfactorily in the presence of others. If the examiner is experienced, and if the child is not timid, it is sometimes possible to make a successful test in the presence of quite a number of auditors, provided they remain silent, refrain from staring, and otherwise conduct themselves with discretion. But not even the veteran examiner can always be sure of the outcome in demonstration testing.

Getting into "rapport."

The examiner's first task is to win the confidence of the child and overcome his timidity. Unless *rapport* has first been established, the results of the first tests given are likely to be misleading. The time and effort necessary for accomplishing this are variable factors, depending upon the personality of both the examiner and the subject. In a majority of cases from three to five minutes should be sufficient, but in a few cases somewhat more time is necessary.

The writer has found that when a strange child is brought to the clinic for examination, it is advantageous to go out of doors with him for a little walk around the university buildings. It is usually possible to return from such a stroll in a few minutes, with the child chattering away as though to an old friend. Another approach is to begin by showing the child some interesting object, such as a toy, or a form-board, or pictures not used in the test. The only danger in this method is that the child is likely to find the object so interesting that he may not be willing to abandon it for the tests, or that his mind will keep reverting to it during the examination.

Still another method is to give the child his seat as soon as he is ushered into the room, and, after a word of greeting, which must be spoken in a kindly tone but without gushiness, to open up a conversation about matters likely to be of interest. The weather, place of residence, pets, sports, games, toys, travels, current events, etc., are suitable topics if rightly employed. When the child has begun to express himself without timidity and it is clear that his confidence has been gained, one may proceed, as though in continuance of the conversation, to inquire the name, age, and school grade. The examiner notes these down in the appropriate blanks, rather unconcernedly, at the same time complimenting the child (unless it is clearly a case of serious retardation) on the fine progress he has made with his studies.

Keeping the child encouraged.

Nothing contributes more to a satisfactory *rapport* than praise of the child's efforts. Under no circumstances should the examiner permit himself to show displeasure at a response, however absurd it may be. In general, the poorer the response, the better satisfied one should appear to be with it. An error is always to be passed by without comment, unless it is painfully evident to the child himself, in which case the examiner will do well to make some excuse for it; e.g., "You are not quite old enough to answer questions like that one; but, never mind, you are doing beautifully," etc. Exclamations like "fine!" "splendid!" etc., should be used lavishly. Almost any innocent deception is permissible which keeps the child interested, confident, and at his best level of effort. The examination should begin with tests that are fairly easy, in order to give the child a little experience with success before the more difficult tests are reached.

The importance of tact.

It goes without saying that children's personalities are not so uniform and simple that we can adhere always to a single stereotyped procedure in working our way into their good graces. Suggestions like the above have their value, but, like rules of etiquette, they must be supported by the tact which comes of intuition and cannot be taught. The address which flatters and pleases one child may excite disgust in another. The examiner must scent the situation and adapt his method to it. One child is timid and embarrassed; another may think his mental powers are under suspicion and so react with sullen obstinacy; a third may be in an angry mood as a result of a recent playground quarrel. Situations like these are, of course, exceptional, but in any case it is necessary to create in the child a certain mood, or indefinable attitude of mind, before the test begins.

Personality of the examiner.

Doubtless there are persons so lacking in personal adaptability that success in this kind of work would be for them impossible. The wooden, mechanical, matter-of-fact and unresponsive personality is as much out of place in the psychological clinic as the traditional bull in the china shop. It would make an interesting study for some one to investigate, by exact methods, the influence on test results of the personality of different examiners who have been equally trained in the methods to be employed and who are equally conscientious in applying them according to rules.

On the whole, differences of this kind are probably not very great among experienced and reasonably competent examiners. Adaptability grows with experience and with increase of self-confidence. After a few score tests there should be no serious failure from inability to get into *rapport* with the child. Even in those rare cases where the child breaks down and cries from timidity, or perhaps refuses to answer out of embarrassment, the difficulty can be overcome by sufficient tact so that the examination may proceed as though nothing had happened.

If the examiner has the proper psychological and personal equipment, the testing of twenty or thirty children forms a fairly satisfactory apprenticeship. Without psychological training, no amount of experience will guarantee absolute accuracy of the results.

The avoidance of fatigue.

Against the validity of intelligence tests it is often argued that the result of an examination depends a great deal on the time of day when it is made, whether in the morning hours when the mind is at its best, or in the afternoon when it is supposedly fatigued. Although no very extensive investigation has been made of this influence, there is no evidence that the ordinary fatigue incident to school work injures the child's performance appreciably. Our tests of 1000 children showed no inferiority of results secured from 1 to 4 P.M., as compared with tests made from 9 to 12 A.M.

An explanation for this is not hard to find. Although school work causes fatigue, in the sense that a part of the child's available supply of mental energy is used up, there is always a reserve of energy sufficient to carry the child through a thirty-to fifty-minute test. The fact that the required tasks are novel and interesting to a high degree insures that the reserve energy will really be brought into play. This principle, of course, has its natural limits. The examiner would avoid testing a child who was exhausted either from work or play, or a child who was noticeably sleepy.

Duration of the examination.

About the only danger of fatigue lies in making the examination too long. Young children show symptoms of weariness much more quickly than older children, and it is therefore fortunate that not so much time is needed for testing them. The following allowances of time will usually be found sufficient:—

Children	3–5	years old	25–30	minutes
"	6–8	" "	30–40	"
"	9–12	" "	40–50	"
"	13–15	" "	50–60	"

This allowance ordinarily includes the time necessary for getting into *rapport* with the child, in addition to that actually consumed in the tests. But the examiner need not expect to hold fast to any schedule. Some subjects respond in a lively manner, others are exasperatingly slow. It is more often the mentally retarded child who answers slowly, but exceptions to this rule are not uncommon. One 8-year-old boy examined by the writer answered so hesitatingly that it required two sittings of nearly an hour each to complete the test. The result, however, showed a mental age of 11½ years, or an I Q of 143.

It is permissible to hurry the child by an occasional "that's fine; now, quickly," etc., but in doing this caution must be exercised, or the child's mental process may be blocked. The appearance of nagging must be carefully avoided. If the test goes so slowly that it cannot be completed in the above limits of time, it is usually best to stop and complete the examination at another time. When this is not possible, it is advisable to take a ten-minute intermission and a little walk out of doors.

Time can be saved by having all the necessary materials close at hand and conveniently arranged. The coins should be kept in a separate purse, and the pictures, colors, stamps, and designs for drawing should be mounted on stiff cardboard which may be punched and kept in a notebook cover. The series of sentences, digits, comprehension questions, fables, etc., should either be mounted in similar fashion, or else printed in full on the record sheets used in the tests. The latter is more convenient.[43] All other materials should be kept where they will not have to be hunted for.

Besides saving valuable time, a little methodical foresight of this kind adds to the success of the test. If the child is kept waiting, the test loses its interest and attention strays. See to it, if possible, that no lull occurs in the performance.

Inexperienced examiners sometimes waste time foolishly by stopping to instruct the child on his failures. This is doubly bad, for besides losing time it makes the child conscious of the imperfection of his responses and creates embarrassment. Adhere to the purpose of the test, which is to ascertain the child's intellectual level, not to instruct him.

Desirable range of testing.

There are two considerations here of equal importance. It is necessary to make the examination thorough, but in the pursuit of thoroughness we must be careful not to produce fatigue or ennui. Unless there is reason to suspect mental retardation, it is usually best to begin with the group of tests just below the child's age. However, if there is a failure in the tests of that group, it is necessary to go back and try all the tests of the previous group. In like manner the examination should be carried up the scale, until a test group has been found in which all the tests are failed.

It must be admitted, however, that because of time limitations and fatigue, it is not always practicable to adhere to this ideal of thoroughness. In testing normal children, little error will result if we go back no farther than the year which yielded only one failure, and if we stop with the year in which there was only one success. *This is the lowest permissible limit of thoroughness.* Defectives are more uneven mentally than normal children, and therefore scatter their successes and failures over a wider range. With such subjects it is absolutely imperative that the test be thorough.

In the case of defectives it is sometimes necessary to begin with random testing, until a rough idea is gained of the mental level. But the skilled observer soon becomes able to utilize symptoms in the child's conversation and conduct and to dispense with most of this preliminary exploration.

Order of giving the tests.

The child's efforts in the tests are sometimes markedly influenced by the order in which they are given. If language tests or memory tests are given first, the child is likely to be embarrassed. More suitable to begin with are those which test knowledge or judgment about objective things, such as the pictures, weights, stamps, bow-knot, colors, coins, counting pennies, number of fingers, right and left, time orientation, ball and field, paper-folding, etc. Tests like naming sixty words, finding rhymes, giving differences or similarities, making sentences, repeating sentences, and drawing are especially unsuitable because they tend to provoke self-consciousness.

The tests as arranged in this revision are in the order which it is usually best to follow, but one should not hesitate to depart from the order given when it seems best in a given case to do so. It is necessary to be constantly alert so that when the child shows a tendency to balk at a given type of test, such as those of memory, language, numbers, drawing, "comprehension," etc., the work can be shifted to more agreeable tasks. When the child is at his ease again, it is usually possible to return to the troublesome tests with better success. In the case of 8-year-old D. C., who is a speech defective but otherwise above normal, it was quite impossible at the first sitting to give such tests as sentence-making, naming sixty words, reading, repeating sentences, giving definitions, etc.; at each test of this type the child's voice broke and he was ready to cry, due, no doubt, to sensitiveness regarding his speech defect. Others do everything willingly except the drawing and copying. The younger children sometimes refuse to repeat the sentences or digits. In all such cases it is best to pass on to something else. After a few minutes the rejected task may be done willingly.

Coaxing to be avoided.

Although we should always encourage the child to believe that he can answer correctly, if he will only try, we must avoid the common practice of dragging out responses by too much urging and coaxing. The sympathies of the examiner tend to lead him into the habit of repeating and explaining the question if the child does not answer promptly. This is nearly always a mistake, for the question is one which should be understood. Besides, explanations and coaxing are too often equivalent to answering the question for the child. It is almost impossible to impress this danger sufficiently upon the untrained examiner. One who is not familiar with the psychology of suggestion may put the answer in the child's mouth without suspecting what he is doing.

Adhering to formula.

It cannot be too strongly emphasized that unless we follow a standardized procedure the tests lose their significance. The danger is chiefly that of unintentionally and unconsciously introducing variations which will affect the meaning of the test. One who has not had a thorough training in the methods of mental testing cannot appreciate how numerous are the opportunities for the unconscious transformation of a test. Many of these are pointed out in the description of the individual tests, but it would be folly to undertake to warn the experimenter against every possible error of this kind. Sometimes the omission or the addition of a single phrase in giving the test will alter materially the significance of the response. Only the trained psychologist can vary the formula without risk of invalidating the result, and even he must be on his guard. All sorts of misunderstandings regarding the correct placing of tests and regarding their accuracy or inaccuracy have come about through the failure of different investigators to follow the same procedure.

One who would use the tests for any serious purpose, therefore, must study the procedure for each and every test until he knows it thoroughly. After that a considerable amount of practice is necessary before one learns to avoid slips. During the early stages of practice it is necessary to refer to the printed instructions frequently in order to check up errors before they have become habitual.

The instructions hitherto available are at fault in not defining the procedure with sufficient definiteness, and it is the purpose of this volume to make good this deficiency as far as possible.

It is too much, however, to suppose that the instructions can be made "fool-proof." With whatever definiteness they may be set forth, situations are sure to arise which the examiner cannot be formally prepared for. There is no limit to the multitude of misunderstandings possible. After testing hundreds of children one still finds new examples of misapprehension. In a few such cases the instruction may be repeated, if there is reason to think the child's hearing was at fault or if some extraordinary distraction has occurred. But unless otherwise stated in the directions, the repetition of a question is ordinarily to be avoided. Supplementary explanations are hardly ever permissible.

In short, numberless situations may arise in the use of a test which may injure the validity of the response, events which cannot always be dealt with by preconceived rule. Accordingly, although we must urge unceasingly the importance of following the standard procedure, it is not to be supposed that formulas are an adequate substitute either for scientific judgment or for common sense.

Scoring.

The exact method of scoring the individual tests is set forth in the following chapters. Reference to the record booklet for use in testing will show that the records are to be kept in detail. Each subdivision of a test should be scored separately, in order that the clinical picture may be as complete as possible. This helps in the final evaluation of the results. It makes much difference, for example, whether success in repeating six digits is earned by repeating all three correctly or only one; or whether the child's lack of success with the absurdities is due to failure on two, three, four, or all of them. Time should be recorded whenever called for in the record blanks.

Recording responses.

Plus and minus signs alone are not usually sufficient. Whenever possible the entire response should be recorded. If the test results are to be used by any other person than the examiner, this is absolutely essential. Any other standard of completeness opens the door to carelessness and inaccuracy. In nearly all the tests, except that of naming sixty words, the examiner will find it possible by the liberal use of abbreviations to record practically the entire response *verbatim*. In doing so, however, one must be careful to avoid keeping the child waiting. Occasionally it is necessary to leave off recording altogether because of the embarrassment sometimes aroused in the child by seeing his answer written down. The writer has met the latter difficulty several times. When for any reason it is not feasible to record anything more than score marks, success may be indicated by the sign +, failure by −, and half credit by ½. An exceptionally good response may be indicated by ++ and an exceptionally poor response by − −. If there is a slight doubt about a success or failure the sign? may be added to the + or −. In general, however, score the response either + or −, avoiding half credit as far as it is possible to do so.

If the entire response is not recorded it is necessary to record at least the score mark for each test *when the test is given*. It must be borne in mind that the scoring is not a purely mechanical affair. Instead, the judgment of the examiner must come into play with every record made. If the scoring is delayed, there is not only the danger of forgetting a response, but the judgment is likely to be influenced by the subject's responses to succeeding questions. Our special record booklet contains wide margins, so that extended notes and observations regarding the child's responses and behavior can be recorded as the test proceeds.

Scattering of successes.

It is sometimes a source of concern to the untrained examiner that the successes and failures should be scattered over quite an extensive range of years. Why, it may be asked, should not a child who has 10-year intelligence answer correctly all the tests up to and including group X, and fail on all the tests beyond? There are two reasons why such is almost never the case. In the first place, the intelligence of an individual is ordinarily not even. There are many different kinds of intelligence, and in some of these the subject is better endowed than in others. A second reason lies in the fact that no test can be purely and simply a test of native intelligence. Given a certain degree of intelligence, accidents of experience and training bring it about that this intelligence will work more successfully with some kinds of material than with others. For both of these reasons there results a scattering of successes and failures over three or four years. The subject fails first in one or two tests of a group, then in two or three tests of the following group, the number of failures increasing until there are no successes at all. Success "tapers off" from 100 per cent to 0. Once in a great while a child fails on several of the tests of a given year and succeeds with a majority of those in the next higher year. This is only an extreme instance of uneven intelligence or of specialized experience, and does not necessarily reflect upon the reliability of the tests for children in general. The method of calculation given above strikes a kind of average and gives the general level of intelligence, which is essentially the thing we want to know.

Supplementary considerations.

It would be a mistake to suppose that any set of mental tests could be devised which would give us complete information about a child's native intelligence. There are no tests which are absolutely pure tests of intelligence. All are influenced to a greater or less degree also by training and by social environment. For this reason, all the ascertainable facts bearing on such influences should be added to the record of the mental examination, and should be given due weight in reaching a final conclusion as to the level of intelligence.

The following supplementary information should be gathered, when possible:—

1. Social status (very superior, superior, average, inferior, or very inferior).
2. The teacher's estimate of the child's intelligence (very superior, superior, average, inferior, or very inferior).
3. School opportunities, including years of attendance, regularity, retardation or acceleration, etc.
4. Quality of school work (very superior, superior, average, inferior, or very inferior).
5. Physical handicaps, if any (adenoids, diseased tonsils, partial deafness, imperfect vision, malnutrition, etc.).

In addition, the examiner will need to take account of the general attitude of the child during the examination. This is provided for in the record blanks under the heading "comments." The comments should describe as fully as possible the conduct and attitude of the child during the examination, with emphasis upon such disturbing factors as fear, timidity, unwillingness to answer, overconfidence, carelessness, lack of attention, etc. Sometimes, also, it is desirable to verify the child's age and to make record of the verification.

Once more let it be urged that no degree of mechanical perfection of the tests can ever take the place of good judgment and psychological insight. Intelligence is too complicated to be weighed, like a bag of grain, by any one who can read figures.

Alternative tests.

The tests designated as "alternative tests" are not intended for regular use. Inasmuch as they have been standardized and belong in the year group where they are placed, they may be used as substitute tests on certain occasions. Sometimes one of the regular tests is spoiled in giving it, or the requisite material for it may not be at hand. Sometimes there may be reason to suspect that the subject has become acquainted with some of the tests. In such cases it is a great convenience to have a few substitutes available.

It is necessary, however, to warn against a possible misuse of alternative tests. *It is not permissible to count success in an alternative test as offsetting failure in a regular test.* This would give the subject too much leeway of failure. There are very exceptional cases, however, when it is legitimate to break this rule; namely, when one of the regular tests would be obviously unfair to the subject being tested. In year X, for example, one of the three alternative tests should be substituted for the reading test (X, 4) in case we are testing a subject who has not had the equivalent of at least two years of school work. In year VIII, it would be permissible to substitute the alternative test of naming six coins, instead of the vocabulary test, in the case of a subject who came from a home where English was not spoken. In VII, it would perhaps not be unfair to substitute the alternative test, in place of the test of copying a diamond, in the case of a subject who, because of timidity or embarrassment, refused to attempt the diamond. But it would be going entirely too far to substitute an alternative test in the place of every regular test which the subject responded to by silence. In the large majority of cases persistent silence deserves to be scored failure.

Certain tests have been made alternatives because of their inferior value, some because the presence of other tests of similar nature in the same year rendered them less necessary.

Finding mental age.

As there are six tests in each age group from III to X, each test in this part of the scale counts 2 months toward mental age. There are eight tests in group XII, which, because of the omission of the 11-year group, have a combined value of 24 months, or 3 months each. Similarly, each of the six tests in XIV has a value of 4 months (24 ÷ 6 = 4). The tests of the "average adult" group are given a value of 5 months each, and those of the "superior adult" group a value of 6 months each. These values are in a sense arbitrary, but they are justified in the fact that they are such as to cause ordinary adults to test at the "average adult" level.

The calculation of mental age is therefore simplicity itself. The rule is: (1) Credit the subject with all the tests below the point where the examination begins (remembering that the examination goes back until a year group has been found in which all the tests are passed); and (2) add to this basal credit 2 months for each test passed successfully up to and including year X, 3 months for each test passed in XII, 4 months for each test passed in XIV, 5 months for each success in "average adult," and 6 months for each success in "superior adult."

For example, let us suppose that a child passes all the tests in VI, five of the six tests in VII, three in VIII, two in IX, and one in X. The total credit earned is as follows:—

	Years	Months
Credit presupposed, years I to V	5	
Credit earned in VI, 6 tests passed, 2 months each	1	
Credit earned in VII, 5 tests passed, 2 months each		10

	Years	Months
Credit earned in VIII, 3 tests passed, 2 months each		6
Credit earned in IX, 2 tests passed, 2 months each		4
Credit earned in X, 1 test passed, 2 months		2
Total credit	7	10

Taking a subject who tests higher, let us suppose the following tests are passed: All in X, six of the eight in XII, two of the six in XIV, and one of the six in "average adult." The total credit is as follows:—

	Years	Months
Credit presupposed, years I to IX	9	
Credit earned in X, 6 tests passed, 2 months each	1	
Credit earned in XII, 6 tests passed, 3 months each	1	6
Credit earned in XIV, 2 tests passed, 4 months each	0	8
Credit earned in "average adult," 1 success, 5 months		5
Total credit	12	7

One other point: If one or more tests of a year group have been omitted, as sometimes happens either from oversight or lack of time, the question arises how the tests which were given in such a year group should be evaluated. Suppose, for example, a subject has been given only four of the six tests in a given year, and that he passes two, or half of those given. In such a case the probability would be that had all six tests been given, three would have been passed; that is, one half of all. It is evident, therefore, that when a test has been omitted, a proportionately larger value should be assigned to each of those given.

If all six tests are given in any year group below XII, each has a value of 2 months. If only four are given, each has a value of 3 months (12 ÷ 4 = 3). If five tests only are given, each has a value of 2.4 months (12 ÷ 5 = 2.4). If in year group XII only six of the eight tests are given, each has a value of 4 months (24 ÷ 6 = 4). If in the "average adult" group only five of the six tests are given, each has a value of 6 months instead of the usual 5 months. In this connection it will need to be remembered that the six "average adult" tests have a combined value of 30 months (6 tests, 5 months each); also that the combined value of the six "superior adult" tests is 36 months (6 × 6 = 36). Accordingly, if only five of the six "superior adult" tests are given, the value of each is 36 ÷ 5 = 7.2 months.

For example, let us suppose that a subject has been tested as follows: All the six tests in X were given and all were passed; only six of the eight in XII were given and five were passed; five of the six in XIV were given and three were passed; five of the six in "average adult" were given and one was passed; five were given in "superior adult" and no credit earned. The result would be as follows:—

	Years	Months
Credit presupposed, years I to IX	9	
Credit earned in X, 6 given, 6 successes	1	
Credit earned in XII, 6 given, 5 passed. Unit value of each test given is 24 ÷ 6 = 4. Total value of the 5 tests passed is 5 × 4 or	1	8
Credit earned in XIV, 5 tests given, 3 passed. Unit value of each of the 5 given is 24 ÷ 5 = 4.8. Value of the 3 passed is 3 × 4.8, or	0	14+
Credit earned in "average adult," 5 tests given, 1 passed. Unit value of the 5 tests given is 30 ÷ 5 = 6. Value of the 1 success	0	6
Credit earned in "superior adult"	0	0
Total credit	13	4+

The calculation of mental age is really simpler than our verbal illustrations make it appear. After the operation has been performed twenty or thirty times, it can be done in less than a half-minute without danger of error.

The use of the intelligence quotient.

As elsewhere explained, the mental age alone does not tell us what we want to know about a child's intelligence status. The significance of a given number of years of retardation or acceleration depends upon the age of the child. A 3-year-old child who is retarded one year is ordinarily feeble-minded; a 10-year-old retarded one year is only a little below normal. The child who at 3 years of age is retarded one year will probably be retarded two years at the age of 6, three years at the age of 9, and four years at the age of 12.

What we want to know, therefore, is the ratio existing between mental age and real age. This is the intelligence quotient, or I Q. To find it we simply divide mental age (expressed in years and months) by real age (also expressed in years and months). The process is easier if we express each age in terms of months alone before dividing. The division can, of course, be performed almost instantaneously and with much less danger of error by the use of a slide rule or a division table. One who has to calculate many intelligence quotients should by all means use some kind of mechanical help.

How to find the I Q of adult subjects.

Native intelligence, in so far as it can be measured by tests now available, appears to improve but little after the age of 15 or 16 years. It follows that in calculating the I Q of an adult subject, it will be necessary to disregard the years he has lived beyond the point where intelligence attains its final development.

Although the location of this point is not exactly known, it will be sufficiently accurate for our purpose to assume its location at 16 years. Accordingly, any person over 16 years of age, however old, is for purposes of calculating I Q considered to be just 16 years old. If a youth of 18 and a man of 60 years both have a mental age of 12 years, the I Q in each case is $12 \div 16$, or .75.

The significance of various values of the I Q is set forth elsewhere.[44] Here it need only be repeated that 100 I Q means exactly average intelligence; that nearly all who are below 70 or 75 I Q are feeble-minded; and that the child of 125 I Q is about as much above the average as the high-grade feeble-minded individual is below the average. For ordinary purposes all who fall between 95 and 105 I Q may be considered as average in intelligence.

Material for use in testing.

It is strongly recommended that in testing by the Stanford revision the regular Stanford record booklets be used. These are so arranged as to make testing accurate, rapid, and convenient. They contain square, diamond, round field, vocabulary list, fables, sentences, digits, and selections for memory tests, the reading selection barred for scoring, the dissected sentences, arithmetical problems, etc. One is required for each child tested.

[45]

FOOTNOTES:

[43] Examiners will find it a great convenience to use the record booklet which has been specially devised for testing with the Stanford revision. It contains all the necessary printed material, including digits, sentences, absurdities, fables, the vocabulary list, the reading selection, the square and diamond for copying, etc., and in addition gives with each test the standard for scoring. It is so arranged as to afford ample room for a *verbatim* record of all the child's responses, and contains other features calculated to make testing easy and accurate. Regarding purchasing of supplies see p. 141.

[44] See Chapter VI.

[45] Houghton Mifflin Company will supply all the printed material needed in the tests, including the lines for the forms for VI, 2, the four pictures for "enumeration," "description," and "interpretation," the pictures for V, 3 and VI, 2, the colors, designs for X, 3, the code for Average Adult 6, and score cards for square, diamond, designs, and ball-and-field.

This is all the material required for the use of the Stanford revision, except the five weights for IX, 2, and V, 1, and the Healy-Fernald Construction Puzzle for X. These may be purchased of C. H. Stoelting & Co., 3037 Carroll Avenue, Chicago. It is not necessary, however, to have the weights and the Construction Puzzle, as the presence of one or more alternative tests in each year makes it possible to substitute other tests instead of those requiring these materials. This saves considerable expense. Apart from these, which may either be made at home (see pages 278, 279) or dispensed with, the only necessary equipment for using the Stanford revision is a copy of this book with the accompanying set of printed matter, and the record booklets. The record booklets are supplied only in packages of 25.

CHAPTER IX
Instructions For Year III

III, 1. Pointing to parts of the body

Procedure. After getting the child's attention, say: *"Show me your nose." "Put your finger on your nose."* Same with eyes, mouth, and hair.

Tact is often necessary to overcome timidity. If two or three repetitions of the instruction fail to bring a response, point to the child's chin or ear and say: *"Is this your nose?" "No?" "Then where is your nose?"* Sometimes, after one has tried two or three parts of the test without eliciting any response, the child may suddenly release his inhibitions and answer all the questions promptly. In case of persistent refusal to respond it is best not to harass the child for an answer, but to leave the test for a while and return to it later. This is a rule which applies generally throughout the scale. In the case of one exceptionally timid little girl, it was impossible to get any response by the usual procedure, but immediately when a doll was shown the child pointed willingly to its nose, eyes, mouth, and hair. The device was successful because it withdrew the child's attention from herself and centered it upon something objective.

Scoring. *Three responses out of four* must be correct. Instead of pointing, the child sometimes responds by winking the eyes, opening the mouth, etc., which is counted as satisfactory.

Remarks. Binet's purpose in this test is to ascertain whether the subject is capable of comprehending simple language. The ability to comprehend and use language is indeed one of the most reliable indications of the grade of mental development. The appreciation of gestures comes first, then the comprehension of language heard, next the ability to repeat words and sentences mechanically, and finally the ability to use language as a means of communication. The present test, however, is not more strictly a test of language comprehension than the others of the 3-year group, and in any case it could not be said to mark the *beginning* of the power to comprehend spoken language. That is fairly well advanced by the age of 2 years. The test closely resembles III, 2 (naming familiar objects), and III, 3 (enumeration of objects in a picture), except that it brings in a personal element and gives some clue to the development of the sense of self. All the data agree in locating the test at year III.

III, 2. Naming familiar objects

Procedure. Use a key, a penny, a closed knife, a watch, and an ordinary lead pencil. The key should be the usual large-sized doorkey, not one of the Yale type. The penny should not be too new, for the freshly made, untarnished penny resembles very little the penny usually seen. Any ordinary pocket knife may be used, and it is to be shown unopened. The formula is, *"What is this?"* or, *"Tell me what this is."*

Scoring. There must be at least *three correct responses out of five*. A response is not correct unless the object is named. It is not sufficient for the child merely to show that he knows its use. A child, for example, may take the pencil and begin to mark with it, or go to the door and insert the key in the lock, but this is not sufficient. At the same time we must not be too arbitrary about requiring a particular name. "Cent" or "pennies" for "penny" is satisfactory, but "money" is not. The watch is sometimes called "a clock" or "a tick-tock," and we shall perhaps not be too liberal if we score these responses *plus*. "Pen" for "pencil," however, is unsatisfactory. Substitute names for "key" and "knife" are rarely given. Mispronunciations due to baby-talk are of course ignored.

Remarks. The purpose of this test is to find out whether the child has made the association between familiar objects and their names. The mental processes necessary to enable the child to pass this test are very elementary, and yet, as far as they go, they are fundamental. Learning the names of objects frequently seen is a form of mental activity in which the normally endowed child of 2 to 4 years finds great satisfaction. Any marked retardation in making such associations is a grave indication of the lack of that spontaneity which is so necessary for the development of the higher grades of intelligence. It would be entirely beside the point, therefore, to question the validity of the test on the ground that a given child may not have been *taught* the names of the objects used. Practically all children 3 years old, however poor their environment, have made the acquaintance of at least three of the five objects, and if intelligence is normal they have learned their names as a result of spontaneous inquiry.

Always use the list of objects here given, because it has been standardized. Any improvised selection would be sure to contain some objects either less or more familiar than those in the standardized list. Note also that three correct responses out of five are sufficient. If we required five correct answers out of six (like Kuhlmann), or three out of three (like Binet, Goddard, and Huey), the test would probably belong at the 4-year level. Binet states that this test is materially harder than that of naming objects in a picture, since in the latter the child selects from a number of objects in the picture those he knows best, while in the former test he must name the objects we have arbitrarily chosen. This difference does not hold, however, if we require only three correct responses out of five for passing the test of naming objects, instead of Binet's three out of three. All else being equal, it is of course easier to recognize and name a real object shown than it is to recognize and name it from a picture.

III, 3. Enumeration of objects in pictures

Procedure. Use the three pictures designated as "Dutch Home," "River Scene," and "Post-Office." Say, "*Now I am going to show you a pretty picture.*" Then, holding the first one before the child, close enough to permit distinct vision, say: "*Tell me what you see in this picture.*" If there is no response, as sometimes happens, due to embarrassment or timidity, repeat the request in this form: "*Look at the picture and tell me everything you can see in it.*" If there is still no response, say: "*Show me the ...*" (naming some object in the picture). Only one question of this type, however, is permissible. If the child answers correctly, say: "*That is fine;*

now tell me everything you see in the picture." From this point the responses nearly always follow without further coaxing. Indeed, if *rapport* has been properly cultivated before the test begins, the first question will ordinarily be sufficient. If the child names one or two things in a picture and then stops, urge him on by saying "*And what else*" Proceed with pictures *b* and *c* in the same manner.

Scoring. The test is passed if the child enumerates as many as *three* objects in *one* picture *spontaneously*; that is, without intervening questions or urging. Anything better than enumeration (as description or interpretation) is also acceptable, but description is rarely encountered before 5 years and interpretation rarely before 9 or 10.[46]

Remarks. The purpose of the test in this year is to find out whether the sight of a familiar object in a picture provokes recognition and calls up the appropriate name.[47] The average child of 3 or 4 years is in what Binet calls "the identification stage"; that is, familiar objects in a picture will be identified but not described, their relations to one another will not be grasped.

In giving the test, always present the pictures in the same order, first Dutch Home, then River Scene, then Post-Office. The order of presentation will no doubt seem to the uninitiated too trivial a matter to insist upon, but a little experience teaches one that an apparently insignificant change in the procedure may exert a considerable influence upon the response. Some pictures tend more strongly than others to provoke a particular type of response. Some lend themselves especially to enumeration, others to description, others to interpretation. The pictures used in the Stanford revision have been selected from a number which have been tried because they are more uniform in this respect than most others in use. However, they are not without their differences, picture *b*, for example, tending more than the others to provoke description.

There seems to be no disagreement as to the proper location of this test.

III, 4. Giving sex

Procedure. If the subject is a boy, the formula is: *"Are you a little boy or a little girl?"* If a girl, *"Are you a little girl or a little boy?"* This variation in the formula is necessary because of the tendency in young children to repeat mechanically the last word of anything that is said to them. If there is no response, say: *"Are you a little girl?"* (if a boy); or, *"Are you a little boy?"* (if a girl). If the answer to the last question is "no" (or a shake of the head), we then say: *"Well, what are you? Are you a little boy or a little girl?"* (or *vice versa*).

Scoring. The response is satisfactory if it indicates that the child has really made the discrimination, but we must be cautious about accepting any other response than the direct answer, "A little girl," or, "A little boy." "Yes" and "no" in response to the second question must be carefully checked up.

Remarks. Binet and Goddard say that 3-year-olds cannot pass this test and that 4-year-olds almost never fail. We can accept the last part of this statement, but not the first part. Nearly all of our 3-year-old subjects succeed with it.

The test probably has nothing to do with sex consciousness, as such. Success in it would seem to depend on the ability to discriminate between familiar class names which are in a certain degree related.

III, 5. Giving the family name

Procedure. The child is asked, *"What is your name?"* If the answer, as often happens, includes only the first name (Walter, for example), say: *"Yes, but what is your other name? Walter what?"* If the child is silent, or if he only repeats the first name, say: *"Is your name Walter ... ?"* (giving a fictitious name, as Jones, Smith, etc.). This question nearly always brings the correct answer if it is known.

Scoring. Simply + or −. No attention is paid to faults of pronunciation.

Remarks. There is unanimous agreement that this test belongs in the 3-year group. Although the child has not had as much opportunity to learn the family name as his first name, he is almost certain to have heard it more or less, and if his intelligence is normal the interest in self will ordinarily cause it to be remembered.

The critic of the intelligence scale need not be unduly exercised over the fact that there may be an occasional child of 3 years who has never heard his family name. We have all read of such children, but they are so extremely rare that the chances of a given 3-year-old being unjustly penalized for this reason are practically negligible. In the second place, contingencies of this nature are throughout the scale consistently allowed for in the percentage of passes required for locating a test. Since (in the year groups below XIV) the individual tests are located at the age level where they are passed by 60 to 70 per cent of unselected children of that age, it follows that the child of average ability *is expected* to fail on about one third of the tests of his age group. The plan of the scale is such as to warrant this amount of leeway. But even granting the possibility that one subject out of a hundred or so may be unjustly penalized for lack of opportunity to acquire the knowledge which the test calls for, the injustice done does not greatly alter the result. A single test affects mental age only to the extent of two months, and the chances of two such injustices occurring with the same child are very slight. Herein lies the advantage of a multiplicity of tests. No test considered by itself is very dependable, but two dozen tests, properly arranged, are almost infinitely reliable.

III, 6. Repeating six to seven syllables

Procedure. Begin by saying: *"Can you say 'mamma'? Now, say 'nice kitty.'"* Then ask the child to say, *"I have a little dog."* Speak the sentence distinctly and with expression, but in a natural voice and not too slowly. If there is no response, the first sentence may be repeated two or three times. Then give the other two sentences: *"The dog runs after the cat,"* and, *"In summer the sun is hot."* A great deal of tact is sometimes necessary to enlist the child's coöperation in this test. If he cannot be persuaded to try, the alternative test of three digits may be substituted.

Scoring. The test is passed if at least *one sentence is repeated without error after a single reading.* "Without error" is to be taken literally; there must be no omission, insertion, or transposition of words. Ignore indistinctness of articulation and defects of pronunciation as long as they do not mutilate the sentence beyond easy recognition.

Remarks. The test does not presuppose that the child should have the ability to make and use sentences like these for purposes of communication, or even that he should know the meaning of all the words they contain. Its purpose is to bring out the ability of the child to repeat a six-syllable series of more or less familiar language sounds. As every one knows, the normal child of 2 or 3 years is constantly imitating the speech of those around him and finds this a great source of delight. Long practice in the semi-mechanical repetition of language sounds is necessary for the learning of speech coördinations and is therefore an indispensable preliminary to the purposeful use of language. High-grade idiots and the lowest grade of imbeciles never acquire much facility in the repetition of language heard. The test gets at one of the simplest forms of mental integration.

Binet says that children of 3 years *never* repeat sentences of ten syllables. This is not strictly true, for six out of nineteen 3-year-olds succeeded in doing so. All the data agree, however, that the *average* child of 3 years repeats only six to seven syllables correctly.

III. Alternative test: repeating three digits

Procedure. Use the following digits: 6–4–1, 3–5–2, 8–3–7. Begin with two digits, as follows: *"Listen; say 4–2." "Now, say 6–4–1." "Now, say 3–5–2,"* etc. Pronounce the digits in a distinct voice and with perfectly uniform emphasis at a rate just a little faster than one per second. Two per second, as recommended by Binet, is too rapid.

Young subjects, because of their natural timidity in the presence of strangers, sometimes refuse to respond to this test. With subjects under 5 or 6 years of age it is sometimes necessary in such cases to re-read the first series of digits several times in order to secure a response. The response thus secured, however, is not counted in scoring, the purpose of the re-reading being merely to break the child's silence. The second and third series may be read but once. With the digits tests above year IV the re-reading of a series is never permissible.

Scoring. Passed if the child repeats correctly, *after a single reading, one series out of the three* series given. Not only must the correct digits be given, but the order also must be correct.

Remarks. Others, on the basis of rather scanty data, have usually located this test at the 4-year level. Our results show that with the procedure described above it is fully as easy as the test of repeating sentences of 6 to 7 syllables.[48]

FOOTNOTES:

[46] See instructions for VII, 2, and XII, 7.

[47] For a discussion of the significance of the different types of response, enumeration, description, and interpretation, see VII, 2, and XII, 7.

[48] See p. 194 *ff.* for further discussion of the digits test.

CHAPTER X
INSTRUCTIONS FOR YEAR IV

IV, 1. Comparison of lines

Procedure. Present the appropriate accompanying card with the lines in horizontal position. Point to the lines and say: *"See these lines. Look closely and tell me which one is longer. Put your finger on the longest one."* We use the superlative as well as the comparative form of *long* because it is often more familiar to young subjects. If the child does not respond, say: *"Show me which line is the biggest."* Then withdraw the card, turn it about a few times, and present it again with the position of the two lines reversed, saying: *"Now show me the longest."* Turn the card again and make a third presentation.

Scoring. All three comparisons must be made correctly; or if only two responses out of three are correct, all three pairs are again shown, just as before, and if there is no error this time, the test is passed. The standard, therefore, is *three correct responses out of three, or five out of six.*

Sometimes the child points, but at no particular part of the card. In such cases it may be difficult to decide whether he has failed to comprehend and to make the discrimination or has only been careless in pointing. It is then necessary to repeat the experiment until the evidence is clear.

Remarks. As noted by Binet, success in this test depends on the comprehension of the verbal directions rather than on actual discrimination of length. The child who would unerringly choose the larger of two pieces of candy might fail on the comparison of lines. However, since the child must correctly compare the lines three times in succession, or at least in five out of six trials, *willingness to attend* also plays a part. The attention of the low-grade imbecile, or even of the normal child of 3 years, is not very obedient to the suggestions of the experimenter. It may be gained momentarily, but it is not easily held to the same task for more than a few seconds. Hence some children who perfectly comprehend this task fail to make a succession of correct comparisons because they are unable or unwilling to bring to bear even the small amount of attention which is necessary. This does not in the least condone the failure, for it is exactly in such voluntary control of mental processes that we find one of the most characteristic differences between bright and dull, or mature and immature subjects.

There has been little disagreement as to the proper location of this test.

IV, 2. Discrimination of forms

Procedure. Use the forms supplied with this book. First, place the circle of the duplicate set at "X", and say: *"Show me one like this,"* at the same time passing the finger around the circumference of the circle. If the child does not respond, say: *"Do you see all of these things?"* (running the finger over the various forms); *"And do you see this one?"* (pointing again to the circle); *"Now, find me another one just like this."* Use the square next, then the triangle, and the others in any order.

Correct the child's first error by saying: *"No, find one just like this"* (again passing the finger around the outline of the form at "X"). Make no comment on errors after the first one, proceeding at once with the next card, but each time the choice is correct encourage the child with a hearty "That's good," or something similar.

Scoring. The test is passed if *seven out of ten* choices, are correct, the first corrected error being counted.

Remarks. In the test of discriminating forms, unlike the test of comparing lines, lack of success is less often due to inability to understand the task than to failure to discriminate. The test may be regarded as a variation of the form-board test. It displays the subject's ability to compare and contrast successive visual perceptions of form. The accurate perception of even a fairly simple form requires the integration of a number of sensory elements into one whole. The forms used in this test have meaning. They are far from nonsense figures even for the (normal) child of 4 years, who has, of course, never heard about "triangles," "squares," "rectangles," etc. The meaning present at this level of intelligence is probably a compound of such factors as appreciation of symmetry and direction, and discrimination of quantity and number.

Another element in success, especially in the latter part of the experiment, is the ability to make an *attentive* comparison between the form shown and the others. The child may be satisfied to point to the first form his eye happens to fall upon. Far from being a legitimate excuse for failure, such an exhibition of inattention and of weakness of the critical faculty is symptomatic of a mental level below 4 years.

In addition to counting the number of errors made, it is interesting to note with what forms they occur. To match the circle with the ellipse or the octagon, for example, is a less serious error than to match it with the square or triangle.

This test was devised and standardized by Dr. Fred Kuhlmann. It is inserted here without essential alteration, except that the size recommended for the forms is slightly reduced and minor changes have been made in the wording of the directions. Our own results are favorable to the test and to the location assigned it by its author.

IV, 3. Counting four pennies

Procedure. Place four pennies in a horizontal row before the child. Say: *"See these pennies. Count them and tell me how many there are. Count them with your finger, this way"* (pointing to the first one on the child's left) —*"One"*—*"Now, go ahead."* If the child simply gives the number (whether right or wrong) without pointing, say: *"No; count them with your finger, this way,"* starting him off as before. Have him count them aloud.

Scoring. The test is passed only if the counting tallies with the pointing. It is not sufficient merely to state the correct number without pointing.

Remarks. Contrary to what one might think, this is not to any great extent a test of "schooling." Practically all children of this age have had opportunity to learn to count as far as four, and with normal children the spontaneous interest in number is such that very few 4-year-olds, even from inferior social environment, fail to pass the test.

While success requires more than the ability to repeat the number names by rote, it does not presuppose any power of calculation or a mastery of the number concepts from one to four. Many children who will readily say, mechanically, "one, two, three, four," when started off, are not able to pass the test. On the other hand, it is not expected that the child who passes will also necessarily understand that four is made up of two two's, or four one's, or three plus one, etc.

Binet, Goddard, and Kuhlmann place this test in the 5-year group, but three separate series of tests made for the Stanford revision, as well as nearly all the statistics available from other sources, show that it belongs at 4 years.

IV, 4. Copying a square

Procedure. Place before the child a cardboard on which is drawn in heavy black lines a square about 1¼ inches on a side.[49] Give the child a pencil and say: "*You see that* (pointing to the square). *I want you to make one just like it. Make it right here* (showing where it is to be drawn). *Go ahead. I know you can do it nicely.*"

Avoid such an expression as, "*I want you to draw a figure like that.*" The child may not know the meaning of either *draw* or *figure*. Also, in pointing to the model, take care not to run the finger around the four sides.

Children sometimes have a deep-seated aversion to drawing on request and a bit of tactful urging may be necessary. Experience and tact will enable the experimenter in all but the rarest cases to come out victorious in these little battles with balky wills. Give three trials, saying each time: "*Make it exactly like this,*" pointing to model. Make sure that the child is in an easy position and that the paper used is held so it cannot slip.

Scoring. The test is passed if at least *one drawing out of the three* is as good as those marked + on the score card. Young subjects usually reduce figures in drawing from copy, but size is wholly disregarded in scoring. It is of more importance that the right angles be fairly well preserved than that the lines should be straight or the corners entirely closed. The scoring of this test should be rather liberal.

Remarks. After the three copies have been made say: *"Which one do you like best?"* In this way we get an idea of the subject's power of auto-criticism, a trait in which the mentally retarded are nearly always behind normal children of their own age. Normal children, when young, reveal the same weakness to a certain extent. It is especially significant when the subject shows complete satisfaction with a very poor performance.

Observe whether the child makes each part with careful effort, looking at the model from time to time, or whether the strokes are made in a haphazard way with only an initial glance at the original. The latter procedure is quite common with young or retarded subjects. Curiously enough, the first trial is more successful than either of the others, due perhaps to a waning of effort and attention.

Note that pencil is used instead of pen and that only one success is necessary. Binet gives only one trial and requires pen. Goddard allows pencil, but permits only one trial. Kuhlmann requires pen and passes the child only when two trials out of three are successful. But these authors locate the test at 5 years. Our results show that nearly three fourths of 4-year-olds succeed with pencil in one out of three trials if the scoring is liberal. It makes a great deal of difference whether pen or pencil is used, and whether two successes are required or only one. No better illustration could be given of the fact that without thoroughgoing standardization of procedure and scoring the best mental test may be misleading as to the degree of intelligence it indicates.

Copying a square is one of three drawing tests used in the Binet scale, the others being the diamond (year VII), and the designs to be copied from memory (year X). These tests do not to any great extent test what is usually known as "drawing ability." Only the square and the diamond tests are strictly comparable with one another, the other having a psychologically different purpose. In none of them does success seem to depend very much on the amount of previous instruction in drawing. To copy a figure like a square or a diamond requires first of all an appreciation of spacial relationships. The figure must be perceived as a whole, not simply as a group of meaningless lines. In the second place, success depends upon the ability to use the visual impression in guiding a rather complex set of motor coördinations. The latter is perhaps the main difficulty, and is one which is not fully overcome, at least for complicated movements, until well toward adult life.

It is interesting to compare the square and the diamond as to relative difficulty. They have the same number of lines and in each case the opposite sides are parallel; but whereas 4-year intelligence is equal to the task of copying a square, the diamond ordinarily requires 7-year intelligence. Probably no one could have foreseen that a change in the angles would add so much to the difficulty of the figure. It would be worth while to devise and standardize still more complicated figures.

IV, 5. Comprehension, first degree

Procedure. After getting the child's attention, say: *"What must you do when you are sleepy?"* If necessary the question may be repeated a number of times, using a persuasive and encouraging tone of voice. No other form of question may be substituted. About twenty seconds may be allowed for an answer, though as a rule subjects of 4 or 5 years usually answer quite promptly or not at all.

Proceed in the same way with the other two questions: *"What ought you to do when you are cold?"* *"What ought you to do when you are hungry?"*

Scoring. There must be *two correct responses out of three.* No one form of answer is required. It is sufficient if the question is comprehended and given a reasonably sensible answer. The following are samples of correct responses:—

a. "Go to bed." "Go to sleep." "Have my mother get me ready for bed." "Lie still, not talk, and I'll soon be asleep."

b. "Put on a coat" (or "cloak," "furs," "wrap up," etc.). "Build a fire." "Run and I'll soon get warm." "Get close to the stove." "Go into the house," or, "Go to bed," may possibly deserve the score *plus*, though they are somewhat doubtful and are certainly inferior to the responses just given.

c. "Eat something." "Drink some milk." "Buy a lunch." "Have my mamma spread some bread and butter," etc.

With the comprehension questions in this year it is nearly always easy to decide whether the response is acceptable, failure being indicated usually either by silence or by an absurd or irrelevant answer. One 8-year-old boy who had less than 4-year intelligence answered all three questions by putting his finger on his eye and saying: "I'd do that." "Have to cry" is a rather common incorrect response.

Remarks. The purpose of these questions is to ascertain whether the child can comprehend the situations suggested and give a reasonably pertinent reply. The first requirement, of course, is to understand the language; the second is to tell how the situation suggested should be met.

The question may be raised whether a given child might not fail to answer the questions correctly and yet have the intelligence to do the appropriate thing if the real situation were present. This is at least conceivable, but since it would not be practicable to make the subject actually cold, sleepy, or hungry in order to observe his behavior, we must content ourselves with suggesting a situation to be imagined. It probably requires more intelligence to tell what one ought to do in a situation which has to be imagined than to do the right thing when the real situation is encountered.

The comprehension questions of this year had not been standardized until the Stanford investigation of 1913–14. Questions *a* and *b* were suggested by Binet in 1905, while *c* is new. They make an excellent test of 4-year intelligence.

IV, 6. Repeating four digits

Procedure. Say: "*Now, listen. I am going to say over some numbers and after I am through, I want you to say them exactly like I do. Listen* *closely and get them just right—4–7–3–9."* Same with 2–8–5–4 and 7–2–6–1. The examiner should consume nearly four seconds in pronouncing each series, and should practice in advance until this speed can be closely approximated. If the child refuses to respond, the first series may be repeated as often as may be necessary to prove an attempt, but *success with a series which has been re-read may not be counted.* The second and third series may be pronounced but once.

Scoring. Passed if the child repeats correctly, *after a single reading, one series out of the three* series given. The order must be correct.

Remarks. The test of repeating four digits was not included by Binet in the scale and seems not to have been used by any of the Binet workers. It is passed by about three fourths of our 4-year-olds.

IV. Alternative test: repeating twelve to thirteen syllables

The three sentences are:—

a. *"The boy's name is John. He is a very good boy."*
b. *"When the train passes you will hear the whistle blow."*
c. *"We are going to have a good time in the country."*

Procedure. Get the child's attention and say: *"Listen, say this: 'Where is kitty?'"* After the child responds, add: *"Now say this ...,"* reading the first sentence in a natural voice, distinctly and with expression. If the child is too timid to respond, the first sentence may be re-read, but in this case the response is not counted. *Re-reading is permissible only with the first sentence.*

Scoring. The test is passed if at least *one sentence is repeated without error after a single reading.* As in the alternative test of year III, we ignore ordinary indistinctness and defects of pronunciation due to imperfect language development, but the sentence must be repeated without addition, omission, or transposition of words.

Remarks. Sentences of twelve syllables had not been standardized previous to the Stanford revision, but Binet locates memory for ten syllables at year V, and others have followed his example. Our own data show that even 4-year-olds are usually able to repeat twelve syllables with the procedure here set forth.

FOOTNOTES:

[49] No material is needed if the regular Stanford record blanks are used, as these all contain the square and diamond.

CHAPTER XI
INSTRUCTIONS FOR YEAR V

V, 1. Comparison of weights

Materials. It is necessary to have two weights, identical in shape, size, and appearance, weighing respectively 3 and 15 grams.[50] If manufactured weights are not at hand, it is easy to make satisfactory substitutes by taking stiff cardboard pill-boxes, about 1¼ inches in diameter, and filling them with cotton and shot to the desired weight. The shot must be embedded in the center of the cotton so as to prevent rattling. After the box has been loaded to the exact weight, the lid should be glued on firmly. If one does not have access to laboratory scales, it is always possible to secure the help of a druggist in the rather delicate task of weighing the boxes accurately. A set of pill-box weights will last through hundreds of tests, if handled carefully, but they will not stand rough usage. The manufactured blocks are more durable, and so more satisfactory in the long run. If the weights are not at hand, the alternative test may be substituted.

Procedure. Place the 3- and 15-gram weights on the table before the child some two or three inches apart. Say: "*You see these blocks. They look just alike, but one of them is heavy and one is light. Try them and tell me which one is heavier.*" If the child does not respond, repeat the instructions, saying this time, "*Tell me which one is the heaviest.*" (Many American children have heard only the superlative form of the adjective used in the comparison of two objects.)

Sometimes the child merely points to one of the boxes or picks up one at random and hands it to the examiner, thinking he is asked to *guess* which is heaviest. We then say: "*No, that is not the way. You must take the boxes in your hands and try them, like this*" (illustrating by lifting with one hand, first one box and then the other, a few inches from the table). Most children of 5 years are then able to make the comparison correctly. Very young subjects, however, or older ones who are retarded, sometimes adopt the rather questionable method of lifting both weights in the same hand at once. This is always an unfavorable sign, especially if one of the blocks is placed in the hand on top of the other block.

After the first trial, the weights are shuffled and again presented for comparison as before, *this time with the positions reversed.* The third trial follows with the blocks in the same position as in the first trial. Some children have a tendency to stereotyped behavior, which in this test shows itself by choosing always the block on a certain side. Hence the necessity of alternating the positions.[51] Reserve commendation until all three trials have been given.

Scoring. The test is passed if *two of the three* comparisons are correct. If there is reason to suspect that the successful responses were due to lucky guesses, the test should be entirely repeated.

Remarks. This test is decidedly more difficult than that of comparing lines (IV, 1). It is doubtful, however, if we can regard the difference as one due primarily to the relative difficulty of visual discrimination and muscular discrimination. In fact, the test with weights hardly taxes sensory discrimination at all when used with children of 5-year intelligence. Success depends, in the first place, on the ability to understand the instructions; and in the second place, on the power to hold the instructions in mind long enough to guide the process of making the comparison. The test presupposes, in elementary form, a power which is operative in all the higher independent processes of thought, the power to neglect the manifold distractions of irrelevant sensations and ideas and to drive direct toward a goal. Here the goal is furnished by the instruction, "Try them and see which is heavier." This must be held firmly enough in mind to control the steps necessary for making the comparison. Ideas of piling the blocks on top of one another, throwing them, etc., must be inhibited. Sometimes the low-grade imbecile starts off in a very promising way, then apparently forgets the instructions (loses sight of the goal), and begins to play with the boxes in a random way. His mental processes are not consecutive, stable, or controlled. He is blown about at the mercy of every gust of momentary interest.

There is very general agreement in the assignment of this test to year V.

V, 2. Naming colors

Materials. Use saturated red, yellow, blue, and green papers, about 2 × 1 inch in size, pasted one half inch apart on white or gray cardboard. For sake of uniformity it is best to match the colors manufactured especially for this test.[52]

Procedure. Point to the colors in the order, red, yellow, blue, green. Bring the finger close to the color designated, in order that there may be no mistake as to which one is meant, and say: *"What is the name of that color?"* Do not say: *"What color is that?"* or, *"What kind of a color is that?"* Such a formula might bring the answer, "The first color"; or, "A pretty color." Still less would it do to say: *"Show me the red," "Show me the yellow,"* etc. This would make it an entirely different test, one that would probably be passed a year earlier than the Binet form of the experiment. Nor is it permissible, after a color has been miscalled, to return to it and again ask its name.

Scoring. The test is passed only if *all* the colors are named correctly and without marked uncertainty. However, prefixing the adjective "dark," or "light," before the name of a color is overlooked.

Remarks. Naming colors is not a test of color discrimination, for that capacity is well developed years below the level at which this test is used. All 5-year-olds who are not color blind discriminate among the four primary colors here used as readily as adults do. As stated by Binet, it is a test of the "verbalization of color perception." It tells us whether the child has associated the names of the four primary colors with his perceptual imagery of those colors.

The *ability* to make simple associations between a sense impression and a name is certainly present in normal children some time before the above color associations are actually made. Many objects of experience are correctly named two or three years earlier, and it may seem at first a little strange that color names are learned so late. But it must be remembered that the child does not have numerous opportunities to observe and hear the names of several colors at once, nor does the designation of colors by their names ordinarily have much practical value for the young child. When he finally learns their names, it is more because of his spontaneous interest in the world of sense. Lack of such spontaneous interest is always an unfavorable sign, and it is not surprising, therefore, that imbecile intelligence has ordinarily never taken the trouble to associate colors with their names. Girls are somewhat superior to boys in this test, due probably to a greater natural interest in colors.

Binet originally placed this test in year VIII, changing it to year VII in the 1911 scale. Goddard places it in year VII, while Kuhlmann omits it altogether. With a single exception, all the actual statistics with normal children justify the location of the test in year V. Bobertag's figures are the exception, opposed to which are Rowe, Winch, Dumville, Dougherty, Brigham, and all three of the Stanford investigations.

The test is probably more subject to the influence of home environment than most of the other tests of the scale, and if the social status of the child is low, failure would not be especially significant until after the age of 6 years. On the whole it is an excellent test.

V, 3. Æsthetic comparison

Use the three pairs of faces supplied with the printed forms. It goes without saying that improvised drawings may not be substituted for Binet's until they have first been standardized.

Procedure. Show the pairs in order from top to bottom. Say: *"Which of these two pictures is the prettiest?"* Use both the comparative and the superlative forms of the adjective. Do not use the question, "Which face is the uglier (ugliest)?" unless there is some difficulty in getting the child to respond. It is not permitted, in case of an incorrect response, to give that part of the test again and to allow the child a chance to correct his answer; or, in case this is done, we must consider only the original response in scoring.

Scoring. The test is passed only if all *three* comparisons are made correctly. Any marked uncertainty is failure. Sometimes the child laughingly designates the ugly picture as the prettier, yet shows by his amused expression that he is probably conscious of its peculiarity or absurdity. In such cases "pretty" seems to be given the meaning of "funny" or "amusing." Nevertheless, we score this response as failure, since it betokens a rather infantile tolerance of ugliness.

Remarks. From the psychological point of view this is a most interesting test. One might suppose that æsthetic judgment would be relatively independent of intelligence. Certainly no one could have known in advance of experience that intellectual retardation would reveal itself in weakness of the æsthetic sense about as unmistakably as in memory, practical judgment, or the comprehension of language. But such is the case. The development of the æsthetic sense parallels general mental growth rather closely. The imbecile of 4-year intelligence, even though he may have lived forty years, has no more chance of passing this test than any other test in year V. It would be profitable to devise and standardize a set of pictures of the same general type which would measure a less primitive stage of æsthetic development.

The present test was located by Binet in year VI and has been retained in that year in other revisions; but three separate Stanford investigations, as well as the statistics of Winch, Dumville, Brigham, Rowe, and Dougherty, warrant its location in year V.

V, 4. Giving definitions in terms of use

Procedure. Use the words: *Chair, horse, fork, doll, pencil,* and *table.* Say: *"You have seen a chair. You know what a chair is. Tell me, what is a chair?"* And so on with the other words, always in the order in which they are named above.

Occasionally there is difficulty in getting a response, which is sometimes due merely to the child's unwillingness to express his thoughts in sentences. The earlier tests require only words and phrases. In other cases silence is due to the rather indefinite form of the question. The child could answer, but is not quite sure what is expected of him. Whatever the cause, a little tactful urging is nearly always sufficient to bring a response. In this test we have not found the difficulty of overcoming silence nearly as great as others have stated it to be. In consecutive tests of 150 5- and 6-year-old children we encountered unbreakable silence with 8 words out of the total 900 (150 × 6). This is less than 1 per cent. But tactful encouragement is sometimes necessary, and it is best to take the precaution of not giving the test until *rapport* has been well established.

The urging should take the following form: *"I'm sure you know what a ... is. You have seen a .... Now, tell me, what is a ... ?"* That is, we merely repeat the question with a word of encouragement and in a coaxing tone of voice. It would not at all do to introduce other questions, like, *"What does a ... look like?"* or, *"What is a ... for?"* *"What do people do with a ... ?"*

Sometimes, instead of attempting a definition (of *doll,* for example), the child begins to talk in a more or less irrelevant way, as "I have a great big doll. Auntie gave it to me for Christmas," etc. In such cases we repeat the question and say, *"Yes, but tell me; what is a doll?"* This is usually sufficient to bring the little chatter-box back to the task.

Unless it is absolutely necessary to give the child lavish encouragement, it is best to withhold approval or disapproval until the test has been finished. If the first response is a poor one and we pronounce it "fine" or "very good," we tempt the child to persist in his low-grade type of definition. By withholding comment until the last word has been defined, we give greater play to spontaneity and initiative.

Scoring. As a rule, children of 5 and 6 years define an object in terms of use, stating what it does, what it is for, what people do with it, etc. Definitions by description, by telling what substance it is made of, and by giving the class to which it belongs are grouped together as "definitions superior to use." It is not before 8 years that two thirds of the children spontaneously give a large proportion of definitions in terms superior to use.

The test is passed in year V if *four words out of the six* are defined in terms of use (or better than use). The following are examples of satisfactory responses:—

> *Chair*: "To sit on." "You sit on it." "It is made of wood and has legs and back," etc.
>
> *Horse*: "To drive." "To ride." "What people drive." "To pull the wagon." "It is big and has four legs," etc.
>
> *Fork*: "To eat with." "To stick meat with." "It is hard and has three sharp things," etc.
>
> *Doll*: "To play with." "What you dress and put to bed." "To rock," etc.
>
> *Pencil*: "To write with." "To draw." "They write with it." "It is sharp and makes a black mark."
>
> *Table*: "To eat on." "What you put the dinner on." "Where you write." "It is made of wood and has legs."

Examples of failure are such responses as the following: "A chair is a chair"; "There is a chair"; or simply, "There" (pointing to a chair). We record such responses without pressing for a further definition. About the only other type of failure is silence.

Remarks. It is not the purpose of this test to find out whether the child knows the meaning of the words he is asked to define. Words have purposely been chosen which are perfectly familiar to all normal children of 5 years. But with young children there is a difference between knowing a word and giving a definition of it. Besides, we desire to find out how the child apperceives the word, or rather the object for which it stands; whether the thing is thought of in terms of use, appearance (shape, size, color, etc.), material composing it, or class relationships.

This test, because it throws such interesting light on the maturity of the child's apperceptive processes, is one of the most valuable of all. It is possible to differentiate at least a half-dozen degrees of excellence in definitions, according to the intellectual maturity of the subject. A volume, indeed, could be written on the development of word definitions and the growth of meanings; but we will postpone further discussion until VIII, 5. Our concern at present is to know that children of 5 years should at least be able to define four of these six words in terms of use.

Binet placed the test in year VI, but our own figures and those of nearly all the other investigations indicate that it is better located in year V.

V, 5. The game of patience

Material. Prepare two rectangular cards, each 2 × 3 inches, and divide one of them into two triangles by cutting it along one of its diagonals.

Procedure. Place the uncut card on the table with one of its longer sides to the child. By the side of this card, a little nearer the child and a few inches apart, lay the two halves of the divided rectangle with their hypothenuses turned from each other as follows:

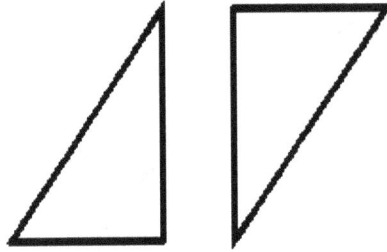

Then say to the child: *"I want you to take these two pieces* (touching the two triangles) *and put them together so they will look exactly like this"* (pointing to the uncut card). If the child hesitates, we repeat the instructions with a little urging. Say nothing about hurrying, as this is likely to cause confusion. Give three trials, of one minute each. If only one trial is given, success is too often a result of chance moves; but luck is not likely to bring two successes in three trials. If the first trial is a failure, move the cut halves back to their original position and say: *"No; put them together so they will look like this"* (pointing to the uncut card). Make no other comment of approval or disapproval. Disregard in silence the inquiring looks of the child who tries to read his success or failure in your face.

If one of the pieces is turned over, the task becomes impossible, and it is then necessary to turn the piece back to its original position and begin over, not counting this trial. Have the under side of the pieces marked so as to avoid the risk of presenting one of them to the child wrong side up.

Scoring. There must be *two successes in three trials*. About the only difficulty in scoring is that of deciding what constitutes a trial. We count it a trial when the child brings the pieces together and (after few or many changes) leaves them in some position. Whether he succeeds after many moves, or leaves the pieces with approval in some absurd position, or gives up and says he cannot do it, his effort counts as one trial. A single trial may involve a number of unsuccessful changes of position in the two cards, but these changes may not consume altogether more than one minute.

Remarks. As aptly described by Binet, the operation has the following elements: "(1) To keep in mind the end to be attained, that is to say, the figure to be formed. It is necessary to comprehend this end and not to lose sight of it. (2) To try different combinations under the influence of this directing idea, which guides the efforts of the child even though he be unconscious of the fact. (3) To judge the formed combination, compare it with the model, and decide whether it is the correct one."

It may be classed, therefore, as one of the many forms of the "combination method." Elements must be combined into some kind of whole under the guidance of a directing idea. In this respect it has something in common with the form-board test, the Ebbinghaus test, and the test with dissected sentences (XII, 4). Binet designates it a "test of patience," because success in it depends upon a certain willingness to persist in a line of action under the control of an idea.

Not all failures in this test are equally significant. A bright child of 5 years sometimes fails, but usually not without many trial combinations which he rejects one after another as unsatisfactory. A dull child of the same age often stops after he has brought the pieces into any sort of juxtaposition, however absurd, and may be quite satisfied with his foolish effort. His mind is not fruitful and he lacks the power of auto-criticism.

It would be well worth while to work out a new and somewhat more difficult "test of patience," but with special care to avoid the puzzling features of the usual games of anagrams. The one given us by Binet is rather easy for year V, though plainly somewhat too difficult for year IV.

V, 6. Three commissions

Procedure. After getting up from the chair and moving with the child to the center of the room, say: *"Now, I want you to do something for me. Here's a key. I want you to put it on that chair over there; then I want you to shut (or open) that door, and then bring me the box which you see over there* (pointing in turn to the objects designated). *Do you understand? Be sure to get it right. First, put the key on the chair, then shut* (open) *the door, then bring me the box* (again pointing). *Go ahead."* Stress the words *first* and *then* so as to emphasize the order in which the commissions are to be executed.

Give the commissions always in the above order. Do not repeat the instructions again or give any further aid whatever, even by the direction of the gaze. If the child stops or hesitates it is never permissible to say: *"What next?"* Have the self-control to leave the child alone with his task.

Scoring. *All three commissions must be executed and in the proper order.* Failure may result, therefore, either from leaving out one or more of the commands or from changing the order. The former is more often the case.

Remarks. Success depends first on the ability to comprehend the commands, and secondly, on the ability to hold them in mind. It is therefore a test of memory, though of a somewhat different kind from that involved in repeating digits or sentences. It is an excellent test, for it throws light on a kind of intelligence which is demanded in all occupations and in everyday life. A more difficult test of the same type ought to be worked out for a higher age level.

Binet originally located this test in year VI, but in 1911 changed it to year VII. This is unfortunate, for the three Stanford investigations, as well as the statistics of all other investigators, show conclusively that it is easy enough for year V.

V. Alternative test: giving age

Procedure. The formula is simply, *"How old are you?"* The child of this age is, of course, not expected to know the date of his birthday, but merely how many years old he is.

Scoring. About the only danger in scoring is in the failure to verify the child's response. Some children give an incorrect answer with perfect assurance, and it is therefore always necessary to verify.

Remarks. Inability to give the age may or may not be significant. If the child has arrived at the age of 7 or 8 years and has had anything like a normal social environment, failure in the test is an extremely unfavorable sign. But if the child is an orphan or has grown up in neglect, ignorance of age has little significance for intelligence. About all we can say is that if a child gives his age correctly, it is because he has had sufficient interest and intelligence to remember verbal statements which have been made concerning him in his presence. He may even pass the test without attaching any definite meaning to the word "year." On the other hand, if he has lived seven or eight years in a normal environment, it is safe to assume that he has heard his age given many times, and failure to remember it would then indicate either a weak memory or a grave inferiority of spontaneous interests, or both. Normal children have a natural interest in the things they hear said about themselves, while the middle-grade imbecile of even 40 years may fail to remember his age, however often he may have heard it stated.

Binet placed the test in year VI of the 1908 series, but omitted it altogether in 1911. Kuhlmann and Goddard also omit it, perhaps wisely. Nevertheless, it is always interesting to give as a supplementary test. Children from good homes acquire the knowledge about a year earlier than those from less favorable surroundings. Unselected children of California ordinarily pass the test at 5 years.

FOOTNOTES:

[50] The weights required for this test, and also for IX, 2, may be purchased of C. H. Stoelting & Co., 3037 Carroll Avenue, Chicago, Illinois.

[51] For discussion of "stereotypy" see p. 203.

[52] Printed cards showing these colors are included in the set of material furnished by the publishers of this book.

CHAPTER XII
INSTRUCTIONS FOR YEAR VI

VI, 1. Distinguishing right and left

Procedure. Say to the child: *"Show me your right hand."* After this is responded to, say: *"Show me your left ear."* Then: *"Show me your right eye."* Stress the words *left* and *ear* rather strongly and equally; also *right* and *eye.* If there is one error, repeat the test, this time with left hand, right ear, and left eye. Carefully avoid giving any help by look of approval or disapproval, by glancing at the part of the body indicated, or by supplementary questions.

Scoring. The test is passed if all three questions are answered correctly, or if, in case of one error, the three additional questions are all answered correctly. The standard, therefore, *is three out of three, or five out of six.*

The chief danger of variation among different examiners in scoring comes from double responses. For example, the child may point first to one ear and then to the other. In all cases of double response, the rule is to count the second response and disregard the first. This holds whether the first response was wrong and the second right, or *vice versa.*

Remarks. It is interesting to follow the child's acquisitions of language distinctions relating to spacial orientation. Other distinctions of this type are those between up and down, above and below, near and far, before and behind, etc. As Bobertag has pointed out, the child first masters such distinctions as up and down, above and below, before and behind, etc., and arrives at a knowledge of right and left rather tardily.

How may we explain the late distinction of right and left as compared with up and down? At least four theories may be advanced: (1) Something depends on the frequency with which children have occasion to make the respective distinctions. (2) It may be explained on the supposition that kinæsthetic sensations are more prominently involved in distinctions of up and down than in distinctions of right and left. It is certainly true that, in distinguishing the two sides of a thing, less bodily movement is ordinarily required than in distinctions of its upper and lower aspects. The former demands only a shift of the eyes, the latter often requires an upward or downward movement of the head. (3) It may be due to the fact that the appearance of an object is more affected by differences in vertical orientation than by those of horizontal orientation. We see an object now from one side, now from the other, and the two aspects easily blend, while the two aspects corresponding to above and below are not viewed in such rapid succession and so remain much more distinct from one another in the child's mind. Or, (4), the difference may be mainly a matter of language. The child undoubtedly hears the words *up* and *down* much oftener than *right* and *left*, and thus learns their meaning earlier. Horizontal distinctions are commonly made in such terms as *this side* and *that side,* or merely by pointing, while in the case of vertical distinctions the words *up* and *down* are used constantly. This last explanation is a very plausible one, but it is very probable that other factors are also involved.

The distinction between right and left has a certain inherent and more or less mysterious difficulty. To convince one's self of this it is only necessary to try a little experiment on the first fifty persons one chances to meet. The experiment is as follows. Say: "I am going to ask you a question and I want you to answer it as quickly as you can." Then ask: "Which is your right hand?" About forty persons out of fifty will answer correctly without a second's hesitation, several will require two or three seconds to respond, while a few, possibly four or five per cent, will grow confused and perhaps be unable to respond for five or ten seconds. Some very intelligent adults cannot possibly tell which is the right or left hand without first searching for a scar or some other distinguishing mark which is known to be on a particular hand. Others resort to incipient movements of writing, and since, of course, every one knows which hand he writes with, the writing movements automatically initiated give the desired clue. One bright little girl of 8 years responded by trying to wink first one eye and then the other. Asked why she did this, she said she knew she could wink her left eye, but not her right! One who is resourceful enough to adopt such an ingenious method is surely not less intelligent than the one who is able to respond by a direct instead of an intermediate association.

It seems that normal people never encounter a corresponding difficulty in distinguishing up and down. The writer has questioned several hundred without finding a single instance, whereas a great many have to employ some intermediate association in order to distinguish right and left. It is the "p's and q's" that children must be told to mind; not the "p's and b's." The former is a horizontal, the latter a vertical distinction.

Considering the difficulty which normal adults sometimes have in distinguishing right and left, is it fair to use this test as a measure of intelligence? We may answer in the affirmative. It is fair because normal adults, notwithstanding momentary uncertainty, are invariably able to make the distinction, if not by direct association, then by an intermediate one. We overlook the momentary confusion and regard only the correctness of the response. Subjects who are below middle-grade imbecile, however long they have lived, seldom pass the test.

This test found a place in year VI of Binet's 1908 scale, but was shifted to year VII in the 1911 revision. The Stanford statistics, and all other available data, with the exception of Bobertag's, justify its retention in year VI. It is possible that the children of different nations do not have equal opportunity and stimulus for learning the distinction between right and left, but the data show that as far as American and English children are concerned we have a right to expect this knowledge in children of 6 years.

VI, 2. Finding omissions in pictures

Procedure. Show the pictures to the child one at a time in the order in which they are lettered, *a, b, c, d*. When the first picture is shown (that with the eye lacking), say: *"There is something wrong with this face. It is not all there. Part of it is left out. Look carefully and tell me what part of the face is not there."* Often the child gives an irrelevant answer; as, "The feet are gone," "The stomach is not there," etc. These statements are true, but they do not satisfy the requirements of the test, so we say: *"No; I am talking about the face. Look again and tell me what is left out of the face."* If the correct response does not follow, we point to the place where the eye should be and say: *"See, the eye is gone."* When picture *b* is shown we say merely: *"What is left out of this face?"* Likewise with picture *c*. For picture *d* we say: *"What is left out of this picture?"* No help of any kind is given unless (if necessary) with the first picture. With the others we confine ourselves to the single question, and the answer should be given promptly, say within twenty to twenty-five seconds.

Scoring. Passed if the omission is correctly pointed out in *three out of four* of the pictures. Certain minor errors we may overlook, such as "eyes" instead of "eye" for the first picture; "nose and one ear" instead of merely "nose" for the third; "hands" instead of "arms" for the fourth, etc. Errors like the following, however, count as failure: "The other eye," or "The other ear" for the first or third; "The ears" for the fourth, etc.

Remarks. The test is one of the two or three dozen forms of the so-called "completion test," all of which have it in common that from the given parts of a whole the missing parts are to be found. The whole to be completed may be a word, a sentence, a story, a picture, a group of pictures, an object, or in fact almost anything. Sometimes all the parts of the whole are given and only the arrangement or order is to be found, as in the test with dissected sentences.

Further discussion of the completion test will be found in connection with test 4, year XII. For the present we will only observe that notwithstanding a certain similarity among the tests of this type, they do not all call into play the same mental processes. The factor most involved may be verbal language coherence, visual perception of form, the association of abstract ideas, etc. To pass Binet's test with mutilated pictures requires, (1) that the parts of the picture be perceived as constituting a whole; and (2) that the idea of a human face or form be so easily and so clearly reproducible that it may act, even before it comes fully into consciousness, as a model or pattern, for the criticism of the picture shown. The younger the child, the less adequate, in this sense, is his perceptual familiarity with common objects. In standardizing a series of "absurd pictures," the writer has found that normal children of 3 years often see nothing wrong in a picture which shows a cat with two legs or a hen with four legs. Such children would, of course, never mistake a cat for a hen. Their trouble lies in the inability to call up in clear form a "free idea" of a cat or a hen for comparison with the perceptual presentation offered by the picture. Middle-grade imbeciles of adult age have much the same difficulty as normal children of 4 years in recognizing mutilations or absurdities in pictures of familiar objects.

Binet first placed this test in year VII, changing it to year VIII in the 1911 revision. In other revisions it has been retained in year VII, although all the available statistics except Bobertag's warrant its location in year VI.

VI, 3. Counting thirteen pennies

Procedure. The procedure is the same as in the test of counting four pennies (year IV, test 3). If the first response contains only a minor error, such as the omission of a number in counting, failure to tally with the finger, etc., a second trial is given.

Scoring. The test is passed if there is *one success in two trials*. Success requires that the counting should tally with the pointing. It is not sufficient merely to state the number of pennies without pointing, for unless the child points and counts aloud we cannot be sure that his correct answer may not be the joint result of two errors in opposite directions and equal; for example, if one penny were skipped and another were counted twice the total result would still be correct, but the performance would not satisfy the requirements.

Remarks. Does success in this test depend upon intelligence or upon schooling? The answer is, intelligence mainly. There are possibly a few normal 6-year-old children who could not pass the test for lack of instruction, but children of this age usually have enough spontaneous interest in numbers to acquire facility in counting as far as 13 without formal teaching. Certainly, inability to do so by the age of 7 years is a suspicious sign unless the child's environment has been extraordinarily unfavorable. On the other hand, feeble-minded adults of the 5-year level usually have to have a great deal of instruction before they acquire the ability to count 13, and many of them are hardly able to learn it at all. So much does our learning depend on original endowment.

Binet originally placed this test in year VII, but moved it to year VI in 1911. All the statistics, without exception, show that this change was justified. Bobertag says that nearly all 7-year-olds who are not feeble-minded can pass it, a statement with which we can fully agree.

VI, 4. Comprehension, second degree

Procedure. The questions used in this year are:—

a. *"What's the thing to do if it is raining when you start to school?"*
b. *"What's the thing to do if you find that your house is on fire?"*
c. *"What's the thing to do if you are going some place and miss your train (car)?"*

Note that the wording of the first part of the questions is slightly different from that in year IV, test 5.

If there is no response, or if the child looks puzzled, the question may be repeated once or twice. The form of the question must not under any circumstances be altered. Question *b*, for example, would be materially changed if we should say: *"Suppose you were to come home from school and find that your house was burning up. What would you do?"* The expression "burning up" would probably be much less likely to suggest calling a fireman than would the words "on fire."

Scoring. *Two out of three* must be answered correctly. The harder the comprehension questions are, the greater the variety of answers and the greater the difficulty of scoring. Because of the difficulty many examiners find in scoring this test, we will list the most common satisfactory, unsatisfactory, and doubtful responses to each question.

(a) If it is raining when you start to school

Satisfactory. "Take umbrella," "Bring a parasol," "Put on rubbers," "Wear an overcoat," etc. This type of response occurred 61 times out of 72 successes. "Have my father bring me" also counts *plus*.

Unsatisfactory. "Go home," "Stay at home," "Stay in the house," "Have the rainbow," "Stay in school," etc. "Stay at home" is the most common failure and might at first seem to the examiner to be a satisfactory response. As a matter of fact, this answer rests on a slight misunderstanding of the question, the import of which is that one is to go to school and it is raining.

Doubtful. "Run" as an answer is a little more troublesome. It may reasonably be scored *plus* if it can be ascertained that the child is accustomed to meet the situation in this way. It is a common response with children in those regions of the Southwest where rains are so infrequent that umbrellas are rarely used. "Bring my lunch" may be considered a satisfactory response in case the child is in the habit of so doing on rainy days.

(b) If you find that your house is on fire

Satisfactory. "Ring the fire alarm," "Call the firemen," "Call for help," "Put water on it," etc.

Unsatisfactory. The most common failure, accounting for nearly half of all, is to suggest finding other shelter; *e.g.*, "Go to the hotel," "Get another house," "Stay with your friends," "Build a new house," etc. Others are: "Tell them you are sorry it burned down," "Be careful and not let it burn again," "Have it insured," "Cry," "Call the policeman," etc.

Doubtful. Instead of suggesting measures to put out the fire, a good many children suggest mere escape or the saving of household articles. Responses of this type are: "Jump out of the windows," "Save yourself," "Get out as fast as you can," "Save the baby," "Get my dolls and jewelry and hurry and get out." These answers are about one seventh as frequent as the perfectly satisfactory ones, and the rule for scoring them is a matter of some importance. Under certain circumstances the logical thing to do would be to save one's self or valuables without wasting time trying to call help. There may be no help in reach, or a fire which the child imagines may be too far along for help to be effective. In order to avoid the possibility of doing a subject an injustice, it may be desirable to score such answers *plus*. We must not be too arbitrary.

(c) If you miss your train

Satisfactory. The answer we expect is, "Wait for another," "Take the next car," or something to that effect. This type of answer includes about 85 per cent of the responses which do not belong obviously in the unsatisfactory group. "Take a jitney" is a modern variation of this response which must be counted as satisfactory.

Unsatisfactory. These are endless. One continues to meet new examples of absurdity, however many children one has tested. The possibilities are literally inexhaustible, but the following are among the most common: "Wait for it to come back," "Have to walk," "Be mad," "Don't swear," "Run and try to catch it," "Try to jump on," "Don't go to that place," "Go to the next station," etc.

Doubtful. The main doubtful response is, "Go home again," "Come back next day and catch another," etc. In small or isolated towns having only one or two trains per day, this is the logical thing to do, and in such cases the score is *plus*. Fortunately, only about one answer in ten gives rise to any difference of opinion among even partly trained examiners.

Remarks. The three comprehension questions of this group were all suggested by Binet in 1905. Only one of them, however, "What would you do if you were going some place and missed your train?" was incorporated in the 1908 or 1911 series, and this was used in year X with seven others much harder. The other two remained unstandardized previous to the Stanford investigation.[53]

VI, 5. Naming four coins

Procedure. Show a nickel, a penny, a quarter, and a dime, asking each time: *"What is that?"* If the child misunderstands and answers, "Money," or "A piece of money," we say: *"Yes, but what do you call that piece of money?"* Show the coins always in the order given above.

Scoring. The test is passed if *three of the four* questions are correctly answered. Any correct designation of a coin is satisfactory, including provincialisms like "two bits" for the 25-cent piece, etc. If the child changes his response for a coin, we count the second answer and ignore the first. No supplementary questions are permissible.

Remarks. Some of the critics of the Binet scale regard this test as of little value, because, they say, the ability to identify pieces of money depends entirely on instruction or other accidents of environment. The figures show, however, that it is not greatly influenced by differences of social environment, although children from poor homes do slightly better with it than those from homes of wealth and culture. The fact seems to be that practically all children by the age of 6 years have had opportunity to learn the names of the smaller coins, and if they have failed to learn them it betokens a lack of that spontaneity of interest in things which we have mentioned so often as a fundamental presupposition of intelligence. It is by no means a test of mere mechanical memory.

This test was given a place in year VII of Binet's 1908 scale, the coins used being the 1-sou, 2-sous, 10-sous, and 5-franc pieces. It was omitted from the Binet 1911 revision and also from that of Goddard. Kuhlmann retains it in year VII. Others, however, have required all four coins to be correctly named, and when this standard is used the test is difficult enough for year VII. Germany has six coins up to and including the 1-mark piece, all of which could be named by 76 per cent of Bobertag's 7-year-olds. With the coins and the standard of scoring used in the Stanford revision the test belongs well in year VI.

VI, 6. Repeating sixteen to eighteen syllables

The sentences are:—

a. *"We are having a fine time. We found a little mouse in the trap."*
b. *"Walter had a fine time on his vacation. He went fishing every day."*
c. *"We will go out for a long walk. Please give me my pretty straw hat."*

Procedure. The instructions should be given as follows: *"Now, listen. I am going to say something and after I am through I want you to say it over just like I do. Understand? Listen carefully and be sure to say exactly what I say."* Then read the first sentence rather slowly, in a distinct voice, and with expression. If the response is not too bad, praise the child's efforts. Then proceed with the second and third sentences, prefacing each with an exhortation to "say exactly what I say."

In this year and in the memory-for-sentences test of later years it is not permissible to re-read even the first sentence. The only reason for allowing a repetition of one of the sentences in the earlier test of this kind was to overcome the child's timidity. With children of 6 years or upward we seldom encounter the timidity which sometimes makes it so hard to secure responses in some of the tests of the earlier years.

Scoring. The test is passed *if at least one sentence out of three is repeated without error, or if two are repeated with not more than one error each.* A single omission, insertion, or transposition counts as an error. Faults of pronunciation are of course overlooked. It is not sufficient that the thought be reproduced intact; the exact language must be repeated. The responses should be recorded *verbatim*. This is easily done if record blanks used for scoring have the sentences printed in full.

Remarks. In this test and in later tests of memory for sentences, it is interesting to ask after each response: *"Did you get it right?"* As in the tests with digits, it is an unfavorable sign when the child is perfectly satisfied with a very poor response.

It is evident that tests of this type give opportunity for different degrees of failure. To repeat only a half or a third of each sentence is much more serious than to make but one error in each sentence (one word omitted, inserted, or misplaced). It would be possible to use the same sentences at three or four different age levels, by setting the appropriate standard for success at each age. If the standard is one sentence out of three repeated with no more than two errors, the test belongs in year V. If we require two absolutely correct responses out of three, the test belongs at about year VII. The shifting standard is rendered unnecessary, however, by the use of other tests of the same kind, easier ones in the lower years and more difficult ones in the upper.

Sentences of sixteen syllables found a place in Binet's 1908 scale and were correctly located in year VI, but later revisions, including that of Binet, have omitted the test.

VI. Alternative test: forenoon and afternoon

Procedure. If it is morning, ask: *"Is it morning or afternoon?"* If it is afternoon, put the question in the reverse form, *"Is it afternoon or morning?"* This precaution is necessary because of the tendency of some children to choose always the latter of two alternatives. Do not cross-question the child or give any suggestion that might afford a clue as to the correct answer.

Scoring. The test is passed if the correct response is given with apparent assurance. If the child says he is not sure but *thinks* it forenoon (or afternoon, as the case may be), we score the response a failure even if the answer happens to be correct. However, this type of response is not often encountered.

Remarks. It is interesting to follow the child's development with regard to orientation in time. This development proceeds much more slowly than we are wont to assume. Certain distinctions with regard to space, as up and down, come much earlier. As Binet remarks, schools sometimes try to teach the events of national history to children whose time orientation is so rudimentary that they do not even know morning from afternoon!

The test has two rather serious faults: (1) It gives too much play to chance, for since only two alternatives are offered, guesses alone would give about fifty per cent of correct responses. (2) We cannot be sure that the verbal distinction between forenoon and afternoon always corresponds the two divisions of the day. It is possible that the temporal discrimination precedes the formation of the correct verbal association.

This test was included in the year VI group of the 1908 scale, but was omitted from the 1911 revision. Nearly all the data except Bobertag's show that it is rather easy for year VI, though too difficult for year V. Bobertag's figures would place the test in year VII. Possibly the corresponding German words are not as easy to learn as our *morning* and *afternoon*.

FOOTNOTES:

[53] For general discussion of the comprehension questions as a test, see p. <u>158</u>.

CHAPTER XIII
INSTRUCTIONS FOR YEAR VII

VII, 1. Giving the number of fingers

Procedure. *"How many fingers have you on one hand?" "How many on the other hand?" "How many on both hands together?"* If the child begins to count in response to any of the questions, say: *"No, don't count. Tell me without counting."* Then repeat the question.

Scoring. Passed *if all three questions are answered correctly and promptly* without the necessity of counting. Some subjects do not understand the question to include the thumbs. We disregard this if the number of fingers exclusive of thumbs is given correctly.

Remarks. Like the two tests of counting pennies, this one, also, throws light on the child's spontaneous interest in numbers. However, the mental processes it calls into play are a little less simple than those required for mere counting. If the child is able to give the number of fingers, it is ordinarily because he has previously counted them and has remembered the result. The memory would hardly be retained but for a certain interest in numbers as such. Middle-grade imbeciles of even adult age seldom remember how many fingers they have, however often they may have been told. They are not able to form accurate concepts of other than the simplest number relationships, and numbers have little interest or meaning for them.

Binet gave this test a place in year VII of the 1908 series, but omitted it in the 1911 revision. Goddard omits it, while Kuhlmann retains it in year VII, where, according to our own figures, it unmistakably belongs. Bobertag finds it rather easy for year VII, though too difficult for year VI.

Our data prove that this test fulfills the requirements of a good test. It shows a rapid but even rise from year V to year VIII in the per cent passing, the agreement among the different testers is extraordinarily close, and it is relatively little influenced by training and social environment. For these reasons, and because it is so easy to give and score with uniformity, it well deserves a place in the scale.

VII, 2. Description of pictures

Procedure. Use the same pictures as in III, 3, presenting them always in the following order: Dutch Home, River Scene, Post-Office. The formula for the test in this year is somewhat different from that of year III. Say: *"What is this picture about? What is this a picture of?"* Use the double question, and follow the formula exactly. It would ruin the test to say: *"Tell me everything you see in this picture,"* for this form of question tends to provoke the enumeration response even with intelligent children of this age.

When there is no response, the question may be repeated as often as is necessary to break the silence.

Scoring. The test is passed if *two of the three* pictures are described or interpreted. Interpretation, however, is seldom encountered at this age. Often the response consists of a mixture of enumeration and description. The rule is that the reaction to a picture should not be scored *plus* unless it is made up chiefly of description (or interpretation).

Study of the following samples of satisfactory responses will give a fairly definite idea of the requirements for satisfactory description:—

Picture (a): satisfactory responses

"The little girl is crying. The mother is looking at her and there is a little kitten on the floor."

"The mother is watching the baby, and the cat is looking at a hole in the floor, and there is a lamp and a table so I guess it's a dining room."

"The little girl has wooden shoes. Her mother is sitting in a chair and has a funny cap on her head. The cat is sitting on the floor and there is a basket by the mother and a table with something on it."

"It's about Holland. The little Dutch girl is crying and the mother is sitting down."

"A little Dutch girl and her mother and that's a kitten, and the little girl has her hand up as if she was doing something to her forehead. She has shoes that curve up in front."

"Dutch lady, and the little baby doesn't want to come to her mother and the cat is looking for some mice."

"The mother is sitting down and the little one has her hands up over her eyes. There's a pail by the mother and a chair with some clothes on it and a table with dishes. And here's a lamp and here's some curtains."

Picture (b): satisfactory responses

"Some people in a boat. The water is high and if they don't look out the boat will tip over."

"Some Indians and a lady and man. They are in a boat on the river and the boat is about to upset, and there are some dead trees going to fall."

"There's a lot of water coming up to drown the people. There are two people in the boat and the boat is sinking."

"There's some people sailing in a canoe and the woman is leaning over on the man because she is afraid."

"There's an Indian and some white people in the boat. I suppose they are out for a ride in a canoe."

"Picture about some man and lady in a canoe and going down to the sea."

"They are taking a boat ride on the ocean and the water is up so high that one of them is scared. Here are some trees and two of them are going to fall down. Here's a little place or bridge you can stand on. The man is touching this one's head and this one has his hand on the cover."

"The water is splashing all over. There's trees on this bank and there's a rock and some trees falling down. The people have a blanket over them."

Picture (c): satisfactory responses

"A man selling eggs and two men reading the paper together and two men watching."

"A few men reading a newspaper and one has a basket of eggs and this one has been fishing."

"There's a man with a basket of eggs and another is reading the paper and a woman is hanging out clothes. There's a house near."

"There's a man trying to read the paper and the others want to read it too. Here's a lady walking up to the barn. There are houses over there and one man has a basket."

"There's a big brick house and five men by it and a man with a basket of eggs and a post-office sign and a lady going home."

"They are all looking at the paper. He is looking over the other man's shoulder and this one is looking at the back of the paper. There's a woman cleaning up her back yard and some coops for hens."

"A man reading a paper, a man with eggs, a woman and a tree and another house. That man has an apron on. This is the post-office."

Unsatisfactory responses are those made up entirely or mainly of enumeration. A phrase or two of description intermingled with a larger amount of enumeration counts *minus*. Sometimes the description is satisfactory as far as it goes, but is exceedingly brief. In such cases a little tactful urging (*"Go ahead,"* etc.) will extend the response sufficiently to reveal its true character.

Remarks. Description is better than enumeration because it involves putting the elements of a picture together in a simple way or noting their qualities. This requires a higher type of mental association (combinative power) than mere enumeration. An unusually complete description indicates relative wealth of mental content and facility of association.

Binet placed this test in year VII, and it seems to have been retained in this location in all revisions except Bobertag's. However, the statistics of various workers show much disagreement. Lack of agreement is easily accounted for by the fact that different investigators have used different series of pictures and doubtless also different standards for success. The pictures used by Binet have little action or detail and are therefore rather difficult for description. On the other hand, the Jingleman-Jack pictures used by Kuhlmann represent such familiar situations and have so much action that even 5- or 6-year intelligence seldom fails with them. The pictures we employ belong without question in year VII.

No better proof than the above could be found to show how ability of a given kind does not make its appearance suddenly. There is no one time in the life of even a single child when the power to describe pictures suddenly develops. On the contrary, pictures of a certain type will ordinarily provoke description, rather than enumeration, as early as 5 or 6 years; others not before 7 or 8 years, or even later.

VII, 3. Repeating five digits

Procedure. Use: 3–1–7–5–9; 4–2–3–8–5; 9–8–1–7–6. Tell the child to listen and to say after you just what you say. Then read the first series of digits at a slightly faster rate than one per second, in a distinct voice, and with perfectly uniform emphasis. *Avoid rhythm.*

In previous tests with digits, it was permissible to re-read the first series if the child refused to respond. In this year, and in the digits tests of later years, this is not permissible. Warning is not given as to the number of digits to be repeated. Before reading each series, get the child's attention. Do not stare at the child during the response, as this is disconcerting. Look aside or at the record sheet.

Scoring. Passed if the child repeats correctly, after a single reading, *one series out of the three* series given. The order must be correct.

Remarks. Psychologically the repetition of digits differs from the repetition of sentences mainly in the fact that digits have less meaning (fewer associations) than the words of a sentence. It is because they are not as well knit together in meaning that three digits tax the memory as much as six syllables making up a sentence.

Testing auditory memory for digits is one of the oldest of intelligence tests. It is easy to give and lends itself well to exact quantitative standardization. Its value has been questioned, however, on two grounds: (1) That it is not a test of pure memory, but depends largely on attention; and (2) that the results are too much influenced by the child's type of imagery. As to the first objection, it is true that more than one mental function is brought into play by the test. The same may be said of every other test in the Binet scale and for that matter of any test that could be devised. It is impossible to isolate any function for separate testing. In fact, the functions called memory, attention, perception, judgment, etc., never operate in isolation. There are no separate and special "faculties" corresponding to such terms, which are merely convenient names for characterizing mental processes of various types. In any test it is "general ability" which is operative, perhaps now *chiefly* in remembering, at another time *chiefly* in sensory discrimination, again in reasoning, etc.

The second objection, that the test is largely invalidated by the existence of imagery types, is not borne out by the facts. Experiments have shown that pure imagery types are exceedingly rare, and that children, especially, are characterized by "mixed" imagery. There are probably few subjects so lacking in auditory imagery as to be placed at a serious disadvantage in this test.

Lengthening a series by the addition of a single digit adds greatly to the difficulty. While four digits can usually be repeated by children of 4 years, five digits belong in year VII and six in year X.

It is always interesting to note the type of errors made. The most common error is to omit one or more of the digits, usually in the first part of the series. If the child's ability is decidedly below the test he may give only the last two or three out of the five or six heard. Substitutions are also quite frequent, and if so many substitutions are made as to give a series quite unlike that which the child has heard, it is an unfavorable sign, indicating weakness of the critical sense which is so often found with low-level intelligence. In case of extreme weakness of the power of auto-criticism, the child in response to the series 9–8–1–7–6–, may say 1–2–3–4–5–6, or perhaps merely a couple of digits like 8–6, and still express complete satisfaction with his absurd response. After each series, therefore, the examiner should say, *"Was it right?"*[54] Very young subjects, however, have a tendency to answer "yes" to any question of this type, and it is therefore best not to call for criticism of a performance below the age of 6 or 7 years.

Digit series of a given length are not always of equal difficulty, and for this reason it is never wise to use series improvised at the moment of the experiment. We must avoid especially series of regularly ascending or descending value, the repetition at regular intervals of a particular digit, and all other peculiarities of arrangement which would favor the grouping of the digits for easier retention.

It remains to mention two or three further cautions in regard to procedure. It is best to begin with a series about one digit below the child's expected ability. If the child has a probable intelligence of about 6 or 7 years, we should begin with four digits; in case of probable 10-year intelligence we begin with five digits, etc. On the other hand, we should avoid beginning too far down, because then the result is too much complicated by the effects of practice and fatigue.

It is not necessary, and often it is not expedient, to give the digits tests of all the different years in succession; that is, without other tests intervening. While this may be permissible with older children, in young children the power of sustained attention is so weak that no single kind of test should occupy more than two or three minutes. Children below 6 or 7 years should ordinarily be given the tests in the order in which they are listed in the record booklet.

In his 1911 revision of the scale Binet unfortunately shifted this test from year VII to year VIII. Goddard follows his example, but Kuhlmann retains it in year VII. The data from more than a dozen leading investigations in America, England, and Germany agree in showing that the test should remain in year VII.

VII, 4. Tying a bow-knot

Procedure. Prepare a shoestring tied in a bow-knot around a stick. The knot should be an ordinary "double bow," with wings not over three or four inches long. Make this ready in advance of the experiment and show the child only the completed knot.

Place the model before the subject with the wings pointing to the right and left, and say: *"You know what kind of knot this is, don't you? It is a bow-knot. I want you to take this other piece of string and tie the same kind of knot around my finger."* At the same time give the child a piece of shoestring, of the same length as that which is tied around the stick, and hold out a finger pointed toward the child and in convenient position for the operation. It is better to have the subject tie the string around the examiner's finger than around a pencil or other object because the latter often falls out of the string and is otherwise awkward to handle.

Some children who assert that they do not know how to tie a bow-knot are sometimes nevertheless successful when urged to try. It is always necessary, therefore, to secure an actual trial.

Scoring. The test is passed if a double bow-knot (both ends folded in) is made *in not more than a minute.* A single bow-knot (only one end folded in) counts half credit, because children are often accustomed to use the single bow altogether. The usual plain common knot, which precedes the bow-knot proper, must not be omitted if the response is to count as satisfactory, for without this preliminary plain knot a bow-knot will not hold and is of no value. To be satisfactory the knot should also be drawn up reasonably close, not left gaping.

Remarks. This test, which had not before been standardized, was suggested to the writer by the late Dr. Huey, who in a conversation once remarked upon the frequent inability of feeble-minded adults to perform the little motor tasks which are universally learned by normal persons in childhood. The test was therefore incorporated in the Stanford trial series of 1913–14 and tried with 370 non-selected children within two months of the 6th, 7th, 8th, or 9th birthday. It was expected that the test would probably be found to belong at about the 8-year level, but it proved to be easy enough for year VII, where 69 per cent of the children passed it. Only 35 per cent of the 6-year-olds succeeded, but after that age the per cent passing increased rapidly to 94 per cent at 9 years.

This little experiment, simple as it is, seems to fulfill reasonably well the requirements of a good test. The main objection which might be brought against it is that it is much subject to the influence of training. If this were true in any marked degree, the mentally retarded children of 7-year intelligence should be expected to succeed better with it than mentally advanced children of the same mental level, since the former would have had at least two or three years more in which to learn the task. A comparison of the two groups, however, shows no great difference. The factor of age, apart from mental age, affects the results so little that it is evident we have here a real test of intelligence.

It would, of course, be easy to imagine a child of 7 years who had not had reasonable opportunity to make the acquaintance of bow-knots or to learn to tie them. But such children are seldom encountered in the ages above 6 or 7. Of 68 7-year-olds who were asked whether they had ever seen a bow-knot ("a knot like that") only two replied in the negative. It cannot be denied, however, that specific instruction and special stimulus to practice do play a certain part. This is suggested by the fact that girls excel the boys somewhat at each age, doubtless because bow-knots play a larger rôle in feminine apparel. Social status affects the results in only a moderate degree, though it might be supposed that poor ragamuffins, on the one hand, and children of the very rich, on the other, would both make a poor showing in this test; the former because of their scanty apparel, the latter because they sometimes have servants to dress them.

The following are probably the chief factors determining success with this test: (1) Interest in common objective things; (2) ability to form permanent associative connections between successive motor coördinations (memory for a series of acts); and (3) skill in the acquisition of voluntary motor control. The last factor is probably much less important than the other two. Motor awkwardness often prolongs the time from the usual ten or fifteen seconds to thirty or forty seconds, but it is rarely a cause of a failure. The important thing is to be able to reproduce the appropriate succession of acts, acts which nearly all children of 7 years, under the joint stimulus of example and spontaneous interest, have before performed or tried to perform.

VII, 5. Giving differences from memory

Procedure. Say: *"What is the difference between a fly and a butterfly?"* If the child does not seem to understand, say: *"You know flies, do you not? You have seen flies? And you know the butterflies! Now, tell me the difference between a fly and a butterfly."* Proceed in the same way with *stone and egg*, and *wood and glass.* A little coaxing is sometimes necessary to secure a response, but supplementary questions and suggestions of every kind are to be avoided. For example, it would not be permissible for the examiner to say: *"Which is larger, a fly or a butterfly?"* This would give the child his cue and he would immediately answer, "A butterfly." The child must be left to find a difference by himself. Sometimes a difference is given, but without any indication as to its direction, as, for example, "One is bigger than the other" (for fly and butterfly). It is then permissible to ask: *"Which is bigger?"*

Scoring. Passed if a real difference is given in *two out of three comparisons*. It is not necessary, however, that an *essential* difference be given; the difference may be trivial, only it must be a real one. The following are samples of satisfactory and unsatisfactory responses:—

Fly and butterfly

Satisfactory. "Butterfly is larger." "Butterfly has bigger wings." "Fly is black and a butterfly is not." "Butterfly is yellow (or white, etc.) and fly is black." "Fly bites you and butterfly don't." "Butterfly has powder on its wings, fly does not." "Fly flies straighter." "Butterfly is outdoors and a fly is in the house." "Flies are more dangerous to our health." "Flies haven't anything to sip honey with." "Butterfly doesn't live as long as a fly." "Butterfly comes from a caterpillar."

Sometimes a double contrast is meant, but not fully expressed; as, "A fly is small and a butterfly is pretty." Here the thought is probably correct, only the language is awkward.

Of 102 correct responses, 70 were in terms of size, or size plus color or form; 12 were in terms of both form and color; 6 in terms of color alone; and the rest scattered among such responses as those mentioned above.

Unsatisfactory. These are mostly misstatements of facts; as: "Fly is bigger." "Fly has legs and butterfly hasn't." "Butterfly has no feet and fly has." "Butterfly makes butter." "Fly is a fly and a butterfly is not." Failures due to misstatement of fact are of endless variety. If an indefinite response is given, like "The fly is different," or "They don't look alike," we ask, *"How is it different?"* or, *"Why don't they look alike?"* It is satisfactory if the child then gives a correct answer.

Stone and egg

Satisfactory. "Stone is harder." "Egg is softer." "Egg breaks easier." "Egg breaks and stone doesn't." "Stone is heavier." "Egg is white and stone is not." "Egg has a shell and stone does not." "Eggs have a white and a yellow in them." "You put eggs in a pudding." "An egg is rounder than a stone." We may also accept statements which are only qualifiedly true; as, "You can break an egg, but not a stone." Likewise double but incomplete comparisons are satisfactory; as, "An egg you fry and a stone you throw," "A stone is tough and an egg you eat," etc.

A little over three fourths of the comparisons made by children of 6, 7, and 8 years are in terms of hardness. The other responses are widely scattered.

Unsatisfactory. "A stone is bigger (or smaller) than an egg." "A stone is square and an egg is round." "An egg is yellow and a stone is white." "Stones are red (or black, etc.) and eggs are white." "An egg is to eat and a stone is to plant." "An egg is round and a stone is sometimes round."

It will be noted that the above responses are partly true and partly false. The error they contain renders them unacceptable. Most of the failures are due to misstatements as to size, shape, or color, but occasionally one meets a bizarre answer.

Wood and glass

Satisfactory. "Glass breaks easier than wood." "Glass breaks and wood does not." "Wood is stronger than glass." "Glass you can see through and wood you can't." "Glass cuts you and wood doesn't." "You get splinters from wood and you don't from glass." "Glass melts and wood doesn't." "Wood burns and glass doesn't." "Wood has bark and glass hasn't." "Wood grows and glass doesn't." "Glass is heavier than wood." "Glass glistens in the sun and wood does not."

An incomplete double comparison is also counted satisfactory; as, "Wood you can burn and glass you can see through."

Unsatisfactory. "Wood is black and glass is white." (Color differences are always unsatisfactory in this comparison unless transparency is also mentioned.) "Glass is square and wood is round." "Glass is bigger than wood" (or *vice versa*). "Wood is oblong and glass is square." "Glass is thin and wood is thick." "Wood is made out of trees and glass out of windows." "There is no glass in wood."

The two most frequent types of failures are misstatements regarding color and thickness. The other failures are widely scattered.

Remarks. The test is one which all the critics agree in commending, largely because it is so little influenced by ordinary school experience. Its excellence lies mainly, however, in the fact that it throws light upon the character of the child's higher thought processes, for thinking means essentially the association of ideas on the basis of differences or similarities. Nearly all thought processes, from the most complex to the very simplest, involve to a greater or less degree one or the other of these two types of association. They are involved in the simple judgments made by children, in the appreciation of puns, in mechanical inventions, in the creation of poetry, in the scientific classification of natural phenomena, and in the origination of the hypotheses of science or philosophy.

The ability to note differences precedes somewhat the ability to note resemblances, though the contrary has sometimes been asserted by logician-psychologists. The difficulty of the test is greatly increased by the fact that the objects to be compared are not present to the senses, which means that the free ideas must be called up for comparison and contrast. Failure may result either from weakness in the power of ideational representation of objects, or from the inadequacy of the associations themselves, or from both. Probably both factors are usually involved.

Intellectual development is especially evident in increased ability to note *essential* differences and likenesses, as contrasted with those which are trivial, superficial, and accidental. To distinguish an egg from a stone on the basis of one being organic, the other inorganic matter requires far higher intelligence than to distinguish them on the basis of shape, color, fragibility, etc. It is not till well toward the adult stage that the ability to give very essential likenesses and differences becomes prominent, and when we get a comparison of this type from a child of 7 or 8 years it is a very favorable sign.

It would be well worth while to standardize a new test of this kind for use in the upper years and especially adapted to display the ability to give essential likenesses and differences. At year VII we must accept as satisfactory any real difference.

One point remains. In the tests of giving differences and similarities, it is well to make note of any tendency to *stereotypy*, by which is meant the mechanical reappearance of the same idea, or element, in successive responses. For example, the child begins by comparing fly and butterfly on the basis of size; as, "A butterfly is bigger than a fly." So far, this is quite satisfactory; but the child with a tendency to stereotypy finds himself unable to get away from the dominating idea of size and continues to make it the basis of the other comparisons: "A stone is larger than an egg," "Wood is larger than glass," etc. In case of stereotypy in all three responses, we should have to score the total response failure even though the idea employed happened to fit all three parts of the question. As a rule it is encountered only with very young children or with older children who are mentally retarded. It is therefore an unfavorable sign.

Although this test has been universally used in year VIII, all the available statistics, with the exception of Bobertag's and Bloch's, indicate that it is decidedly too easy for that year. Binet himself says that nearly all 7-year-olds pass it. Goddard finds 97 per cent passing at year VIII, and Dougherty 90 per cent at year VI. With the standard of scoring given in the present revision, and with the substitution of *stone and egg* instead of the more difficult *paper and cloth*, the test is unquestionably easy enough for year VII.

VII, 6. Copying a diamond

Procedure. On a white cardboard draw in heavy black lines a diamond with the longer diagonal three inches and the shorter diagonal an inch and a half. The specially prepared record booklet contains the diamond as well as many other conveniences.

Place the model before the child with the longer diagonal pointing directly toward him, and giving him *pen and ink* and paper, say: *"I want you to draw one exactly like this."* Give three trials, saying each time: *"Make it exactly like this one."* In repeating the above formula, merely point to the model; do not pass the fingers around its edge.

Unlike the test of copying a square in year IV, there is seldom any difficulty in getting the child to try this one. By the age of 7 the child has grown much less timid and has become more accustomed to the use of writing materials.

Note whether the child draws each part carefully, looking at the model from time to time, or whether the strokes are made in a more or less haphazard manner with only an initial glance at the original.

After each trial, say to the child: *"Is it good?"* And after the three copies have been made say: *"Which one is the best?"* Retarded children are sometimes entirely satisfied with the most nondescript drawings imaginable, but they are more likely correctly to pick out the best of three than to render a correct judgment about the worth of each drawing separately.

Scoring. The test is passed if *two of the three* drawings are at least as good as those marked satisfactory on the score card. The diamond should be drawn approximately in the correct position, and the diagonals must not be reversed. Disregard departures from the model with respect to size.

Remarks. The test is a good one. Age and training, apart from intelligence, affect it only moderately. There are few adult imbeciles of 6-

year intelligence who are able to pass it, while but few subjects who have reached the 8-year level fail on it.[55]

This test was located in year VII of the 1908 scale, but was shifted to year VI in Binet's 1911 revision. The change was without justification, for Binet expressly states, both in 1908 and 1911, that only half of the 6-year-olds succeed with it. The large majority of investigations have given too low a proportion of successes at 6 years to warrant its location at that age, particularly if pen is required instead of pencil. Location at year VI would be warranted only on the condition that the use of pencil be permitted and only one success required in three trials.

VII, Alternative test 1: naming the days of the week

Procedure. Say: *"You know the days of the week, do you not? Name the days of the week for me."* Sometimes the child begins by naming various annual holidays, as Christmas, Fourth of July, etc. Perhaps he has not comprehended the task; at any rate, we give him one more trial by stopping him and saying: *"No; that is not what I mean. I want you to name the days of the week."* No supplementary questions are permissible, and we must be careful not to show approval or disapproval in our looks as the child is giving his response.

If the days have been named in correct order, we check up the response to see whether the real order of days is known or whether the names have only been repeated mechanically. This is done by asking the following questions: *"What day comes before Tuesday?"* *"What day comes before Thursday?"* *"What day comes before Friday?"*

Scoring. The test is passed if, within *fifteen seconds*, the days of the week are *all named in correct order*, and if the child succeeds in at least *two of the three check questions*. We disregard the point of beginning.

Remarks. The test has been criticized as too dependent on rote memory. Bobertag says a child may pass it without having any adequate conception of "week," "yesterday," "day before yesterday," etc. This criticism holds if the test is given according to the older procedure, but does not apply with the procedure above recommended. The "checking-up" questions enable us at once to distinguish responses that are given by rote from those which rest upon actual knowledge.

The test has been shown to be much more influenced by age, apart from intelligence, than most other tests of the scale. Notwithstanding this fault, it seems desirable to keep the test, at least as an alternative, because it forms one of a group which may be designated as tests of time orientation. The others of this group are: "*Distinguishing forenoon and afternoon*" (VI), "*Giving the date*" and "*Naming the months*" (IX). It would be well if we had even more of this type, for interest in the passing of time and in the names of time divisions is closely correlated with intelligence. One reason for the inferiority of the dull and feeble-minded in tests of this type is that their mental associations are weaker and less numerous. The greater poverty of their associations brings it about that their remembered experiences are less definitely located in time with reference to other events.

The test was located in year IX of the 1908 scale, but was omitted from the 1911 revision. Kuhlmann also omits it, while Goddard places it in year VIII. The statistics from every American investigation, however, warrant its location in year VII. It may be located in year VIII only on the condition that the child be required to name the days backwards, and that within a rather low time limit.

VII, Alternative test 2: repeating three digits reversed

Procedure. The digits used are: 2–8–3; 4–2–7; 5–9–6. The test should be given after, but not immediately after, the tests of repeating digits forwards.

Say to the child: *"Listen carefully. I am going to read some numbers again, but this time I want you to say them backwards. For example, if I should say 1–2–3, you would say 3–2–1. Do you understand?"* When it is evident that the child has grasped the instructions, say: *"Ready now; listen carefully, and be sure to say the numbers backwards."* Then read the series at the same rate and in the same manner as in the other digits tests. It is not permissible to re-read any of the series.

If the first series is repeated forwards instead of backwards series exhort the child to listen carefully and to be sure to repeat the numbers backwards.

Scoring. The test is passed if *one series out of three* is repeated backwards without error.

Remarks. The test of repeating digits backwards was suggested by Bobertag in 1911, but appears not to have been used or standardized previous to the Stanford investigation.

It is very much harder to repeat a series of digits backwards in the direct order at year VII, and six at year X. Reversing the order places three digits in year VII, four in year X, five in year XII, and six in "average adult." Even intelligent adults sometimes have difficulty in repeating six digits backwards, once in three trials.

As a test of intelligence this test is better than that of repeating digits in the direct order. It is less mechanical and makes a much heavier demand on attention. The digits must be so firmly fixated in memory that they can be held there long enough to be told off, one by one, backwards.

Feeble-minded children find this test especially difficult, perhaps mainly because of its element of novelty. School children are often asked to write numbers dictated by the teacher, and even the very dull acquire a certain proficiency in doing so; but the test of repeating digits backwards requires a certain facility in adjusting to a new task, exactly the sort of thing in which the feeble-minded are so markedly deficient.

As a rule the response consumes much more time than in the other digits test. This is particularly true when the series to be repeated backwards contains four or more digits. The chance of success is greatly increased if the subject first thinks the series through two or three times in the direct order before attempting the reverse order. The subject who responds immediately is likely to begin correctly, but to give the first part of the original series in the direct order. For example, 6–5–2–8 is given 8–2–6–5.

Sometimes the child gives one or two numbers and then stops, having completely lost the rest of the series in the stress of adjusting to the novel and relatively difficult task of beginning with the final digit. In such cases the feeble-minded are prone to fill in with any numbers they may happen to think of. A good method for the subject is to break the series up into groups and to give each group separately. Thus, 6–5–2–8 is given 8–2 (pause) 5–6. As a rule only the more intelligent subjects adopt this method. One 12-year-old girl attending high school was able to repeat eight digits backwards by the aid of this device.

It would be well worth while to investigate the relation of this test to imagery type. Such a study would have to make use of adult subjects trained in introspection. It would seem that success might be favored by the ability to translate the auditory impression into visual imagery, so that the remembered numbers could be read off as from a book; but this may or may not be the case. At any rate, success seems to depend largely upon the ability to manipulate mental imagery.

The degree of certainty as to the correctness of the response is usually much less than in repeating digits forwards.

FOOTNOTES:

[54] *"Was it wrong?"* is not an equivalent question and should not be used.

[55] For further discussion of drawing tests, see V, 1, and X, 3.

CHAPTER XIV
INSTRUCTIONS FOR YEAR VIII

VIII, 1. The ball-and-field test (Score 2, inferior plan)

Procedure. Draw a circle about two and one half inches in diameter, leaving a small gap in the side next the child. Say: *"Let us suppose that your baseball has been lost in this round field. You have no idea what part of the field it is in. You don't know what direction it came from, how it got there, or with what force it came. All you know is that the ball is lost somewhere in the field. Now, take this pencil and mark out a path to show me how you would hunt for the ball so as to be sure not to miss it. Begin at the gate and show me what path you would take."*[56]

Give the instructions always as worded above. Avoid using an expression like, *"Show me how you would walk around in the field"*; the word *around* might suggest a circular path.

Sometimes the child merely points or tells how he would go. It is then necessary to say: *"No; you must mark out your path with the pencil so I can see it plainly."* Other children trace a path only a little way and stop, saying: "Here it is." We then say: *"But suppose you have not found it yet. Which direction would you go next?"* In this way the child must be kept tracing a path until it is evident whether any plan governs his procedure.

Scoring. The performances secured with this test are conveniently classified into four groups, representing progressively higher types. The first two types represent failures; the third is satisfactory at year VIII, the fourth at year XII. They may be described as follows:—

Type a (failure). The child fails to comprehend the instructions and either does nothing at all or else, perhaps, takes the pencil and makes a few random strokes which could not be said to constitute a search.

Type b (also failure). The child comprehends the instructions and carries out a search, but without any definite plan. Absence of plan is evidenced by the crossing and re-crossing of paths, or by "breaks."

A break means that the pencil is lifted up and set down in another part of the field. Sometimes only two or three fragments of paths are drawn, but more usually the field is pretty well filled up with random meanderings which cross each other again and again. Other illustrations of type *b* are: A single straight or curved line going direct to the ball, short haphazard dashes or curves, bare suggestion of a fan or spiral.

Type c (satisfactory at year VIII). A successful performance at year VIII is characterized by the presence of a plan, but one ill-adapted to the purpose. That some forethought is exercised is evidenced, (1) by fewer crossings, (2) by a tendency either to make the lines more or less parallel or else to give them some kind of symmetry, and (3) by fewer breaks. The possibilities of type *c* are almost unlimited, and one is continually meeting new forms. We have distinguished more than twenty of these, the most common of which may be described as follows:—

1. Very rough or zigzag circles or similarly imperfect spirals.
2. Segments of curves joined in a more or less symmetrical fashion.
3. Lines going back and forth across the field, joined at the ends and not intended to be parallel.
4. The "wheel plan," showing lines radiating from near the center of the field toward the circumference.
5. The "fan plan," showing a number of lines radiating (usually) from the gate and spreading out over the field.
6. "Fan ellipses" or "fan spirals" radiating from the gate like the lines just described.
7. The "leaf plan," "rib plan," or "tree plan," with lines branching off from a trunk line like ribs, veins of a leaf, or branches of a tree.
8. Parallel lines which cross at right angles and mark off the field like a checkerboard.
9. Paths making one or more fairly symmetrical geometrical figures, like a square, a diamond, a star, a hexagon, etc.
10. A combination of two or more of the above plans.

Type d (satisfactory at year XII). Performances of this type meet perfectly, or almost perfectly, the logical requirements of the problem. The paths are almost or quite parallel, and there are no intersections or breaks. The possibilities of type *d* are fewer and embrace chiefly the following:—

1. A spiral, perfect or almost perfect, and beginning either at the gate or at the center of the field.
2. Concentric circles.
3. Transverse lines, parallel or almost so, and joined at the ends.

Up to about 4 years most children failed entirely to comprehend the task. By the age of 6 years the task is usually understood, but the search is conducted without plan. Type *c* is not attained by two thirds before the mental level of 8 years, and score 3 ordinarily not until 11 or 12 years.

Grading presents some difficulties because of occasional border-line performances which have a value almost midway between the types *b* and *c* or between *c* and *d*. Frequent reference to the scoring card will enable the examiner, after a little experience, to score nearly all the doubtful performances satisfactorily.

Remarks. The ball-and-field problem may be called a test of practical judgment. Unlike a majority of the other tests, it gives the subject a chance to show how well he can meet the demands of a real, rather than an imagined, situation. Tests like this, involving practical adjustments, are valuable in rounding out the scale, which, as left by Binet, placed rather excessive emphasis on abstract reasoning and the comprehension of language. The test requires little time and always arouses the child's interest.

Our analysis of the responses of nearly 1500 subjects shows that improvement with increasing mental age is steady and fairly rapid. Occasionally, however, one meets a high-grade performance with children of 6 or 7 years, and a low-grade performance with adults of average intelligence. Like all the other tests of the scale, it is unreliable when used alone.

VIII, 2. Counting backwards from 20 to 1

Procedure. Say to the child: *"You can count backwards, can you not? I want you to count backwards for me from 20 to 1. Go ahead."* In the great majority of cases this is sufficient; the child comprehends the task and begins. If he does not comprehend, and is silent, or starts in, perhaps, to count forwards from 1 or 20, say: *"No; I want you to count backwards from 20 to 1, like this: 20–19–18, and clear on down to 1. Now, go ahead."*

Insist upon the child trying it even though he asserts he cannot do it. In many such cases an effort is crowned with success. Say nothing about hurrying, as this confuses some subjects. Prompting is not permissible.

Scoring. The test is passed if the child counts from 20 to 1 *in not over forty seconds and with not more than a single error* (one omission or one transposition). Errors which the child spontaneously corrects are not counted as errors.

Remarks. The statistics on this test agree remarkably well. It is plainly too easy for year IX, and no one has found it easy enough for year VII. The main lack of uniformity has been in the adherence to a time limit. Binet required that the task be completed in twenty seconds, and Goddard and most others adhere rather strictly to this rule. Kuhlmann, however, allows thirty seconds if there is no error and twenty seconds if one error is committed. We agree with Bobertag that owing to the nature of this test we should not be pedantic about the time. While a majority of children who are able to count backwards do the task in twenty seconds, there are some intelligent but deliberate subjects who require as much as thirty-five or forty seconds. If the counting is done with assurance and without stumbling, there is no reason why we should not allow even forty seconds. Beyond this, however, our generosity should not go, because of the chance it would give for the use of special devices such as counting forwards each time to the next number wanted.

It may be said that counting backwards is a test of schooling, and to a certain extent this is true. It is reasonable to suppose that special training would enable the child to pass the test a little earlier than he would otherwise be able to do, though it is doubtful whether many children below 7 years of age have had enough of such training to influence the performance very materially. On the other hand, when the child has reached an intelligence level of 8 or at most 9 years, he is ordinarily able to count from 20 to 1 whether he has ever tried it before or not.

What psychological factors are involved in this test? It presupposes, in the first place, the ability to count from 1 to 20. But this alone does not guarantee success in counting backwards. Something more is required than a mere rote memory for the number names in their order from 1 up to 20. The quantitative relationships of the numbers must also be apprehended if the task is to be performed smoothly without a great deal of special training. In addition to being reasonably secure in his knowledge of the number relationships involved, the child must be able to give sustained attention until the task is completed. His mental processes must be dominated by the guiding idea, "count backwards." Associations which do not harmonize with this aim, or which fail to further it, must be inhibited. Even momentary relaxation of attention means a loss of directive force in the guiding idea and the dominance of better known associations which may be suggested by the task, but are out of harmony with it. Thus, if a child momentarily loses sight of the end after counting backwards successfully from 20 to 14, he is likely to be overpowered by the law of habit and begin counting forwards, 14–15–16–17, etc. We may regard the test, therefore, as a test of attention, or prolonged thought control. The ability to exercise unbroken vigilance for a period of twenty or thirty seconds is rarely found below the level of 7- or 8-year intelligence.

VIII, 3. Comprehension, third degree

The questions for this year are:—

a. *"What's the thing for you to do when you have broken something which belongs to some one else?"*

b. *"What's the thing for you to do when you notice on your way to school that you are in danger of being tardy?"*

c. *"What's the thing for you to do if a playmate hits you without meaning to do it?"*

The procedure is the same as in previous comprehension questions.[57] Each question may be repeated once or twice, but its form must not be changed. No explanations are permissible.

Scoring:—

Question a (If you have broken something)

Satisfactory responses are those suggesting either restitution or apology, or both. Confession is not satisfactory unless accompanied by apology. The following are satisfactory: "Buy a new one." "Pay for it." "Give them something instead of it." "Have my father mend it." "Apologize." "Tell them I'm sorry, that I did not mean to break it," etc. Of 92 correct answers, 76 suggested restitution, while 16 suggested apology, or apology and restitution.

Unsatisfactory. "Tell them I did it." "Go tell my mother." "Feel sorry." "Be ashamed." "Pick it up," etc. Mere confession accounts for over 20 per cent of all failures.

Question b (In danger of being tardy)

Satisfactory. The expected response is, "Hurry," "Walk faster," or something to that effect. One bright city boy said he would take a car. Of the answers not obviously incorrect, nearly 95 per cent suggest hurrying. The rule ordinarily recommended is to grade all other responses *minus*. But this rule is too sweeping to be followed blindly. One who would use intelligence tests must learn to discriminate. "I would go back home and not go to school that day" is a good answer in those cases (fortunately rare) in which children are forbidden by the teacher to enter the schoolroom if tardy. "Go back home and get mother to write an excuse" would be good policy if by so doing the child might escape the danger of incurring an extreme penalty. When teachers inflict absurd penalties for unexcused tardiness, it is the part of wisdom for children to incur no risks! When such a response is given, it is well to inquire into the school's method of dealing with tardiness and to score the response accordingly.

Unsatisfactory. "Go to the principal." "Tell the teacher I couldn't help it." "Have to get an excuse." "Go to school anyway." "Get punished." "Not do it again." "Not play hooky." "Start earlier next time," etc.

Lack of success results oftenest from failure to get the exact shade of meaning conveyed by the question. It is implied, of course, that something is to be done at once to avoid tardiness; but the subject of dull comprehension may suggest a suitable thing to do in case tardiness has been incurred. Hence the response, "I would go to the principal and explain." Answers of this type are always unsatisfactory.

Question c (Playmate hits you)

Satisfactory responses are only those which suggest either excusing or overlooking the act. These ideas are variously expressed as follows: "I would excuse him" (about half of all the correct answers). "I would say 'yes' if he asked my pardon." "I would say it was all right." "I would take it for a joke." "I would just be nice to him." "I would go right on playing." "I would take it kind-hearted." "I would not fight or run and tell on him." "I would not blame him for it." "Ask him to be more careful," etc.

Unsatisfactory responses are all those not of the above two types; as: "I would hit them back." "I would not hit them back, but I would get even some other way." "Tell them not to do it again." "Tell them to 'cut it out.'" "Tell him it's a wrong thing to do." "Make him excuse himself." "Make him say he's sorry." "Would not play with him." "Tell my mamma." "I would ask him why he did it." "He'd say 'excuse me' and I'd say 'thank you.'" "He should excuse me." "He is supposed to say 'excuse me.'"

Remarks. All three comprehension questions of this year were used by Binet, Goddard, Huey, and others in year X; two of them in the "easy series" and one in the "hard series." The Stanford data show that they belong at the 8-year level on the standard of scoring above set forth. The three differ little among themselves in difficulty, but all of them are decidedly easier than the other five used by Binet. It would be absurd to go on using the comprehension questions as Binet bunched them, eight together, ranging in difficulty from one which is easy enough for 6-year intelligence ("What's the thing to do if you miss your train?") to one which is hard for the 12-year level ("Why is a bad act done when one is angry more excusable than the same act done when one is not angry?").

VIII, 4. Giving similarities; two things

Procedure. Say to the child: *"I am going to name two things which are alike in some way, and I want you to tell me how they are alike. Wood and coal: in what way are they alike?"* Proceed in the same manner with:—

> *An apple and a peach.*
> *Iron and silver.*
> *A ship and an automobile.*

After the first pair the formula may be abbreviated to *"In what way are ... and ... alike?"* It is often necessary to insist a little if the child is silent or says he does not know, but in doing this we must avoid supplementary questions and suggestions. In giving the first pair, for example, it would not be permissible to ask such additional questions as, *"What do you use wood for? What do you use coal for? And now, how are wood and coal alike?"* This is really putting the answer in the child's mouth. It is only permissible to repeat the original question in a persuasive tone of voice, and perhaps to add: *"I'm sure you can tell me how ... and ... are alike,"* or something to that effect.

A very common mistake which the child makes is to give differences instead of similarities. This tendency is particularly strong if test 5, year VII (giving differences), has been given earlier in the sitting, but it happens often enough in other cases also to suggest that finding differences is, to a much greater extent than finding similarities, the child's preferred method of making a comparison. When a difference is given, instead of a similarity, we say: *"No, I want you to tell me how they are alike. In what way are ... and ... alike?"* Unless the child is of rather low intelligence level this is sufficient, but the mentally retarded sometimes continue to give differences persistently in spite of repeated admonitions, or if they cease to do so for one or two comparisons, they are likely to repeat the mistake in the latter part of the test.

Scoring. The test is passed if a likeness is given in *two out of four* comparisons. We accept as satisfactory any real likeness, whether fundamental or superficial, though, of course, the more essential the resemblance, the better indication it is of intelligence. The following are samples of satisfactory and unsatisfactory answers:—[58]

(a) Wood and coal

Satisfactory. "Both burn." "Both keep you warm." "Both are used for fuel." "Both are vegetable matter." "Both come from the ground." "Can use them both for running engines." "Both hard." "Both heavy." "Both cost money."

Of 80 correct answers, 64, or 80 per cent, referred in one way or another to combustibility.

Unsatisfactory. Most frequent is the persistent giving of a difference instead of a similarity. This accounts for a little over half of all the failures. About half of the remainder are cases of inability to give any response. Incorrect statements with regard to color are rather common. Sample failures of this type are: "Both are black," or "Both the same color." Other failures are: "Both are dirty on the outside;" "You can't break them;" "Coal burns better;" "Wood is lighter than coal," etc.

(b) An apple and a peach

Satisfactory. "Both are round." "Both the same shape." "They are about the same color." "Both nearly always have some red on them." "Both good to eat." "Can make pies of both of them." "Both can be cooked." "Both mellow when they are ripe." "Both have a stem" (or seeds, skin, etc.). "Both come from trees." "Can be dried in the same way." "Both are fruits." "Both green (in color) when they are not ripe."

Of 82 correct answers, 25 per cent mention color; 25 per cent, form; 22 per cent, edibility; 20 per cent, having stem, seed, or skin; and 5 per cent, that both grow on trees.

Unsatisfactory. "Both taste the same." "Both have a lot of seeds." "Both have a fuzzy skin." "An apple is bigger than a peach." "One is red and one is white," etc.

Again, over 50 per cent of the failures are due to giving differences and about 18 per cent to silence.

(c) Iron and silver

Satisfactory. "Both are metals" (or mineral). "Both come out of the ground." "Both cost money." "Both are heavy." "Both are hard." "Both can be melted." "Both can be bent." "Both used for utensils." "You manufacture things out of both of them." "Both can be polished."

These are named most frequently in the following order: (1) hardness, (2) origin from the ground, (3) heaviness, (4) use in making things.

Unsatisfactory. "Both thin" (or thick). "Sometimes they are the same shape." "Both the same color." "A little silver and lots of iron weigh the same." "Both made by the same company." "They rust the same." "You can't eat them" (!)[59]

Of 60 failures, 32 were due to giving differences and 14 to silence or unwillingness to hazard a reply.

(d) A ship and an automobile

Satisfactory. "Both means of travel." "Both go." "You ride in them." "Both take you fast." "They both use fuel." "Both run by machinery." "Both have a steering gear." "Both have engines in them." "Both have wood in them." "Both can be wrecked." "Both break if they hit a rock."

About 45 per cent of the answers are in terms of running or travel, 37 per cent in terms of machinery or structure, the rest scattered.

Unsatisfactory. "Both black" (or some other color). "Both very big." "They are made alike." "Both run on wheels." "Ship is for the water and automobile for the land." "Ship goes on water and an automobile sometimes goes in water." "An auto can go faster." "Ship is run by coal and automobile by gasoline."

Of 51 failures, 32 were due to giving differences and 14 to failure to reply.

Remarks. The test of finding similarities was first used by Binet in 1905. Our results show that it is fully as satisfactory as the test of giving differences. The test reveals in a most interesting way one of the fundamental weaknesses of the feeble mind. Young normal children, say of 7 or 8 years, often fail to pass, but it is the feeble-minded who give the greatest number of absurd answers and who also find greatest difficulty in resisting the tendency to give differences.[60]

VIII, 5. Giving definitions superior to use

Procedure. The words for this year are *balloon, tiger, football,* and *soldier*. Ask simply: *"What is a balloon?"* etc.

If it appears that any of the words are not familiar to the child, substitution may be made from the following: *automobile, battle-ship, potato, store.*

Make no comments on the responses until all the words have been given. In case of silence or hesitation in answering, the question may be repeated with a little encouragement; but supplementary questions are never in order. Ordinarily there is no difficulty in securing a response to the definition test of this year. The trouble comes in scoring the response.

Scoring. The test is passed if two of the four words are defined in terms superior to use. "Superior to use" includes chiefly: (*a*) Definitions which describe the object or tell something of its nature (form, size, color, appearance, etc.); (*b*) definitions which give the substance or the materials or parts composing it; and (*c*) those which tell what class the object belongs to or what relation it bears to other classes of objects.

It is possible to distinguish different grades of definitions in each of the above classes. A definition by description (type *a*) may be brief and partial, mentioning only one or two qualities or characteristics, or it may be relatively rich and complete. Likewise with definitions of type *b*. Classificatory definitions (type *c*) are of particularly uneven value, the lowest order being those which subsume the object to be defined under a remote class and give few if any characteristics to distinguish it from other members of the same class; as, for example, "A football is a thing you can have fun with," or, "A soldier is a person." The best classificatory definitions are those which subsume the object under the next higher class and give the more essential traits (perhaps a number of them) which distinguish the object from others of the class named; as, for example, "A tiger is a large animal like a cat; it lives in the jungle and eats men and other animals," or, "A soldier is a man who goes to war." These shades of distinction give interesting and valuable clues to the maturity and richness of the apperceptive processes, but for purposes of scoring it is necessary merely to decide whether the definition is given in terms superior to use.

The following are samples of satisfactory definitions, those for each word being arranged roughly in the order of their value from excellent to barely passing:—

(a) Balloon

Satisfactory. "A balloon is a means of traveling through the air." "It is a kind of airship, made of cloth and filled with air so it can go up." "It is big and made of cloth. It has gas in it and carries people up in a basket that's fastened on to the bottom." "It is a thing you hold by a string and it goes up." "It is like a big bag with air in it." "It is a big thing that goes up."

Unsatisfactory. "To go up in the air." "What you go up in." "When you go up." "They go up in it." "It's full of gas." "To carry you up." "A balloon is a balloon," etc. "It is big." "They go up," etc.

(b) Tiger

Satisfactory. "It is a wild animal of the cat family." "It is an animal that's a cousin to the lion." "It is an animal that lives in the jungle." "It is a wild animal." "It looks like a big cat." "It lives in the woods and eats flesh." "Something that eats people."

Unsatisfactory. "To eat you up." "To kill people." "To travel in the circus." "What eats people." "It is a tiger," etc. "You run from it," etc.

(c) Football

Satisfactory. "It is a leather bag filled with air and made for kicking." "It is a ball you kick." "It is a thing you play with." "It is made of leather and is stuffed with air." "It is a thing you kick." "It is brown and filled with air." "It is a thing shaped like a watermelon."

Unsatisfactory. "To kick." "To play with." "What they play with." "Boys play with it." "It's filled with air." "It is a football." "It is a basket ball." "It is round." "You kick it."

(d) Soldier

Satisfactory. "A man who goes to war." "A brave man." "A man that walks up and down and carries a gun." "It is a man who minds his captain and stands still and walks straight." "It is a man who goes to war and shoots." "It is a man who stands straight and marches."

Unsatisfactory. "To shoot." "To go to war." "It is a soldier." "A soldier that marches." "He fights." "He shoots." "What fights," etc. "When you march and shoot."

Silence accounts for only a small proportion of the failures with children of 8, 9, and 10 years.

Remarks. The "use definitions" sometimes given at this age are usually of slightly better quality than those given in year V. Younger children more often use the infinitive form, "to play with" (doll), "to drive" (horse), "to eat on" (table), etc. Use definitions of this year more often begin with "they," or "what"; as, "they go up in it" (balloon), "they kick it" (football), etc.

Why, it may be asked, is the use definition regarded as inferior to the descriptive or the classificatory definition? Is not the use to which an object may be put the most essential thing about it, for the child at least? Is it not more important to know that a fork is to eat with than to be able to name the material it is made of? Is not the use primary and does it not determine most of the physical characteristics of the object?

The above questions may sound reasonable, but they are based on poor psychology. We must rest our case upon the facts. The first lesson which the student of child psychology must learn is that it is unsafe to set up criteria of intelligence, of maturity, or of any other mental trait on the basis of theoretical considerations. Experiment teaches that normal children of 5 or 6 years, also older feeble-minded persons of the 5-year intelligence level, define objects in terms of use; also that normal children of 8 or 9 years and older feeble-minded persons of this mental level have for the most part developed beyond the stage of use definitions into the descriptive or classificatory stage. An ounce of fact is worth a ton of theory.

The test has usually been located in year IX, with the requirement of three successes out of five trials and with somewhat more rigid scoring of the individual definitions. When only two successes are required in four trials, and when scored leniently, the test belongs at the 8-year level.

VIII, 6. Vocabulary; twenty definitions, 3600 words

Procedure. Use the list of words given in the record booklet. Say to the child: "*I want to find out how many words you know. Listen; and when I say a word you tell me what it means.*" If the child can read, give him a printed copy of the word list and let him look at each word as you pronounce it.

The words are arranged approximately (though not exactly) in the order of their difficulty, and it is best to begin with the easier words and proceed to the harder. With children under 9 or 10 years, begin with the first. Apparently normal children of 10 years may safely be credited with the first ten words without being asked to define them. Apparently normal children of 12 may begin with word 16, and 15-year-olds with word 21. Except with subjects of almost adult intelligence there is no need to give the last ten or fifteen words, as these are almost never correctly defined by school children. A safe rule to follow is to continue until eight or ten successive words have been missed and to score the remainder *minus* without giving them.

The formula is as follows: "What is an *orange*?" "What is a *bonfire*?" "*Roar*; what does *roar* mean?" "*Gown*; what is a *gown*?" "What does *tap* mean?" "What does *scorch* mean?" "What is a *puddle*?" etc.

Some children at first show a little hesitation about answering, thinking that a strictly formal definition is expected. In such cases a little encouragement is necessary; as: "*You know what a bonfire is. You have seen a bonfire. Now, what is a bonfire?*" If the child still hesitates, say: "*Just tell me in your own words; say it any way you please. All I want is to find out whether you know what a bonfire is.*" Do not torture the child, however, by undue insistence. If he persists in his refusal to define a word which he would ordinarily be expected to know, it is better to pass on to the next one and to return to the troublesome word later. Above all, avoid helping the child by illustrating the use of a word in a sentence. Adhere strictly to the formula given above. If the definition as given does not make it clear whether the child has the correct idea, say: "*Explain,*" or, "*I don't understand; explain what you mean.*"

Encourage the child frequently by saying: "That's fine. You are doing beautifully. You know lots of words," etc. Never tell the child his definition is not correct, and never ask for a different definition.

Avoid saying anything which would suggest a model form of definition, as the type of definition which the child spontaneously chooses throws interesting light on the degree of maturity of the apperceptive processes. Record all definitions *verbatim* if possible, or at least those which are exceptionally good, poor, or doubtful.

Scoring. Credit a response in full if it gives one correct meaning for the word, regardless of whether that meaning is the most common one, and regardless of whether it is the original or a derived meaning. Occasionally half credit may be given, but this should be avoided as far as possible.

To find the entire vocabulary, multiply the number of words known by 180. (This list is made up of 100 words selected by rule from a dictionary containing 18,000 words.) Thus, the child who defines 20 words correctly has a vocabulary of 20 × 180 = 3600 words; 50 correct definitions would mean a vocabulary of 9000 words, etc. The following are the standards for different years, as determined by the vocabulary reached by 60 to 65 per cent of the subjects of the various mental levels:—

8 years	20 words	vocabulary 3,600
10 years	30 words	vocabulary 5,400
12 years	40 words	vocabulary 7,200
14 years	50 words	vocabulary 9,000
Average adult	65 words	vocabulary 11,700
Superior adult	75 words	vocabulary 13,500

Although the form of the definition is significant, it is not taken into consideration in scoring. The test is intended to explore the range of ideas rather than the evolution of thought forms. When it is evident that the child has one fairly correct meaning for a word, he is given full credit for it, however poorly the definition may have been stated.

While there is naturally some difficulty now and then in deciding whether a given definition is correct, this happens much less frequently than one would expect. In order to get a definite idea of the extent of error due to the individual differences among examiners, we have had the definitions of 25 subjects graded independently by 10 different persons. The result showed an average difference below 3 in the number of definitions scored *plus*. Since these subjects attempted on an average about 60 words, the average number of doubtful definitions per subject was below 5 per cent of the number attempted.

An idea of the degree of leniency to be exercised may be had from the following examples of definitions, which are mostly of low grade, but acceptable unless otherwise indicated:—

1. *Orange.* "An orange is to eat." "It is yellow and grows on a tree." (Both full credit.)
2. *Bonfire.* "You burn it outdoors." "You burn some leaves or things." "It's a big fire." (All full credit.)
3. *Roar.* "A lion roars." "You holler loud." (Full credit.)
4. *Gown.* "To sleep in." "It's a nightie." "It's a nice gown that ladies wear." (All full credit.)
5. *Puddle.* "You splash in it." "It's just a puddle of water." (Both full credit.)
6. *Straw.* "It grows in the field." "It means wheat-straw." "The horses eat it." (All full credit.)
7. *Rule.* "The teacher makes rules." "It means you can't do something." "You make marks with it," i.e., a ruler, often called a *rule* by school children. (All full credit.)
8. *Afloat.* "To float on the water." "A ship floats." (Both full credit.)

9. *Eyelash.* If the child says, "It's over the eye," tell him to point to it, as often the word is confused with *eyebrow*.

10. *Copper.* "It's a penny." "It means some copper wire." (Both full credit.)

11. *Health.* "It means good health or bad health." "It means strong." (Both full credit.)

12. *Guitar.* "You play on it." (Full credit.)

13. *Mellow.* If the child says, "It means a mellow apple," ask what kind of apple that would be. For full credit the answer must be "soft," "mushy," etc.

14. *Pork.* If the answer is "meat," ask what animal it comes from. Half credit if wrong animal is named.

15. *Plumbing.* "You fix pipes." (Full credit.)

16. *Southern.* If the answer is "Southern States," or "Southern California," say: *"Yes; but what does 'southern' mean?"* Do not credit unless explanation is forthcoming.

17. *Noticeable.* "You notice a thing." (Full credit.)

18. *Civil.* "Civil War." (Failure unless explained.) "It means to be nice." (Full credit.)

19. *Treasury.* Give half credit for definitions like "Valuables," "Lots of money," etc.; i.e., if the word is confused with *treasure*.

20. *Ramble.* "To go about fast." (Half credit.)

21. *Nerve.* Half credit if the slang use is defined, "You've got nerve," etc.

22. *Majesty.* "What you say to a king." (Full credit.)

23. *Sportive.* "To like sports." (Half credit.) "Playful" or "happy." (Full credit.)

24. *Hysterics.* "You laugh and cry at the same time." "A kind of sickness." "A kind of fit." (All full credit.)

25. *Repose.* "You pose again." (Failure.)

26. *Coinage.* "A place where they make money." (Half credit.)

27. *Dilapidated.* "Something that's very old." (Half credit.)

28. *Conscientious.* "You're careful how you do your work." (Full credit.)

29. *Artless.* "No art." (Failure unless correctly explained.)

30. *Priceless.* "It has no price." (Failure.)

31. *Promontory.* "Something prominent." (Failure unless child can explain what it refers to.)

32. *Milksop.* "You sop up milk." (Failure.)

33. *Harpy.* "A kind of bird." (Full credit.)

34. *Exaltation.* "You feel good." (Full credit.)

35. *Retroactive.* "Acting backward." (Full credit.)

36. *Theosophy.* "A religion." (Full credit.)

It is seen from the above examples that a very liberal standard has been used. Leniency in judging definitions is necessary because the child's power of expression lags farther behind his understanding than is true of adults, and also because for the young subject the word has a relatively less unitary existence.

Remarks. Our vocabulary test was derived by selecting the last word of every sixth column in a dictionary containing approximately 18,000 words, presumably the 18,000 most common words in the language. The test is based on the assumption that 100 words selected according to some arbitrary rule will be a large enough sampling to afford a fairly reliable index of a subject's entire vocabulary. Rather extensive experimentation with this list and others chosen in a similar manner has proved that the assumption is justified. Tests of the same 75 individuals with five different vocabulary tests of this type showed that the average difference between two tests of the same person was less than 5 per cent. This means that any one of the five tests used is reliable enough for all practical purposes. It is of no special importance that a given child's vocabulary is 8000 rather than 7600; the significance lies in the fact that it is approximately 8000 and not 4000, 12,000, or some other widely different number.

It may seem to the reader almost incredible that so small a sampling of words would give a reliable index of an individual's vocabulary. That it does so is due to the operation of the ordinary laws of chance. It is analogous to predicting the results of an election when only a small proportion of the ballots have been counted. It is known that a ballot box contains 600 votes, and if when only 30 have been counted it is found that they are divided between two candidates in the proportion of 20 and 10, it is safe to predict that a complete count will give the two candidates approximately 400 and 200 respectively.[61] In 1914 about 1,000,000 votes were cast for governor in California, and when only 10,000 votes had been counted, or a hundredth of all, it was announced and conceded that Governor Johnson had been reëlected by the 150,000 plurality. The completed count gave him 188,505 plurality. The error was less than 4 per cent of the total vote.

The vocabulary test has a far higher value than any other single test of the scale. Used with children of English-speaking parents (with children whose home language is not English it is of course unreliable), it probably has a higher value than any three other tests in the scale. Our statistics show that in a large majority of cases the vocabulary test alone will give us an intelligence quotient within 10 per cent of that secured by the entire scale. Out of hundreds of English-speaking children we have not found one testing significantly above age who had a significantly low vocabulary; and correspondingly, those who test much below age never have a high vocabulary.

Occasionally, however, a subject tests somewhat higher or lower in vocabulary than the mental age would lead us to expect. This is often the case with dull children in cultured homes and with very intelligent children whose home environment has not stimulated language development. But even in these cases we are not seriously misled, for the dull child of fortunate home surroundings shows his dullness in the quality of his definitions if not in their quantity; while the bright child of illiterate parents shows his intelligence in the aptness and accuracy of his definitions.

We have not worked out a satisfactory method of scoring the quality of definitions in our vocabulary test, but these differences will be readily observed by the trained examiner. Definitions in terms of use and definitions which are slightly inaccurate or hazy are quite characteristic of the lower mental ages. Children of the lower mental age have also a tendency to venture wild guesses at words they do not know. This is especially characteristic of retarded subjects and is another example of their weakness of auto-criticism. One feeble-minded boy of 12 years, with a mental age of 8 years, glibly and confidently gave definitions for every one of the hundred words. About 70 of the definitions were pure nonsense.

This vocabulary test was arranged and partially standardized by Mr. H. G. Childs and the writer in 1911. Many experiments since then have proved its value as a test of intelligence.

VIII, Alternative test 1: naming six coins

Procedure is exactly as in VI, 5 (naming four coins). The dollar should be shown before the half-dollar.

Scoring. *All six coins must be correctly named.* If a response is changed the rule is to count the second answer and ignore the first.

Remarks. Binet used nine pieces and required knowledge of all at year X (1908), but at year IX in the 1911 revision. Most other workers have used the same method, with the test located in either year IX or year X.

VIII, Alternative test 2: writing from dictation

Procedure. Give the child pen, ink, and paper, place him in a comfortable position for writing, and say: *"I want you to write something for me as nicely as you can. Write these words: 'See the little boy.' Be sure to write it all: 'See the little boy.'"*

Do not dictate the words separately, but give the sentence as a whole. Further repetition of the sentence is not permissible, as ability to remember what has been dictated is a part of the test. Copy, of course, must not be shown.

Scoring. Passed if the sentence is written legibly enough to be easily recognized, and if no word has been omitted. Ordinary mistakes of spelling are disregarded. The rule is that the mistake in spelling must not mutilate the word beyond easy recognition. The performance may be graded by the use of Thorndike's handwriting scale. The handwriting of 8-year-old children who have been in school not less than one year or more than two usually falls between quality 7 and quality 9 on this scale, but we shall, perhaps, not be too liberal if we consider a performance satisfactory which does not grade below quality 6, provided it is not seriously mutilated by errors, omissions, etc.[62]

Remarks. This test found a place in year VIII of Binet's 1908 scale, but has been omitted from all the other revisions, including Binet's own. Bobertag did not even regard the test as worthy of a trial. The universal criticism has been that it is a test of schooling rather than of intelligence. That the performance depends, in a certain sense, upon special instruction is self-evident. Without such instruction no child of 8 years, however intelligent, would be able to pass the test. Nature does not give us a conventionalized language, either written or spoken. It must be acquired. It is also true that a high-grade feeble-minded child, say 8 years of age and of 6-year intelligence, is sometimes (though not always) able to pass the test after two years of school instruction. It is exceedingly improbable, however, that a feeble-minded subject with less than 6-year intelligence will ever be able to pass this test, however long he remains in school.

The conclusions to be drawn from these facts are as follows: (1) Inability to pass the test should not be counted against the child unless it is known that he has had at least a full year of the usual school instruction. (2) Ability to pass the test after only two years of school instruction is almost certain proof that the child has reached a mental level of at least 6 years. (3) Failure to pass the test must be regarded as a grave symptom in the case of the child 9 or more years of age who is known to have attended school as much as two years. (4) For mental levels higher than 8 years the test has hardly any diagnostic value, since feeble-minded persons of 8- or 9-year intelligence can usually be taught to write quite legibly.

If the limitations above set forth are kept in mind, the test is by no means without value, and is always worth giving as a supplementary test. Learning to write simple sentences from dictation is no mean accomplishment. It demands, in the first place, a fairly complete mastery of rather difficult muscular coördinations. Moreover, these coördinations must be firmly associated with the corresponding letters and words, for if the writing coördinations are not fairly automatic, so much attention will be required to carry them out that the child will not be able to remember what he has been told to write. The necessity of remembering the passage acts as a distraction, and writing from dictation is therefore a more difficult task than writing from copy.

FOOTNOTES:

[56] The Stanford record booklet contains the circle ready for use.

[57] See IV, 5, and VI, 4.

[58] For aid in classifying the responses in this and certain other tests the writer is indebted to Miss Grace Lyman.

[59] One is here reminded of the puzzling conundrum, "Why is a brick like an elephant?" The answer being, "Because neither can climb a tree!" A response of this type states a fact, but because of its bizarre nature should hardly be counted satisfactory.

[60] For further discussion of the processes involved, see VII, 5.

[61] Supposing the ballots to have been shuffled.

[62] See scoring card for samples of satisfactory and unsatisfactory performances.

CHAPTER XV
INSTRUCTIONS FOR YEAR IX

IX, 1. Giving the date

Procedure. Ask the following questions in order:—

a. *"What day of the week is it to-day?"*
b. *"What month is it?"*
c. *"What day of the month is it?"*
d. *"What year is it?"*

If the child misunderstands and gives the day of the month for the day of the week, or *vice versa*, we merely repeat the question with suitable emphasis, but give no other help.

Scoring. An error of three days in either direction is allowed for *c*, but *a*, *b*, and *d* must all be given correctly. If the child makes an error and spontaneously corrects it, the change is allowed, but corrections must not be called for or suggested.

Remarks. Binet originally located this test in year IX, but unfortunately moved it to year VIII in the 1911 revision. Kuhlmann, Goddard, and Huey all retain it in year IX, where, according to our own data, it unquestionably belongs. With the exception of Binet's 1911 results, the statistics for the test are in remarkably close agreement for children in France, Germany, England, and Eastern and Western United States. It seems that practically all children in civilized countries have ample opportunity to learn the divisions of the year, month, and week, and to become oriented with respect to these divisions. Special instruction is doubtless capable of hastening time orientation to a certain degree, but not greatly. Binet tells of a French *école maternelle* attended by children 4 to 6 years of age, where instruction was given daily in regard to the date, and yet not a single one of the children was able to pass this test. This is a beautiful illustration of the futility of precocious teaching. In spite of well-meant instruction, it is not until the age of 8 or 9 years that children have enough comprehension of time periods, and sufficient interest in them, to keep very close track of the date. Failure to pass the test at the age of 10 or 11 years is a decidedly unfavorable sign, unless the error is very slight.

The fact that normal adults are occasionally unable to give the day of the month is no argument against the validity of the test, since the system of tests is so constructed as to allow for accidental failures on any particular test. As a matter of fact, very nearly 100 per cent of normal 12-year-old children pass this test.

The unavoidable fault of the test is its lack of uniformity in difficulty at different dates. It is easier for school children to give the day of the week on Monday or Friday than on Tuesday, Wednesday, or Thursday. Mistakes in giving the day of the month are less likely to occur at the beginning or end of the month than at any other time, while mistakes in naming the month are most likely to occur then.

It is interesting to compare the four parts of this test in regard to difficulty. Binet and Bobertag both state that ability to name the year comes last, but they give no figures. Our own data show that the four parts of the test are of almost exactly the same difficulty and that this is true at all ages.

IX, 2. Arranging five weights

Use the five weights, 3, 6, 9, 12, and 15 grams. Be sure that the weights are identical in appearance. The weights may be made as described under V, 1, or they may be purchased of C. H. Stoelting & Co., Chicago, Illinois. If no weights are at hand one of the alternative tests may be substituted.

Procedure. Place the five boxes on the table in an irregular group before the child and say: *"See the boxes. They all look alike, don't they? But they are not alike. Some of them are heavy, some are not quite so heavy, and some are still lighter. No two weigh the same. Now, I want you to find the heaviest one and place it here. Then find the one that is just a little lighter and put it here. Then put the next lighter one here, and the next lighter one* *here, and the lightest of all at this end* (pointing each time at the appropriate spot). *Do you understand?"* Whatever the child answers, in order to make sure that he does understand, we repeat the instructions thus: *"Remember now, that no two weights are the same. Find the heaviest one and put it here, the next heaviest here, and lighter, lighter, until you have the very lightest here. Ready; go ahead."*

It is best to follow very closely the formula here given, otherwise there is danger of stating the directions so abstractly that the subject could not comprehend them. A formula like *"I want you to arrange the blocks in a gradually decreasing series according to weight"* would be Greek to most children of 10 years.

If the subject still seems at a loss to know what to do, the instructions may be again repeated. But no further help of any kind may be given. Do not tell the subject to take the blocks one at a time in the hand and try them, and do not illustrate by hefting the blocks yourself. It is a part of the test to let the subject find his own method.

Give three trials, shuffling the boxes after each. Do not repeat the instructions before the second and third trials unless the subject has used an absurd procedure in the previous trial.

Scoring. The test is passed if the blocks are arranged in the correct order *twice out of three trials*. Always record the order of arrangement and note the number and extent of displacement. Obviously an arrangement like 12–6–15–3–9 is very much more serious than one like 15–12–6–9–3, but we require that two trials be absolutely without error.

Scoring is facilitated if the blocks are marked on the bottom so that they may be easily identified. It is then necessary to exercise some care to see that the subject does not examine the bottom of the blocks for a clue as to the correct order.

Remarks. Binet originally located this test in year IX, but in his 1911 revision changed it to year VIII. Other revisions have retained it in year IX. The correct location depends upon the weights used and upon the procedure and scoring. Kuhlmann uses weights of 3, 9, 18, 27, 36, and 45 grams, and this probably makes the test easier. Bobertag tried two sets of boxes, one set being of larger dimensions than the other. The larger gave decidedly the more errors. If we require only one success in three trials the test could be located a year or two lower in the scale, while three successes as a standard would require that it be moved upward possibly as much as two years.

Much depends also on whether the child is left to find his own method, and on this there has been much difference of procedure. Kuhlmann, Bobertag, and Wallin illustrate the correct method of making the comparison by first hefting and arranging the weights while the subject looks on. We prefer to keep the test in its original form, and with the procedure and scoring we have used it is well located in year IX.

Wallin carries his assistance still further by saying, after the first block has been placed, "Now, find the heaviest of the four," and after the second has been placed, "Now, find the heaviest of the three," etc. Finally, when the arrangement has been made, he tells the subject to try them again to make sure the order is correct, allowing the subject to make whatever changes he thinks necessary. This procedure robs the test of its most valuable features. The experiment was not devised primarily as a test of sensory discrimination, for it has long been recognized that individuals who have developed as far as the 9- or 10-year level of intelligence are ordinarily but little below normal in sensory capacity.

Psychologically, the test resembles that of comparing weights in V, 1. Success depends, in the first place, upon the correct comprehension of the task and the setting of a goal to be attained; secondly, upon the choice of a suitable method for realizing the goal; and finally, upon the ability to keep the end clearly in consciousness until all the steps necessary for its attainment have been gone through. Elementary as are the processes involved, they represent the prototype of all purposeful behavior. The statesman, the lawyer, the teacher, the physician, the carpenter, all in their own way and with their own materials, are continually engaged in setting goals, choosing means, and inhibiting the multitudinous appeals of irrelevant and distracting ideas.

In this experiment the subject may fail in any one of the three requirements of the test or in all of them. (1) He may not comprehend the instructions and so be unable to set the goal. (2) Though understanding what is expected of him, he may adopt an absurd method of carrying out the task. Or (3) he may lose sight of the end and begin to play with the blocks, stacking them on top of one another, building trains, tossing them about, etc. Sometimes the guiding idea is not completely lost, but is weakened or rendered only partially operative. In such a case the subject may compare some of the blocks carefully, place others without trying them at all, but continue in his half-rational, half-irrational procedure until all the blocks have been arranged.

It is essential, therefore, to supplement the mere record of success or failure by jotting down a brief but accurate description of the performance. Note any hesitation or inability to grasp the instructions. Note especially any absurd procedure, such as placing all the blocks without hefting any of them, comparing only some of them, holding them up and shaking them, hefting two at once in the same hand, etc. The ideal method, of course, is to try all the blocks carefully before placing any of them, then to make a tentative arrangement, and finally, to correct this tentative arrangement by means of individual comparisons. A slight departure from this method does not always bring failure, but it renders success less probable. As a rule it is only the very intelligent children of 10 years who think to test out their first arrangement by making a final and additional trial of each block in turn. Contrary to what might be supposed, success is slightly favored by hefting the blocks successively with one hand rather than by taking one in each hand for simultaneous comparison, but as the child cannot be expected to know this, we must regard the two methods as equally logical.

The test of arranging weights has met universal praise. Its special advantage is that it tests the subject's intelligence in the manipulation of *things* rather than his capacity for dealing with *abstractions*. It tests his ability to do something rather than his ability to express himself in language. It throws light upon certain factors of motor adaptation and practical judgment which play a great part in the everyday life of the average human being. It depends as little upon school, perhaps, as any other test of the scale, and it is readily usable with children of all nations without danger of being materially altered in translation Moreover, it is always an interesting test for the child. Bobertag goes so far as to say that any 8- or 9-year child who passes this test cannot possibly be feeble-minded. This may be true; but the converse is hardly the case; that is, the failure of older children is by no means certain proof of mental retardation. The same observation, however, applies equally well to many other of the Binet tests, some of which correlate more closely with true mental age than this one. A rather considerable fraction of normal 12-year-olds fail on it, and it is in fact somewhat less dependable than certain other tests if we wish to differentiate between 9-year and 11-year intelligence. But it is a test we could ill afford to eliminate.[63]

IX, 3. Making change

Procedure. Ask the following questions in the order here given:—

a. *"If I were to buy 4 cents worth of candy and should give the storekeeper 10 cents, how much money would I get back?"*
b. *"If I bought 13 cents worth and gave the storekeeper 15 cents, how much would I get back?"*
c. *"If I bought 4 cents worth and gave the storekeeper 25 cents, how much would I get back?"*

Coins are not used, and the subject is not allowed the help of pencil and paper. If the subject forgets the statement of the problem, it is permissible to repeat it once, but only once. The response should be made in ten or fifteen seconds for each problem.

Scoring, The test is passed if *two out of three* problems are answered correctly in the allotted time. In case two answers are given to a problem, we follow the usual rule of counting the second and ignoring the first.

Remarks. Problems of this nature, when thoroughly standardized, are extremely valuable as tests of intelligence. The difficulty of the test, as we have used it, does not lie in the subtraction of 4 from 10, 12 from 15, etc. Such subtractions, when given as problems in subtraction, are readily solved by practically all normal 8-year-olds who have attended school as much as two years. The problems of the test have a twofold difficulty: (1) The statement of the problem must be comprehended and held in mind until the solution has been arrived at; (2) the problem is so stated that the subject must himself select the fundamental operation which applies. The latter difficulty is somewhat the greater of the two, addition sometimes being employed instead of subtraction.

It is just such difficulties as this that prove so perplexing to the feeble-minded. High-grade defectives, although they require more than the usual amount of drill and are likely to make occasional errors, are nevertheless capable of learning to add, subtract, multiply, and divide fairly well. Their main trouble comes in deciding which of these operations a given problem calls for. They can master routine, but as regards initiative, judgment, and power to reason they are little educable. The psychology and pedagogy of mental deficiency is epitomized in this statement.

There has been little disagreement as to the proper location of the test of making change, but various procedures have been employed. Coins have generally been employed, in which case the subject is actually allowed to make the change. Most other revisions have also given only a single problem, usually 4 cents out of 20 cents, or 4 out of 25, or 9 out of 25. It is evident that these are not all of equal difficulty. There is general agreement, however, that normal children of 9 years should be able to make simple change.

IX, 4. Repeating four digits reversed

The series are 6–5–2–8; 4–9–3–7; 3–6–2–9.
Procedure and scoring. Exactly as in VII, alternate test 2.[64]

IX, 5. Using three words in a sentence

Procedure The words used are:—

a. *Boy, ball, river.*
b. *Work, money, men.*
c. *Desert, rivers, lakes.*

Say: *"You know what a sentence is, of course. A sentence is made up of some words which say something. Now, I am going to give you three words, and you must make up a sentence that has all three words in it. The three words are 'boy,' 'ball,' 'river.' Go ahead and make up a sentence that has all three words in it."* The others are given in the same way.

Note that the subject is not shown the three words written down, and that the reply is to be given orally.

If the subject does not understand what is wanted, the instruction may be repeated, but it is not permissible to illustrate what a sentence is by giving one. There must be no preliminary practice.

A curious misunderstanding which is sometimes encountered comes from assuming that the sentence must be constructed entirely of the three words given. If it appears that the subject is stumbling over this difficulty, we explain: *"The three words must be put with some other words so that all of them together will make a sentence."*

Nothing is said about hurrying, but if a sentence is not given within one minute the rule is to count that part of the test a failure and to proceed to the next trio of words.

Give only one trial for each part of the test.

Do not specially caution the child to avoid giving more than one sentence, as this is implied in the formula used and should be understood.

Scoring. The test is passed if *two of the three* sentences are satisfactory. In order to be satisfactory a sentence must fulfill the following requirements: (1) It must either be a simple sentence, or, if compound, must not contain more than two distinct ideas; and (2) it must not express an absurdity.

Slight changes in one or more of the key words are disregarded, as *river* for *rivers*, etc.

The scoring is difficult enough to justify rather extensive illustration.

(a) Boy, ball, river

Satisfactory. An analysis of 128 satisfactory responses gave the following classification:—

1. Simple sentence containing a simple subject and a simple predicate; as: "The boy threw his ball into the river." "The boy lost his ball in the river." "The boy's ball fell into the river." "The boy swam into the river after his ball," etc. This group contains 76 per cent of the correct responses.

2. A sentence with a simple subject and a compound predicate; as: "A boy went to the river and took his ball with him." About 8 per cent of all were of this type.

3. A complex sentence containing a relative clause (2 per cent only); as: "The boy ran after his ball which was rolling toward the river."

4. A compound sentence containing two independent clauses (about 14 per cent); as: "The boy had a ball and he lost it in the river."

Unsatisfactory. The failures fall into four chief groups:—

1. Sentences with three clauses (or else three separate sentences).

2. Sentences containing an absurdity.

3. Sentences which omit one of the key words.

4. Silence, due ordinarily to inability to comprehend the task.

Group 1 includes 78 per cent of the failures; group 2, about 12 per cent; and group 3 and 4 about 5 per cent each. Samples of group 1 are: "There was a boy, and he bought a ball, and it fell into the river." "I saw a boy, and he had a ball, and he was playing by the river." Illustration of an absurd sentence, "The boy was swimming in the river and he was playing ball."

(b) Work, money, men

Satisfactory:—

1. Sentence with a simple subject and simple predicate (including 75 per cent of 116 satisfactory responses); as: "Men work for their money." "Men get money for their work," etc.

2. A complex sentence with a relative clause (12 per cent of correct answers); as: "Men who work earn much money." "It is easy for men to earn money if they are willing to work," etc.

3. A compound sentence with two independent, coördinate clauses (13 per cent); as: "Men work and they earn money." "Some men have money and they do not work."

Unsatisfactory:—

1. Three clauses; as: "I know a man and he has money, and he works at the store."

2. Sentences which are absurd or meaningless; as: "Men work with their money."

3. Omission of one of the words.

4. Inability to respond.

(c) Desert, rivers, lakes

Satisfactory:—

1. Sentences with a simple subject and a simple predicate (including 84 per cent of 126 correct answers); as: "There are no rivers or lakes in the desert." "The desert has one river and one

lake," etc.

2. A complex sentence with a relative clause (only 2 per cent); as: "In the desert there was a river which flowed into a lake."

3. A compound sentence with two independent, coördinate clauses (11 per cent); as: "We went to the desert, and it had no rivers or lakes."

4. A compound, complex sentence (3 per cent of all); as: "There was a desert, and near by there was a river that emptied into a lake."

Unsatisfactory:—

1. Sentences with three clauses (40 per cent of all failures); as: "A desert is dry, rivers are long, lakes are rough."

2. Sentences containing an absurdity (12 per cent of the failures): as: "a desert is dry, rivers are long, lakes are filled with swimming boys." "The lake went through the desert and the river." "There was a desert and rivers and lakes in the forest." "The desert is full of rivers and lakes."

3. Omission of one of the words (40 per cent of the failures).

4. Inability to respond (8 per cent).

Remarks. The test of constructing a sentence containing given words was first used by Masselon and is known as "the Masselon experiment." Meumann, who used it in a rather extended experiment,[65] finds it a good test of intelligence and a reliable index as to the richness, definiteness, and maturity of the associative processes. As Meumann shows, it is instructive to study the qualitative differences between the responses of bright and dull children, apart from questions of sentence structure. These differences are especially discernible in (*a*) the logical qualities of the associations, and (*b*) the definiteness of statement. As regards (*a*), bright children are much more likely to use the given words as keystones in the construction of a sentence which would be logically suggested by them. For example, *donkey, blows*, suggest some such sentence as, "The donkey receives blows because he is lazy." In like manner we have found that the words *work, money, men* usually suggest to the more intelligent children a sentence like "Men work for their money" (or "because they need money," etc.), while the dull child is more likely to give some such sentence as "The men have work and they don't have much money." That is, the sentence of the dull child, even though correct in structure and free enough from outright absurdity to satisfy the standard of scoring which we have set forth, is likely to express ideas which are more or less nondescript, ideas not logically suggested by the set of words given.

The experiment is one of the many forms of the "completion test," or "the combination method." As we have already noted, the power to combine more or less separate and isolated elements into a logical whole is one of the most essential features of intelligence. The ability to do so in a given case depends, in the first place, upon the number and logical quality of the associations which have previously been made with each of the given elements separately, and in the second place, upon the readiness with which these ideational stores yield up the particular associations necessary for weaving the given words into some kind of unity. The child must pass from what is given to what is not given but merely suggested. This requires a certain amount of invention. Scattered fragments must be conceived as the skeleton of a thought, and this skeleton, or partial skeleton, must be assembled and made whole. The task is analogous to that which confronts the palæontologist, who is able to reconstruct, with a high degree of certainty, the entire skeleton of an extinct animal from the evidence furnished by three or four fragments of bones. It is no wonder, therefore, that subjects whose ideational stores are scanty, and whose associations are based upon accidental rather than logical connections, find the test one of peculiar difficulty. Invention thrives in a different soil.

Binet located this test in year X. Goddard and Kuhlmann assign it the same location, though their actual statistics agree closely with our own. Our procedure makes the test somewhat easier than that of Binet, who gave only one trial and used the somewhat more difficult words *Paris, river, fortune*. Others have generally followed the Binet procedure, merely substituting for Paris the name of a city better known to the subject. Binet's requirement of a written response also makes the test harder.

Perhaps the greatest obstacle to uniformity in the use of the test comes from the difficulty of scoring, particularly in deciding whether the sentence contains enough absurdity to disqualify it, and whether it expresses three separate ideas or only two. It is hoped that the rather large variety of sample responses which we have given will reduce these difficulties to a minimum.

An additional word is necessary in regard to what constitutes an absurdity in (*b*). A sentence like "There are some rivers and lakes in the desert" is not an absurdity in certain parts of Western United States. In Professor Ordahl's tests at Reno, Nevada, many children whose intelligence was altogether above suspicion gave this reply. The statement is, indeed, perfectly true for the semi-arid region in the vicinity of Reno known as "the desert." On the other hand, such sentences as "The desert is full of rivers and lakes," or "There are forty rivers and lakes in the desert," can hardly be considered satisfactory. Similar difficulties are presented by (*c*), though not so frequently. "Men who work do not have money" expresses, unfortunately, more truth than nonsense.

IX, 6. Finding rhymes

Procedure. Say to the child: *"You know what a rhyme is, of course. A rhyme is a word that sounds like another word. Two words rhyme if they end in the same sound. Understand?"* Whether the child says he understands or not, we proceed to illustrate what a rhyme is, as follows: *"Take the two words 'hat' and 'cat.' They sound alike and so they make a rhyme. 'Hat,' 'rat,' 'cat,' 'bat' all rhyme with one another."*

That is, we first explain what a rhyme is and then we give an illustration. A large majority of American children who have reached the age of 9 years understand perfectly what a rhyme is, without any illustration. A few, however, think they understand, but do not; and in order to insure that all are given equal advantage it is necessary never to omit the illustration.

After the illustration say: *"Now, I am going to give you a word and you will have one minute to find as many words as you can that rhyme with it. The word is 'day.' Name all the words you can think of that rhyme with 'day.'"*

If the child fails with the first word, before giving the second we repeat the explanation and give sample rhymes for *day*; otherwise we proceed without further explanation to *mill* and *spring*, saying, *"Now, you have another minute to name all the words you can think of that rhyme with 'mill,'* etc. Apart from the mention of "one minute" say nothing to suggest hurrying, as this tends to throw some children into mental confusion.

Scoring. Passed if in *two out of the three* parts of the experiment the child finds *three words* which rhyme with the word given, the time limit for each series being *one minute*. Note that in each case there must be three words in addition to the word given. These must be real words, not meaningless syllables or made-up words. However, we should be liberal enough to accept such words as *ding* (from "ding-dong ") for *spring, Jill* (see "Jack and Jill") for *mill, Fay* (girl's name) for *day,* etc.

Remarks. At first thought it would seem that the demands made by this test upon intelligence could not be very great. Sound associations between words may be contrasted unfavorably with associations like those of cause and effect, part to whole, whole to part, opposites, etc. But when we pass from *a-priori* considerations to an examination of the actual data, we find that the giving of rhymes is closely correlated with general intelligence.

The 9-year-olds who test at or above 10 years nearly always do well in finding rhymes, while 9-year-olds who test as low as 8 years seldom pass. When a test thus shows high correlation with the scale as a whole, we must either accept the test as valid or reject the scale altogether. While the feeble-minded do not do as well in this test as normal children of corresponding mental age, the percentage successes for them rises rapidly between mental age 8 and mental age 10 or 11.

Closer psychological analysis of the processes involved will show why this is true. To find rhymes for a given word means that one must hunt out verbal associations under the direction of a guiding idea. Every word has innumerable associations and many of these tend, in greater or less degree, to be aroused when the stimulus word is given. In order to succeed with the test, however, it is necessary to inhibit all associations which are not relevant to the desired end. The directing idea must be held so firmly in mind that it will really direct the thought associations. Besides acting to inhibit the irrelevant, it must create a sort of magnetic stress (to borrow a figure from physics) which will give dominance to those associative tendencies pointing in the right direction. Even the feeble-minded child of imbecile grade has in his vocabulary a great many words which rhyme with *day, mill,* and *spring.* He fails on the test because his verbal associations cannot be subjugated to the influence of a directing idea. The end to be attained does not dominate consciousness sufficiently to create more than a faint stress. Instead of a single magnetic pole there is a conflict of forces. The result is either chaos or partial success. *Mill* may suggest *hill,* and then perhaps the directing idea becomes suddenly inoperative and the child gives *mountain, valley,* or some other irrelevant association. The lack of associations, however, is a more frequent cause of failure than inability to inhibit the irrelevant.

If any one supposes that finding rhymes does not draw upon the higher mental powers, let him try the experiment upon himself in various stages of mental efficiency, say at 9 A.M., when mentally refreshed by a good night of sleep and again when fatigued and sleepy. Poets questioned by Galton on this point all testified to the greater difficulty of finding rhymes when mentally fatigued. In this and in many other respects the mental activities of the fatigued or sleepy individual approach the type of mentation which is normal to the feeble-minded.

It is important to note that adults make a less favorable showing in this test than normal children of corresponding mental age, Mr. Knollin's "hoboes" of 12-year intelligence doing hardly as well as school children of 10-year intelligence. Those who are habitually employed in school exercises probably acquire an adeptness in verbal associations which is later gradually lost in the preoccupations of real life.

There has been more disagreement as to the proper location of this test than of any other test of the Binet scale. Binet placed it in year XII of the 1908 scale, but shifted it to year XV in 1911. Kuhlmann retains it in year XII, while Goddard drops it down to year XI. However, when we examine the actual statistics for normal children we do not find very marked disagreement, and such disagreement as is present can be largely accounted for by variations in procedure and by differing conclusions drawn from identical data. In the first place, Binet gave but one trial. This, of course, makes the test much harder than when three trials are given and only two successes are required. To make one trial equal in difficulty to three trials we should perhaps need to demand only two rhymes, instead of three, in the one trial. In the second place, the word used by Binet (*obeissance*) is much harder than one-syllable words like *day, mill,* and *spring.* Finally, the wide shift of the test from year XII to year XV was not justified by the statistics of Binet himself, and the figures of Kuhlmann and Goddard are really in exceptionally close agreement with our own, notwithstanding the fact that Goddard required three successes instead of two. In four series of tests, considered together, we have found 62 per cent passing at year IX, 81 per cent at year X, 83 per cent at year XI, and 94 per cent at year XII.

IX, Alternative test 1: naming the months

Procedure. Simply ask the subject to *"name all the months of the year."* Do not start him off by naming one month; give no look of approval or disapproval as the months are being named, and make no suggestions or comments of any kind.

When the months have been named, we "check up" the performance by asking: *"What month comes before April?" "What month comes before July?" "What month comes before November?"*

Scoring. Passed if the months are named in about *fifteen or twenty seconds with no more than one error* of omission, repetition, or displacement, and if *two out of the three check questions* are answered correctly. Disregard place of beginning.

Remarks. Some are inclined to consider this test of little value, because of its supposed dependence on accidental training. With this opinion we cannot fully agree. The arguments already given in favor of the retention of naming the days of the week (year VII), apply equally well in the present case. It has been shown, however, that age, apart from intelligence, does have some effect on the ability to name the months.

Defective adults of 9-year intelligence do about as well with it as normal children of 10-year intelligence.

The test appears in year X of Binet's 1908 scale and in year IX of the 1911 revision. Goddard places it correctly in year IX, while Kuhlmann and Bobertag have omitted it.

IX, Alternative test 2: counting the value of stamps

Procedure. Place before the subject a cardboard on which are pasted three 1-cent and three 2-cent stamps arranged as follows: 111222. Be sure to lay the card so that the stamps will be right side up for the child. Say: *"You know, of course, how much a stamp like this costs* (pointing to a 1-cent stamp). *And you know how much one like this costs* (pointing to a 2-cent stamp). *Now, how much money would it take to buy all these stamps?"*

Do not tell the individual values of the stamps if these are not known, for it is a part of the test to ascertain whether the child's spontaneous curiosity has led him to find out and remember their values. If the individual values are known, but the first answer is wrong, a second trial may be given. In such cases, however, it is necessary to be on guard against guessing.

If the child merely names an incorrect sum without saying anything to indicate how he arrived at his answer, it is well to tell him to figure it up aloud. *"Tell me how you got it."*

Scoring. Passed if the correct value is given in not over fifteen seconds.

Remarks. The value of this test may be questioned on two grounds: (1) That it has an ambiguous significance, since failure to pass it may result either from incorrect addition or from lack of knowledge of the individual values of the stamps; (2) that familiarity with stamps and their values is so much a matter of accident and special instruction that the test is not fair.

Both criticisms are in a measure valid. The first, however, applies equally well to a great many useful intelligence tests. In fact, it is only a minority in which success depends on but one factor. The other criticism has less weight than would at first appear. While it is, of course, not impossible for an intelligent child to arrive at the age of 9 years without having had reasonable opportunity to learn the cost of the common postage stamps, the fact is that a large majority have had the opportunity and that most of those of normal intelligence have taken advantage of it. It is necessary once more to emphasize the fact that in its method of locating a test the Binet system makes ample allowance for "accidental" failures.

Like the tests of naming coins, repeating the names of the days of the week or the months of the year, giving the date, tying a bow-knot, distinguishing right and left, naming the colors, etc., this one also throws light on the child's spontaneous interest in common objects. It is mainly the children of deficient intellectual curiosity who do not take the trouble to learn these things at somewhere near the expected age.

The test was located in year VIII of the Binet scale. However, Binet used coins, three single and three double sous. Since we do not have either a half-cent or a 2-cent coin, it has been necessary to substitute postage stamps. This changes the nature of the test and makes it much harder. It becomes less a test of ability to do a simple sum, and more a test of knowledge as to the value of the stamps used. That the test is easy enough for year VIII when it can be given in the original form is indicated by all the French, German, and English statistics available, but four separate series of Stanford tests agree in finding it too hard for year VIII when stamps are substituted and the test is carried out according to the procedure described above.

FOOTNOTES:

[63] Compare with V, 1.

[64] See discussion, p. 207 *ff.*

[65] "Ueber eine neue Methode der Intelligenzprüfung und über den Wert der Kombinationsmethoden," in *Zeitschrift für Pädagogische Psychologie und Experimentelle Pädagogik* (1912), pp. 145–63.

CHAPTER XVI
INSTRUCTIONS FOR YEAR X

X, 1. Vocabulary (thirty definitions, 5400 words)

Procedure and scoring as in <u>VIII, 6</u>. At year X, thirty words should be correctly defined.

X, 2. Detecting absurdities

Procedure. Say to the child: *"I am going to read a sentence which has something foolish in it, some nonsense. I want you to listen carefully and tell me what is foolish about it."* Then read the sentences, rather slowly and in a matter-of-fact voice, saying after each: *"What is foolish about that?"* The sentences used are the following:—

a. *"A man said: 'I know a road from my house to the city which is downhill all the way to the city and downhill all the way back home.'"*
b. *"An engineer said that the more cars he had on his train the faster he could go."*
c. *"Yesterday the police found the body of a girl cut into eighteen pieces. They believe that she killed herself."*
d. *"There was a railroad accident yesterday, but it was not very serious. Only forty-eight people were killed."*
e. *"A bicycle rider, being thrown from his bicycle in an accident, struck his head against a stone and was instantly killed. They picked him up and carried him to the hospital, and they do not think he will get well again."*

Each should ordinarily be answered within thirty seconds. If the child is silent, the sentence should be repeated; but no other questions or suggestions of any kind are permissible. Such questions as *"Could the road be downhill both ways?"* or, *"Do you think the girl could have killed herself?"* would, of course, put the answer in the child's mouth. It is even best to avoid laughing as the sentence is read.

Owing to the child's limited power of expression it is not always easy to judge from the answer given whether the absurdity has really been detected or not. In such cases ask him to explain himself, using some such formula as: *"I am not sure I know what you mean. Explain what you mean. Tell me what is foolish in the sentence I read."* This usually brings a reply the correctness or incorrectness of which is more apparent, while at the same time the formula is so general that it affords no hint as to the correct answer. Additional questions must be used with extreme caution.

Scoring. Passed if the absurdity is detected in *four out of the five* statements. The following are samples of satisfactory and unsatisfactory answers:—

(a) The road downhill

Satisfactory. "If it was downhill to the city it would be uphill coming back." "It can't be downhill both directions." "That could not be." "That is foolish. (Explain.) Because it must be uphill one way or the other." "That would be a funny road. (Explain.) No road can be like that. It can't be downhill both ways."

Unsatisfactory. "Perhaps he took a little different road coming back." "I guess it is a very crooked road." "Coming back he goes around the hill." "The man lives down in a valley." "The road was made that way so it would be easy." "Just a road. I don't see anything foolish." "He should say, 'a road which goes.'"

(b) What the engineer said

Satisfactory. "If he has more cars he will go slower." "It is the other way. If he wants to go faster he mustn't have so many cars." "The man didn't mean what he said, or else it was a slip of the tongue." "That's the way it would be if he was going downhill." "Foolish, because the cars don't help pull the train." "He ought to say *slower*, not *faster*."

Unsatisfactory. "A long train is nicer." "The engine pulls harder if the train has lots of cars." "That's all right. I suppose he likes a big train." "Nothing foolish; when I went to the city I saw a train that had lots of cars and it was going awfully fast." "He should have said, 'the faster I can *run*.'"

(c) The girl who was thought to have killed herself

Satisfactory. "She could not have cut herself into eighteen pieces." "She would have been dead before that." "She might have cut two or three pieces off, but she couldn't do the rest." (Laughing) "Well, she may have killed herself; but if she did it's a sure thing that some one else came along after and chopped her up." "That policeman must have been a fool. (Explain.) To think that she could chop herself into eighteen pieces."

Unsatisfactory. "*Think* that she killed herself; they *know* she did." "They can't be sure. Some one may have killed her." "It was a foolish girl to kill herself." "How can they tell who killed her?" "No girl would kill herself unless she was crazy." "It ought to read: 'They think that she committed suicide.'"

(d) The railroad accident

Satisfactory. "That was very serious." "I should like to know what you would call a serious accident!" "You could say it was not serious if two or three people were killed, but forty-eight,—that is serious."

Unsatisfactory. "It was a foolish mistake that made the accident." "They couldn't help it. It was an accident." "It might have been worse." "Nothing foolish; it's just sad."

(e) The bicycle rider

Satisfactory. "How could he get well after he was already killed?" "Why, he's already dead." "No use to take a dead man to the hospital." "They ought to have taken him to a grave-yard!"

Unsatisfactory. "Foolish to fall off of a bicycle. He should have known how to ride." "They ought to have carried him home. (Why?) So his folks could get a doctor." "He should have been more careful." "Maybe they can cure him if he isn't hurt very bad." "There's nothing foolish in that."

Remarks. The detection of absurdities is one of the most ingenious and serviceable tests of the entire scale. It is little influenced by schooling, and it comes nearer than any other to being a test of that species of mother-wit which we call common sense. Like the "comprehension questions," it may be called a test of judgment, using this term in the colloquial and not in the logical sense. The stupid person, whether depicted in literature, proverb, or the ephemeral joke column, is always (and justly, it would seem) characterized by a huge tolerance for absurd contradictions and by a blunt sensitivity for the fine points of a joke. Intellectual discrimination and judgment are inferior. The ideas do not cross-light each other, but remain relatively isolated. Hence, the most absurd contradictions are swallowed, so to speak, without arousing the protest of the critical faculty. The latter, indeed, is only a name for the tendency of intellectually irreconcilable elements to clash. If there is no clash, if the elements remain apart, it goes without saying that there will be no power of criticism.

The critical faculty begins its development in the early years and strengthens *pari passu* with the growing wealth of inter-associations among ideas; but in the average child it is not until the age of about 10 years that it becomes equal to tasks like those presented in this test. Eight-year intelligence hardly ever scores more than two or three correct answers out of five. By 12, the critical ability has so far developed that the test is nearly always passed. It is an invaluable test for the higher grades of mental deficiency.

As a test of the critical powers Binet first used "trap questions"; as, for example, "Is snow red or black?" The results were disappointing, for it was found that owing to timidity, deference, and suggestibility normal children often failed on such questions. Deference is more marked in normal than in feeble-minded children, and it is because of the influence of this trait that it is necessary always to forewarn the subject that the sentence to be given contains nonsense.

Binet located the test in year XI of the 1908 scale, but changed it to year X in 1911. Goddard and Kuhlmann retain it in year XI. The large majority of the statistics, including those of Goddard and Kuhlmann, warrant the location of the test in year X. Not all have used the same absurdities, and these have not been worded uniformly. Most have required three successes out of five, but Bobertag and Kuhlmann require three out of four; Bobertag's procedure is also different in that he does not forewarn the child that an absurdity is to follow.

The present form of the test is the result of three successive refinements. It will be noted that we have made two substitutions in Binet's list of absurdities. Those omitted from the original scale are: *I have three brothers—Paul, Ernest, and myself,*" and, "*If I were going to commit suicide I would not choose Friday, because Friday is an unlucky day and would bring me misfortune.*" The last has a puzzling feature which makes it much too hard for year X, and the other is objectionable with children who are accustomed to hear a foreign language in which the form of expression used in the absurdity is idiomatically correct.

The two we have substituted for these objectionable absurdities are, "The road downhill" and "What the engineer said." The five we have used, though of nearly equal difficulty, are here listed in the order from easiest to hardest. Our series as a whole is slightly easier than Binet's.

X, 3. Drawing designs from memory

Procedure. Use the designs shown on the accompanying printed form. If copies are used they must be exact in size and shape. Before showing the card say: *"This card has two drawings on it. I am going to show them to you for ten seconds, then I will take the card away and let you draw from memory what you have seen. Examine both drawings carefully and remember that you have only ten seconds."*

Provide pencil and paper and then show the card for ten seconds, holding it at right angles to the child's line of vision and with the designs in the position given in the plate. Have the child draw the designs immediately after they are removed from sight.

Scoring. The test is passed if *one of the designs is reproduced correctly and the other about half correctly.* "Correctly" means that the *essential plan* of the design has been grasped and reproduced. Ordinary irregularities due to lack of motor skill or to hasty execution are disregarded. "Half correctly" means that some essential part of the design has been omitted or misplaced, or that parts have been added.

The sample reproductions shown on the scoring card will serve as a guide. It will be noted that an inverted design, or one whose right and left sides have been transposed, is counted only half correct, however perfect it many be in other respects; also that design *b* is counted only half correct if the inner rectangle is not located off center.

Remarks. Binet states that the main factors involved in success are "attention, visual memory, and a little analysis." The power of rapid analysis would seem to be the most important, for if the designs are analyzed they may be reproduced from a verbal memory of the analysis. Without some analysis it would hardly be possible to remember the designs at all, as one of them contains thirteen lines and the other twelve. The memory span for unrelated objects is far too limited to permit us to grasp and retain that number of unrelated impressions. Success is possible only by grouping the lines according to their relationships, so that several of them are given a unitary value and remembered as one. In this manner, the design to the right, which is composed of twelve lines, may be reduced to four elements: (1) The outer rectangle; (2) the inner rectangle; (3) the off-center position of the inner rectangle; and (4) the joining of the angles. Of course the child does not ordinarily make an analysis as explicit as this; but analysis of some kind, even though it be unconscious, is necessary to success.

Ability to pass the test indicates the presence, in a certain definite amount, of the tendency for the contents of consciousness to fuse into a meaningful whole. Failure indicates that the elements have maintained their unitary character or have fused inadequately. It is seen, therefore, that the test has a close kinship with the test of memory for sentences. The latter, also, permits the fusion or grouping of impressions according to meaning, with the result that five or six times as many meaningful syllables as nonsense syllables or digits can be retained.

Binet had many more failures on design *a* than on design *b*. This was probably due to the fact that he showed the designs with our *b* to the left. A majority of subjects, probably because of the influence of reading habits, examine first the figure to the left, and because of the short time allowed for the inspection are unable to devote much time to the design at the right. We have placed the design of greater intrinsic difficulty at the left, with the result that the failures are almost equally divided between the two.

Binet used this test in his unstandardized series of 1905, omitted it in 1908, but included it in the 1911 revision, locating it in year X. Except for Goddard, who recommends year XI, there is rather general agreement that the test belongs at year X. Our own data show that it may be placed either at year X or year XI, according as the grading is rigid or lenient.

X, 4. Reading for eight memories

Material. We use Binet's selection, slightly adapted, as follows:—

New York, September 5th. A fire last night burned three houses near the center of the city. It took some time to put it out. The loss was fifty thousand dollars, and seventeen families lost their homes. In saving a girl, who was asleep in a bed, a fireman was burned on the hands.

The copy of the selection used by the subject should be printed in heavy type and should not contain the bars dividing it into memories. The Stanford record booklet contains the selection in two forms, one suitable for use in scoring, the other in heavy type to be read by the subject.

Procedure. Hand the selection to the subject, who should be seated comfortably in a good light, and say: *"I want you to read this for me as nicely as you can."* The subject must read aloud.

Pronounce all the words which the subject is unable to make out, not allowing more than five seconds' hesitation in such a case.

Record all errors made in reading the selection, and the exact time. By "error" is meant the omission, substitution, transposition, or mispronunciation of one word.

The subject is not warned in advance that he will be asked to report what he has read, but as soon as he has finished reading, put the selection out of sight and say: *"Very well done. Now, I want you to tell me what you read. Begin at the first and tell everything you can remember."* After the subject has repeated everything he can recall and has stopped, say: *"And what else? Can you remember any more of it?"* Give no other aid of any kind. It is of course not permissible, when the child stops, to prompt him with such questions as, *"And what next? Where were the houses burned? What happened to the fireman?"* etc. The report must be spontaneous.

Now and then, though not often, a subject hesitates or even refuses to try, saying he is unable to do it. Perhaps he has misunderstood the request and thinks he is expected to repeat the selection word for word, as in the tests of memory for sentences. We urge a little and repeat: *"Tell me in your own words all you can remember of it."* Others misunderstand in a different way, and thinking they are expected to tell merely what the story is about, they say: "It was about some houses that burned." In such cases we repeat the instructions with special emphasis on the words *all you can remember*.

Scoring. The test is passed *if the selection is read in thirty-five seconds with not more than two errors, and if the report contains at least eight "memories."* By underscoring the memories correctly reproduced, and by interlineations to show serious departures from the text, the record can be made complete with a minimum of trouble.

The main difficulty in scoring is to decide whether a memory has been reproduced correctly enough to be counted. Absolutely literal reproduction is not expected. The rule is to count all memories whose thought is reproduced with only minor changes in the wording. "It took quite a while" instead of "it took some time" is satisfactory; likewise, "got burnt" for "was burned"; "who was sleeping" for "who was asleep"; "are homeless" for "lost their homes"; "in the middle" for "near the center"; "a big fire" for "a fire," etc.

Memories as badly mutilated as the following, however, are not counted: "A lot of buildings" for "three houses;" "a man" for "a fireman"; "who was sick" for "who was asleep"; etc. Occasionally we may give half credit, as in the case of "was seventeen thousand dollars" for "was fifty thousand dollars"; "and fifteen families" for "and seventeen families," etc.

Remarks. Are we warranted in using at all as a measure of intelligence a test which depends as much on instruction as this one does? Many are inclined to answer this question in the negative. The test has been omitted from the revisions of Goddard, Kuhlmann, and Binet himself. As regards Binet's earlier test of reading for two memories, in year VIII, there could hardly be any difference of opinion. The ability to read at that age depends so much on the accident of environment that the test is meaningless unless we know all about the conditions which have surrounded the child.

The use of the test in year X, however, is a very different matter. There are comparatively few children of that age who will fail to pass it for lack of the requisite school instruction. Children of 10 years who have attended school with reasonable regularity for three years are practically always able to read the selection in thirty-five seconds and without over two mistakes unless they are retarded almost to the border-line of mental deficiency. Of our 10-year-olds who failed to meet the test, only a fourth did so because of inability to meet the reading requirements as regards time or mistakes. The remaining failures were caused by inadequate report, and most of these subjects were of the distinctly retarded group.

We may conclude, therefore, that given anything approaching normal educational advantages, the test is really a measure of intelligence. Used with due caution, it is perhaps as valuable as any other test in the scale. It is only necessary, in case of failure, to ascertain the facts regarding the child's educational opportunities. Even this precaution is superfluous in case the subject tests as low as 8 years by the remainder of the scale. A safe rule is to omit the test from the calculation of mental age if the subject has not attended school the equivalent of two or three years.

It has been contended by some that tests in which success depends upon language mastery cannot be real tests of intelligence. By such critics language tests have been set over against intelligence tests as contrasting opposites. It is easy to show, however, that this view is superficial and psychologically unsound. Every one who has an acquaintance with the facts of mental growth knows that language mastery of some degree is the *sine qua non* of conceptual thinking. Language growth, in fact, mirrors the entire mental development. There are few more reliable indications of a subject's stage of intellectual maturity than his mastery of language.

The rate of reading, for example, is a measure of the rate of association. Letters become associated together in certain combinations making words, words into word groups and sentences. Recognition is for the most part an associative process. Rapid and accurate association will mean ready recognition of the printed form. Since language units (whether letters, words, or word groups) have more or less preferred associations according to their habitual arrangement into larger units, it comes about that in the normal mind under normal conditions these preferred sequences arouse the apperceptive complex necessary to make a running recognition rapid and easy. It is reasonable to suppose that in the subnormal mind the habitual common associations are less firmly fixed, thus diminishing the effectiveness of the ever-changing apperceptive expectancy. Reading is, therefore, largely dependent on what James calls the "fringe of consciousness" and the "consciousness of meaning." In reading connected matter, every unit is big with a mass of tendencies. The smaller and more isolated the unit, the greater is the number of possibilities. Every added unit acts as a modifier limiting the number of tendencies, until we have finally, in case of a large mental unit, a fairly manageable whole. When the most logical and suitable of these associations arise easily from subconsciousness to consciousness, recognition is made easy, and their doing so will depend on whether the habitual relations of the elements have left permanent traces in the mind.

The reading of the subnormal subject bears a close analogy to the reading of nonsense matter by the normal person. It has been ascertained by experiment that such reading requires about twice as much time as the reading of connected matter. This is true for the reason that out of thousands of associations possible with each word, no particular association is favored. The apperceptive expectancy, practically *nil* in the reading of nonsense material, must be decidedly deficient in all poor reading.

Furthermore, in the case of the ordinary reader there is a feeling of rightness or wrongness about the thought sequences. That less intelligent subjects have this sense of fitness to a much less degree is evidenced by their passing over words so mutilated in pronunciation as to deprive them of all meaning. The transposition of letters and words, and the failure to observe marks of punctuation, point to the same thing. In other words, all the reading of the stupid subject is with material which to him is more or less nonsensical.[66]

A little observation will convince one that mentally retarded subjects, even when they possess a reasonable degree of fluency in recognizing printed words, do not sense shades of meaning. Their reading is by small units. Words and phrases do not fuse into one mental content, but remain relatively unconnected. The expression is monotonous and the voice has more of the unnatural "schoolroom" pitch. They read more slowly, more often misplace the emphasis, and miscall more words. In short, one who has psychological insight and is acquainted with reading standards can easily detect the symptoms of intellectual inferiority by hearing a dull subject read a brief selection.

The giving of memories is also significant. Feeble-minded adults who have been well schooled are sometimes able to read the words of the text fairly fluently, but are usually unable to give more than a scanty report of what has been read. The scope of attention has been exhausted in the mere recognition and pronouncing of words. In general, the greater the mechanical difficulties which a subject encounters, the less adequate is his report of memories.

The test has, however, one real fault. School children have a certain advantage in it over older persons *of the same mental age* whose school experience is less recent. Adult subjects tend to give their report in less literal form. It is necessary, therefore, to give credit for the reproduction of the ideas of the passage rather than for strictly literal "memories."

The selection we have used is, with minor changes, the same as Binet's. His selection was divided into nineteen memories. The one here given has twenty-one memories. Binet used the test both in year VIII and year IX, requiring two memories at year VIII and six memories at year IX. When we require eight memories, as we have done, the test becomes difficult enough for non-selected school children of 10 years. Location in year X seems preferable, because it insures that the child will almost certainly have had the schooling requisite for learning to read a selection of this difficulty, even if he has started to school at a later age than is customary. Naturally, placing the test higher in the scale makes it more a test of report and less a test of ability to recognize and pronounce printed words.

X, 5. Comprehension, fourth degree

The questions for this year are:—

a. *"What ought you to say when some one asks your opinion about a person you don't know very well?"*
b. *"What ought you to do before undertaking (beginning) something very important?"*
c. *"Why should we judge a person more by his actions than by his words?"*

The **procedure** is the same as for the previous comprehension tests. Each question may be repeated, but its form must not be changed. It is not permissible to make any explanation whatever as to the meaning of the question, except to substitute *beginning* for *undertaking* when (*b*) seems not to be comprehended.

Scoring. *Two out of the three* questions must be answered satisfactorily. Study of the following classified responses should make scoring fairly easy in most cases:—

(a) When some one asks your opinion

Satisfactory. "I would say I don't know him very well" (42 per cent of the correct answers). "Tell him what I know and no more" (34 per cent of correct answers). "I would say that I'd rather not express any opinion about him" (20 per cent of the correct answers). "Tell him to ask some one else." "I would not express any opinion."

Unsatisfactory. Unsatisfactory responses are due either to failure to grasp the import of the question, or to inability to suggest the appropriate action demanded by the situation.

The latter form of failure is the more common; e.g.: "I'd say they are nice." "Say you like them." "Say what I think." "Say it's none of their business." "Tell them I mind my own business." "Say I would get acquainted with them." "Say that I don't talk about people." "Say I didn't know how he looked." "Tell them you ought not to say such things; you might get into trouble." "I wouldn't say anything." "I would try to answer." "Say I did not know his name," etc.

The following are samples of failure due to mistaking the import of the question: "I'd say, 'How do you do?'" "Say, 'I'm glad to meet you.'"

(b) Before undertaking something important

Satisfactory responses fall into the following classes:—

1. Brief statement of preliminary consideration; as: "Think about it." "Look it over." "Plan it all out." "Make your plans." "Stop and think," etc.

2. Special emphasis on preliminary preparation and correct procedure; as: "Find out the best way to do it." "Find out what it is." "Get everything ready." "Do every little thing that would help you." "Get all the details you can." "Take your time and figure it out," etc.

3. Asking help; as: "Ask some one to help you who knows all about it." "Pray, if you are a Christian." "Ask advice," etc.

4. Preliminary testing of ability, self-analysis, etc.; as: "Try something easier first." "Practice and make sure I could do it." "Learn how to do it," etc.

5. Consider the wisdom or propriety of doing it: "Think whether it would be best to do it." "See whether it would be possible."

About 65 per cent of the correct responses belong either to group (1) or (2), about 20 per cent to group (3), and most of the remainder to group (4).

Unsatisfactory responses are of the following types:—

1. Due to mistaking the import of the question; e.g.: "Ask for it." "Ought to say please." "Ask whose it is." Replies of this kind can be nearly all eliminated by repeating the question, using *beginning* instead of *undertaking*.

2. Replies more or less absurd or irrelevant; as: "Promise to do your best." "Wash your face and hands." "Get a lot of insurance." "Dress up and take a walk." "Tell your name." "Know whether it's correct." "Begin at the beginning." "Say you will do it." "See if it's a fake." "Go to school a long time." "Pass an examination." "Do what is right." "Add up and see how much it will cost." "Say I would do it." "Just start doing it." "Go away." "Consult a doctor." "See if you have time," etc.

(c) Why we should judge a person more by his actions than by his words

Satisfactory responses fall into the following classes:—

1. Words and deeds both mentioned and contrasted in reliability; as: "Actions speak louder than words" (this in 8 per cent of successes). "You can tell more by his actions than by his words." "He might talk nice and do bad things." "Sometimes people say things and don't do them." "It's not what you say but what you do that counts." "Talk is cheap; when he does a thing you can believe it." "People don't do everything they say." "A man might steal but talk like a nice man." Over 45 per cent of all correct responses belong to group (1).

2. Acts stressed without mention of words; as: "You can tell by his actions whether he is good or not." "If he *acts* nice he *is* nice." "Actions show for themselves." Group (2) contains about 25 per cent of the correct responses.

3. Emphasis on unreliability of words; as: "You can't tell by his words, he might lie or boast." "Because you can't always believe what people say." (Group (3) contains 15 per cent of the correct responses.)

4. Responses which state that a man's deeds are sometimes better than his words; as: "He might talk ugly and still not do bad things." "Some really kind-hearted people scold and swear." "A man's words may be worse than his deeds," etc. Group (4) contains over 10 per cent of the correct responses.

Unsatisfactory responses are usually due to inability to comprehend the meaning of the question. If there is a complete lack of comprehension the result is either silence or a totally irrelevant response. If there is partial comprehension of the question the response may be partially relevant, but fail to make the expected distinction.

The following are sample failures: "You could tell by his words that he was educated." "It shows he is polite if he acts nice." "Sometimes people aren't polite." "Actions show who he might be." "Acts may be foolish." "Words ain't right." "A man might be dumb." "A fellow don't know what he says." "Some people can talk, but don't have control of themselves." "You can tell by his acts whether he goes with bad people." "If he doesn't act right you know he won't talk right." "Actions show if he has manners." "Might get embarrassed and not talk good." "He may not know how to express his thoughts." "He might be a rich man but a poor talker." "He might say the wrong thing and afterwards be sorry for it," etc. (The last four are nearer correct than the others, but they fall just short of expressing the essential contrast.)

Remarks. For discussion of the comprehension questions as a test of intelligence, see page 158.

Binet used eight questions, three "easy" and five "difficult," and required that five out of eight be answered correctly in year X. The eight were as follows:—

1. What to do when you have missed your train.
2. When you have been struck by a playmate, etc.
3. When you have broken something, etc.
4. When about to be late for school.
5. When about to undertake something important.
6. Why excuse a bad act committed in anger more readily than a bad act committed without anger.
7. What to do if some one asks your opinion, etc.
8. Why can you judge a person better by his actions, etc.

As we have shown, questions 1, 2, 3, and 4 are much too easy for year X. Question 6 is hard enough for year XII. We have omitted it because it was not needed and is not entirely satisfactory.

X, 6. Naming sixty words

Procedure. Say: *"Now, I want to see how many different words you can name in three minutes. When I say ready, you must begin and name the words as fast as you can, and I will count them. Do you understand? Be* *sure to do your very best, and remember that just any words will do, like 'clouds,' 'dog,' 'chair,' 'happy'—Ready; go ahead!"*

The instructions may be repeated if the subject does not understand what is wanted. As a rule the task is comprehended instantly and entered into with great zest.

Do not stare at the child, and do not say anything as the test proceeds unless there is a pause of fifteen seconds. In this event say: *"Go ahead, as fast as you can. Any words will do."* Repeat this urging after every pause of fifteen seconds.

Some subjects, usually rather intelligent ones, hit upon the device of counting or putting words together in sentences. We then break in with: *"Counting* (or *sentences,* as the case may be) *not allowed. You must name separate words. Go ahead."*

Record the individual words if possible, and mark the end of each half-minute. If the words are named so rapidly that they cannot be taken down, it is easy to keep the count by making a pencil stroke for each word. If the latter method is employed, repeated words may be indicated by making a cross instead of a single stroke. Always make record of repetitions.

Scoring. The test is passed if *sixty* words, exclusive of repetitions, are named in three minutes. It is not allowable to accept twenty words in one minute or forty words in two minutes as an equivalent of the expected score. Only real words are counted.

Remarks. Scoring, as we have seen, takes account only of the number of words. It is instructive, however, to note the kind of words given. Some subjects, more often those of the 8- or 9-year intelligence level, give mainly isolated, detached words. As well stated by Binet, "Little children exhaust an idea in naming it. They say, for example, *hat,* and then pass on to another word without noticing that hats differ in color, in form, have various parts, different uses and accessories, and that in enumerating all these they could find a large number of words."

Others quickly take advantage of such relationships and name many parts of an object before leaving it, or name a number of other objects belonging to the same class. *Hat,* for example, suggests *cap, hood, coat, shirt, shoes, stockings*, etc. *Pencil* suggests *book, slate, paper, desk, ink, map, school-yard, teacher*, etc. Responses of this type may be made up of ten or a dozen plainly distinct word groups.

Another type of response consists in naming only objects present, or words which present objects immediately suggest. It is unfortunate that this occurs, since rooms in which testing is done vary so much with respect to furnishings. The subject who chooses this method is obviously handicapped if the room is relatively bare. One way to avoid this influence is to have all subjects name the words with eyes closed, but the distraction thus caused is sometimes rather disturbing. It is perhaps best for the present to adhere to the original procedure, and to follow the rule of making tests in a room containing few furnishings in addition to the necessary table and chairs.

A fourth type of response is that including a large proportion of unusual or abstract words. This is the best of all, and is hardly ever found except with subjects who are above the 11-year intelligence level.

It goes without saying that a response need not belong entirely to any one of the above types. Most responses, in fact, are characterized by a mixture of two or three of the types, one of them perhaps being dominant.

Though not without its shortcomings, the test is interesting and valuable. Success in it does not, as one might suppose, depend solely upon the size of the vocabulary. Even 8-year-olds ordinarily know the meaning of more than 3000 words, and by 10 years the vocabulary usually exceeds 5000 words, or eighty times as many as the child is expected to name in three minutes. The main factors in success are two, (1) richness and variety of previously made associations with common words; and (2) the readiness of these associations to reinstate themselves. The young or the retarded subject fishes in the ocean of his vocabulary with a single hook, so to speak. He brings up each time only one word. The subject endowed with superior intelligence employs a net (the idea of a class, for example) and brings up a half-dozen words or more. The latter accomplishes a greater amount and with less effort; but it requires intelligence and will power to avoid wasting time with detached words.

One is again and again astonished at the poverty of associations which this test discloses with retarded subjects. For twenty or thirty seconds such children may be unable to think of a single word. It would be interesting if at such periods we could get a glimpse into the subject's consciousness. There must be some kind of mental content, but it seems too vague to be crystallized in words. The ready association of thoughts with definite words connotes a relatively high degree of intellectual advancement. Language forms are the short-hand of thought; without facile command of language, thinking is vague, clumsy, and ineffective. Conversely, vague mental content entails language shortage.

Occasionally a child of 11- or 12-year intelligence will make a poor showing in this test. When this happens it is usually due either to excessive embarrassment or to a strange persistence in running down all the words of a given class before launching out upon a new series. Occasionally, too, an intelligent subject wastes time in thinking up a beautiful list of big or unusual words. As stated by Bobertag, success is favored by a certain amount of "intellectual nonchalance," a willingness to ignore sense and a readiness to break away from a train of associations as soon as the "point of diminishing returns" has been reached. This doubtless explains why adults sometimes make such a surprisingly poor showing in the test. They have less "intellectual nonchalance" than children, are less willing to subordinate such considerations as completeness and logical connection to the demands of speed. Knollin's unemployed men of 12- to 13-year intelligence succeeded no better than school children of the 10-year level.

We do not believe, however, that this fault is serious enough to warrant the elimination of the test. The fact is that in a large majority of cases the score which it yields agrees fairly closely with the result of the scale as a whole. Subjects more than a year or two below the mental age of 10 years seldom succeed. Those more than a year or two above the 10-year level seldom fail.

There is another reason why the test should be retained, it often has significance beyond that which appears in the mere number of words given. The naming of unusual and abstract words is an instance of this. An unusually large number of repetitions has symptomatic significance in the other direction. It indicates a tendency to mental stereotypy, so frequently encountered in testing the feeble-minded. The proportion of repetitions made by normal children of the 10- or 11-year intelligence level rarely exceeds 2 or 3 per cent of the total number of words named; those of older retarded children of the same level occasionally reach 6 or 8 per cent.

It is conceivable, of course, that a more satisfactory test of this general nature could be devised; such, for example, as having the subject name all the words he can of a given class (four-footed animals, things to eat, articles of household furniture, trees, birds, etc.). The main objection to this form of the test is that the performance would in all probability be more influenced by environment and formal instruction than is the case with the test of naming sixty words.

One other matter remains to be mentioned; namely, the relative number of words named in the half-minute periods. As would be expected, the rate of naming words decreases as the test proceeds. In the case of the 10-year-olds, we find the average number of words for the six successive half-minutes to be as follows:—

18, 12½, 10½, 9, 8½, 7.

Some subjects maintain an almost constant rate throughout the test, others rapidly exhaust themselves, while a very few make a bad beginning and improve as they go. As a rule it is only the very intelligent who improve after the first half-minute. On the other hand, mentally retarded subjects and very young normals exhaust themselves so quickly that only a few words are named in the last minute.

Binet first located this test in year XI, but shifted it to year XII in 1911. Goddard and Kuhlmann retain it in year XI, though Goddard's statistics suggest year X as the proper location, and Kuhlmann's even suggest year IX. Kuhlmann, however, accepts fifty words as satisfactory in case the response contains a considerable proportion of abstract or unusual words. All the American statistics except Rowe's agree in showing that the test is easy enough for year X.

X, Alternative test 1: repeating six digits

The digit series used are 3–7–4–8–5–9; and 5–2–1–7–4–6.

The **procedure** and **scoring** are the same as in VII, 3, except that only two trials are given, one of which must be correct. The test is somewhat too easy for year 10 when three trials are given.

The test of repeating six digits did not appear in the Binet scale and seems not to have been standardized until inserted in the Stanford series.

X, Alternative test 2: repeating twenty to twenty-two syllables

The sentences for this year are:—

a. *"The apple tree makes a cool, pleasant shade on the ground where the children are playing."*
b. *"It is nearly half-past one o'clock; the house is very quiet and the cat has gone to sleep."*
c. *"In summer the days are very warm and fine; in winter it snows and I am cold."*

Procedure and **scoring** exactly as in VI, 6.

Remarks. It is interesting to note that five years of mental growth are required to pass from the ability to repeat sixteen or eighteen syllables (year VI) to the ability to repeat twenty or twenty-two syllables. Similarly in memory for digits. Five digits are almost as easy at year VII as six at year X. Two explanations are available: (1) The increased difficulty may be accounted for by a relatively slow growth of memory power after the age of 6 or 7 years; or (2) the increase in difficulty may be real, expressing an inner law as to the behavior of the memory span in dealing with material of increasing length. Both factors are probably involved.

This is another of the Stanford additions to the scale. Average children of 10 years ordinarily pass it, but older, retarded children of 10-year mental age make a poorer showing. In the case of mentally retarded adults, especially, the verbal memory is less exact than that of school children of the same mental age.

X, Alternative test 3: construction puzzle A (Healy and Fernald)

Material. Use the form-board pictured on page 279. This may be purchased of C. H. Stoelting & Co., Chicago, Illinois. A home-made one will do as well if care is taken to get the dimensions exact. Quarter-inch wood should be used. The inside of the frame should be 3 × 4 inches, and the dimensions of the blocks should be as follows: 1³⁄₁₆ × 3; 1 × 1½; 1 × 2¾; 1 × 1½; 1¼ × 2.

Procedure. Place the frame on the table before the subject, the short side nearest him. The blocks are placed in an irregular position on the side of the frame away from the subject. Take care that the board with the blocks in place is not exposed to view in advance of the experiment.

Say: "*I want you to put these blocks in this frame so that all the space will be filled up. If you do it rightly they will all fit in and there will be no space left over. Go ahead.*"

Do not tell the subject to see how quickly he can do it. Say nothing that would even suggest hurrying, for this tends to call forth the trial-and-error procedure even with intelligent subjects.

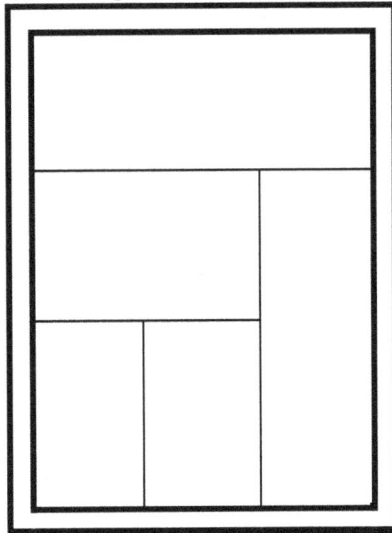

Scoring. The test is passed if the child succeeds in fitting the blocks into place *three times in a total time of five minutes for the three trials.*

The method of procedure is fully as important as the time, but is not so easily scored in quantitative terms. Nevertheless, the examiner should always take observations on the method employed, noting especially any tendency to make and to repeat moves which lead to obvious impossibilities; i.e., moves which leave a space obviously unfitted to any of the remaining pieces. Some subjects repeat an absurd move many times over; others make an absurd move, but promptly correct it; others, and these are usually the bright ones, look far enough ahead to avoid error altogether.

Remarks. This test was devised by Professor Freeman, was adapted slightly by Healy and Fernald, and was first standardized by Dr. Kuhlmann. Miss Gertrude Hall has also standardized it, but on a different procedure from that described above.[67]

The test has a lower correlation with intelligence than most of the other tests of the scale. Many bright children of 10-year intelligence adopt the trial-and-error method and have little success, while retarded older children of only 8-year intelligence sometimes succeed. Age, apart from intelligence, seems to play an important part in determining the nature of the performance. A favorable feature of the test, however, is the fact that it makes no demand on language ability and that it brings into play an aspect of intelligence which is relatively neglected by the remainder of the scale. For this reason it is at least worth keeping as an alternative test.

FOOTNOTES:

[66] See "Genius and Stupidity," by Lewis M. Terman, in *Pedagogical Seminary*, September, 1906, p. 340 *ff.*

[67] *Eugenics and Social Welfare Bulletin*, No. 5, The State Board of Charities, Albany, New York.

CHAPTER XVII
INSTRUCTIONS FOR YEAR XII

XII, 1. Vocabulary (forty definitions, 7200 words)

Procedure and **scoring** as in previous vocabulary tests.[68] In this case forty words must be defined.

XII, 2. Defining abstract words

Procedure. The words to be defined are *pity, revenge, charity, envy,* and *justice*. The formula is, *"What is pity? What do we mean by pity?"* and so on with the other words. If the meaning of the response is not clear, ask the subject to explain what he means. If the definition is in terms of the word itself, as "Pity means to pity someone," "Revenge is to take revenge," etc., it is then necessary to say: *"Yes, but what does it mean to pity some one?"* or, *"What does it mean to take revenge?"* etc. Only supplementary questions of this kind are permissible.

Scoring. The test is passed if *three of the five* words are satisfactorily defined. The definition need not be strictly logical nor the language elegant. It is sufficient if the definition shows that the meaning of the word is known. Definitions which define by means of an illustration are acceptable. The following are samples of satisfactory and unsatisfactory responses:—

(a) Pity

Satisfactory. "To be sorry for some one." "To feel compassion." "To have sympathy for a person." "To feel bad for some one." "It means you help a person out and don't like to have him suffer." "To have a feeling for people when they are treated wrong." "If anybody gets hurt real bad you pity them." "It's when you feel sorry for a tramp and give him something to eat." "If some one is in trouble and you know how it feels to be in that condition, you pity him." "You see something that's wrong and have your feeling aroused."

Of 130 correct responses, 85, or 65 per cent, defined *pity* as "to feel sorry for some one," or words to that effect. Less than 10 per cent defined by means of illustration.

Unsatisfactory. "To think of the poor." "To be good to others." "To help." "It means sorrow." "Mercy." "To cheer people up." "It means 'What a pity!'" "To be ashamed." "To be sick or poor." "It's when you break something."

Apart from inability to reply, which accounts for nearly one fourth of the failures, there is no predominant type of unsatisfactory response.

(b) Revenge

Satisfactory. "To get even with some one." "To get back on him." "To do something to the one who has done something to you." "To hurt them back." "To pay it back," or "Do something back." "To do something mean in return." "To square up with a person." "When somebody slaps you, you slap back." "You kill a person if he does something to you."

The expression "to get even" was found in 42 per cent of 120 correct answers; "to pay it back," or "To do something back," in 20 per cent; "To get back on him," in 17 per cent. About 8 per cent were illustrations.

Unsatisfactory. "To be mad." "You try to hurt them." "To fight." "You hate a person." "To kill them." "It means hateful." "To try again." "To think evil of some one." "To hate some one who has done you wrong." "To let a person off." "To go away from something."

Inability to reply accounts for a little over 40 per cent of the failures.

(c) Charity

Satisfactory. "To give to the poor." "To help those who are needy." "It is charity if you are poor and somebody helps you." "To give to somebody without pay."

Of 110 correct replies, 72 per cent were worded substantially like the first or second given above.

Unsatisfactory. "A person who helps the poor." "A place where poor people get food and things." "It is a good life." "To be happy." "To be poor." "Charity is being treated good." "It is to be charitable." "Charity is selling something that is not worth much." "It means to be good" or "to be kind."

When the last named response is given, we should say: "*Explain what you mean.*" If this brings an amplification of the response to "It means to do things for the poor," or the equivalent, the score is *plus.* "Charity means love" is also *minus* if the statement cannot be further explained and is merely rote memory of the passage in the 13th chapter of 1st Corinthians. Simply "To help" or "To give" is unsatisfactory. Half of the failures are due to inability to reply.

(d) Envy

Satisfactory. "You envy some one who has something you want." "It's the way you feel when you see some one with something nicer than you have." "It's when a poor girl sees a rich girl with nice dresses and things." "You hate some one because they've got something you want." "Jealousy" (satisfactory if subject can explain what *jealousy* means; otherwise it is *minus*). "It's when you see a person better off than you are."

Nearly three fourths of the correct responses say in substance, "You envy a person who has something you want." Most of the others are concrete illustrations.

Unsatisfactory. "To hate some one," or simply "To hate." "You don't like 'em." "Bad feeling toward any one." "To be a great man or woman." "Not to be nice to people." "What we do to our enemies."

Inability to respond accounts for 55 per cent of the failures.

(e) Justice

Satisfactory. "To give people what they deserve." "It means that everybody is treated the same way, whether he is rich or poor." "It's what you get when you go to court." "If one does something and gets punished, that's justice." "To do the square thing." "To give everybody his dues." "Let every one have what's coming to him." "To do the right thing by any one." "If two people do the same thing and they let one go without punishing, that is not justice."

Approximately 38 per cent of 102 correct responses referred to treating everybody the same way; 25 per cent to "doing the square thing", 12 per cent were concrete illustrations; and 4 per cent were definitions of what justice is not.

Unsatisfactory. "It means to have peace." "It is where they have court." "It's the Courthouse." "To be honest." "Where one is just" (*minus*, unless further explained). "To do right" (*minus*, unless in explaining *right* the subject gives a definition of *justice*).

It is very necessary, in case of such answers as "Justice is to do right," "To be just," etc., that the subject be urged to explain further what he means. "To do right" includes nearly 12 per cent of all answers, and is given by the very brightest children. Most of these are able, when urged, to complete the definition in a satisfactory manner.

Remarks. The reader may be surprised that the ability to define common abstract words should develop so late. Most children who have had anything like ordinary home or school environment have doubtless heard all of these words countless times before the age of 12 years. Nevertheless, the statistics from the test show unmistakably that before this age such words have but limited and vague meaning. Other vocabulary studies confirm this fact so completely that we may say there is hardly any trait in which 12- to 14-year intelligence more uniformly excels that of the 9- or 10-year level.

This is readily understandable when we consider the nature of abstract meanings and the intellectual processes by which we arrive at them. Unlike such words as *tree, house,* etc., the ideas they contain are not the immediate result of perceptual processes, in which even childish intelligence is adept, but are a refined and secondary product of relationships between other ideas. They require the logical processes of comparison, abstraction, and generalization. One cannot see justice, for example, but one is often confronted with situations in which justice or injustice is an element; and given a certain degree of abstraction and generalization, out of such situations the idea of justice will gradually be evolved.

The formation and use of abstract ideas, of one kind or another, represent, *par excellence*, the "higher thought processes." It is not without significance that delinquents who test near the border-line of mental deficiency show such inferior ability in arriving at correct generalizations regarding matters of social and moral relationships. We cannot expect a mind of defective generalizing ability to form very definite or correct notions about justice, law, fairness, ownership rights, etc.; and if the ideas themselves are not fairly clear, the rules of conduct based upon them cannot make a very powerful appeal.[69]

Binet used the words *charity*, *justice*, and *kindness*, and required two successes. In the 1911 revision he shifted the test from year XI to year XII, where it more nearly belongs. Goddard also places it in year XII and uses Binet's words, translating *bonté*, however, as *goodness* instead of *kindness*. Kuhlmann retains the test in year XI and adds *bravery* and *revenge*, requiring three correct definitions out of five. Bobertag uses *pity*, *envy*, and *justice*, requires two correct definitions, and finds the test just hard enough for year XII.

After using the words *goodness* and *kindness* in two series of tests, we have discarded them as objectionable in that they give rise to so many doubtful definitions. Even intelligent children often say: "Goodness means to do something good," "Kindness means to be kind to some one," etc. These definitions in a circle occur less than half as often with *pity*, *revenge*, and *envy*, which are also superior to *charity* and *justice* in this respect.

The relative difficulty of our five words is indicated by the order in which we have listed them in the test (i.e., beginning with the easiest and ending with the hardest). On the standard of three correct definitions, these words fit very accurately in year XII.

XII, 3. The ball-and-field test (superior plan)

Procedure, as in year VIII, test 1.

Scoring. Score 3 (or superior plan) is required for passing in year XII.

[70]

XII, 4. Dissected sentences

The following disarranged sentences are used:—

FOR THE STARTED AN WE COUNTRY EARLY AT HOUR

TO ASKED PAPER MY TEACHER CORRECT I MY

A DEFENDS DOG GOOD HIS BRAVELY MASTER

These should be printed in type like that used above. The Stanford record booklet contains the sentences in convenient form.

It is not permissible to substitute written words or printed script, as that would make the test harder. All the words should be printed in caps in order that no clue shall be given as to the first word in a sentence. For a similar reason the period is omitted.

Procedure. Say: *"Here is a sentence that has the words all mixed up so that they don't make any sense. If the words were changed around in the right order they would make a good sentence. Look carefully and see if you can tell me how the sentence ought to read."*

Give the sentences in the order in which they are listed in the record booklet. Do not tell the subject to see how quickly he can do it, because with this test any suggestion of hurrying is likely to produce a kind of mental paralysis. If the subject has no success with the first sentence in one minute, read it off correctly for him, somewhat slowly, and pointing to each word as it is spoken. Then proceed to the second and third, allowing one minute for each.

Give no further help. It is not permissible, in case an incorrect response is given, to ask the subject to try again, or to say: *"Are you sure that is right?" "Are you sure you have not left out any words?"* etc. Instead, maintain absolute silence. However, the subject is permitted to make as many changes in his response as he sees fit, provided he makes them spontaneously and within the allotted time. Record the entire response.

Once in a great while the subject misunderstands the task and thinks the only requirement is to use all the words given, and that it is permitted to add as many other words as he likes. It is then necessary to repeat the instructions and to allow a new trial.

Scoring. *Two sentences out of three must be correctly given within the minute allotted to each.* It is understood, of course, that if the first sentence has to be read for the subject, both the other responses must be given correctly.

A sentence is not counted correct if a single word is omitted, altered, or inserted, or if the order given fails to make perfect sense.

Certain responses are not absolutely incorrect, but are objectionable as regards sentence structure, or else fail to give the exact meaning intended. These are given half credit. Full credit on one, and half credit on each of the other two, is satisfactory. The following are samples of satisfactory and unsatisfactory responses:—

(a)

Satisfactory.

"We started for the country at an early hour."
"At an early hour we started for the country."
"We started at an early hour for the country."

Unsatisfactory.

"We started early at an hour for the country."
"Early at an hour we started for the country."
"We started early for the country."

Half credit.

"For the country at an early hour we started."
"For the country we started at an early hour."

(b)

Satisfactory.

"I asked my teacher to correct my paper."

Unsatisfactory.

"My teacher asked to correct my paper."
"To correct my paper I asked my teacher."

Half credit.

"My teacher I asked to correct my paper."

(c)

Satisfactory.

"A good dog defends his master bravely."
"A good dog bravely defends his master."

Unsatisfactory.

"A dog defends his master bravely."
"A bravely dog defends his master."
"A good dog defends his bravely master."
"A good brave dog defends his master."

Half credit.

"A dog defends his good master bravely."
"A dog bravely defends his good master."
"A good master bravely defends his dog."

Remarks. This is an excellent test. It involves no knowledge which may not be presupposed at the age in which it is given, and success therefore depends very little on experience. The worst that can be urged against it is that it may possibly be influenced to a certain extent by the amount of reading the subject has done. But this has not been demonstrated. At any rate, the test satisfies the most important requirement of a test of intelligence; namely, the percentage of successes increases rapidly and steadily from the lower to the higher levels of mental age.

This experiment can be regarded as a variation of the completion test. Binet tells us, in fact, that it was directly suggested by the experiment of

Ebbinghaus. As will readily be observed, however, it differs to a certain extent from the Ebbinghaus completion test. Ebbinghaus omits parts of a sentence and requires the subject to supply the omissions. In this test we give all the parts and require the formation of a sentence by rearrangement. The two experiments are psychologically similar in that they require the subject to relate given fragments into a meaningful whole. Success depends upon the ability of intelligence to utilize hints, or clues, and this in turn depends on the logical integrity of the associative processes. All but the highest grade of the feeble-minded fail with this test.

This test is found in year XI of Binet's 1908 series and in year XII of his 1911 revision. Goddard and Kuhlmann retain it in the original location. That it is better placed in year XII is indicated by all the available statistics with normal children, except those of Goddard. With this exception, the results of various investigators for year XII are in remarkably close agreement, as the following figures will show:—

Per cent passing at year XII	
Binet	66
Kuhlmann	68
Bobertag	78
Dougherty	64
Strong	72
Léviste and Morlé	70
Stanford series (1911)	62
Stanford series (1913)	57
Stanford series (1914)	62
Princeton data	61

This agreement is noteworthy considering that no two experiments seem to have used exactly the same arrangement of words, and that some have presented the words of a sentence in a single line, others in two or three lines. A single line would appear to be somewhat easier.

XII, 5. Interpretation of fables (score 4)

The following fables are used:—

(a) Hercules and the Wagoner

A man was driving along a country road, when the wheels suddenly sank in a deep rut. The man did nothing but look at the wagon and call loudly to Hercules to come and help him. Hercules came up, looked at the man, and said: "Put your shoulder to the wheel, my man, and whip up your oxen." Then he went away and left the driver.

(b) The Milkmaid and her Plans

A milkmaid was carrying her pail of milk on her head, and was thinking to herself thus: "The money for this milk will buy 4 hens; the hens will lay at least 100 eggs; the eggs will produce at least 75 chicks; and with the money which the chicks will bring I can buy a new dress to wear instead of the ragged one I have on." At this moment she looked down at herself, trying to think how she would look in her new dress; but as she did so the pail of milk slipped from her head and dashed upon the ground. Thus all her imaginary schemes perished in a moment.

(c) The Fox and the Crow

A crow, having stolen a bit of meat, perched in a tree and held it in her beak. A fox, seeing her, wished to secure the meat, and spoke to the crow thus: "How handsome you are! and I have heard that the beauty of your voice is equal to that of your form and feathers. Will you not sing for me, so that I may judge whether this is true?" The crow was so pleased that she opened her mouth to sing and dropped the meat, which the fox immediately ate.

(d) The Farmer and the Stork

A farmer set some traps to catch cranes which had been eating his seed. With them he caught a stork. The stork, which had not really been stealing, begged the farmer to spare his life, saying that he was a bird of excellent character, that he was not at all like the cranes, and that the farmer should have pity on him. But the farmer said: "I have caught you with these robbers, and you will have to die with them."

(e) The Miller, His Son, and the Donkey

A miller and his son were driving their donkey to a neighboring town to sell him. They had not gone far when a child saw them and cried out: "What fools those fellows are to be trudging along on foot when one of them might be riding." The old man, hearing this, made his son get on the donkey, while he himself walked. Soon, they came upon some men. "Look," said one of them, "see that lazy boy riding while his old father has to walk." On hearing this, the miller made his son get off, and he climbed on the donkey himself. Farther on they met a company of women, who shouted out: "Why, you lazy old fellow, to ride along so comfortably while your poor boy there can hardly keep pace by the side of you!" And so the good-natured miller took his boy up behind him and both of them rode. As they came to the town a citizen said to them, "Why, you cruel fellows! You two are better able to carry the poor little donkey than he is to carry you." "Very well," said the miller, "we will try." So both of them jumped to the ground, got some ropes, tied the donkey's legs to a pole and tried to carry him. But as they crossed the bridge the donkey became frightened, kicked loose and fell into the stream.

Procedure. Present the fables in the order in which they are given above. The method is to say to the subject:

"You know what a fable is? You have heard fables?" Whatever the answer, proceed to explain a fable as follows: *"A fable, you know, is a little story, and is meant to teach us a lesson. Now, I am going to read a fable to you. Listen carefully, and when I am through I will ask you to tell me what lesson the fable teaches us. Ready; listen."* After reading the fable, say: *"What lesson does that teach us?"* Record the response *verbatim* and proceed with the next as follows: *"Here is another. Listen again and tell me what lesson this fable teaches us,"* etc.

As far as possible, avoid comment or commendation until all the fables have been given. If the first answer is of an inferior type and we express too much satisfaction with it, we thereby encourage the subject to continue in his error. On the other hand, never express dissatisfaction with a response, however absurd or *malapropos* it may be. Many subjects are anxious to know how well they are doing and continually ask, "Did I get that one right?" It is sufficient to say, "You are getting along nicely," or something to that effect. Offer no comments, suggestions, or questions which might put the subject on the right track. This much self-control is necessary if we would make the conditions of the test uniform for all subjects.

The only occasion when a supplementary question is permissible is in case of a response whose meaning is not clear. Even then we must be cautious and restrict ourselves to some such question as, *"What do you mean?"* or, *"Explain; I don't quite understand what you mean."* The scoring of fables is somewhat difficult at best, and this additional question is often sufficient to place the response very definitely in the right or wrong column.

Scoring. Give score 2, i.e., 2 points, for a correct answer, and 1 for an answer which deserves half credit. The test is passed in year XII *if 4 points are earned*; that is, if two responses are correct or if one is correct and two deserve half credit.

Score 2 means that the fable has been correctly interpreted and that the lesson it teaches has been stated in general terms.

There are two types of response which may be given half credit. They include (1) the interpretations which are stated in general terms and are fairly plausible, but are not exactly correct; and (2) those which are perfectly correct as to substance, but are not generalized.

We overlook ordinary faults of expression and regard merely the essential meaning of the response.

The only way to explain the method is by giving copious illustrations. If the following sample responses are carefully studied, a reasonable degree of expertness in scoring fables may be acquired with only a limited amount of actual practice. The sampling may appear to the reader needlessly prolix, but experience has taught us that in giving directions for the scoring of tests error always lies on the side of taking too much for granted.

(a) Hercules and the Wagoner

Full credit; score 2. "God helps those who help themselves." "Do not depend on others." "Help yourself before calling for help." "It teaches that we should rely upon ourselves."

The following are not quite so good, but are nevertheless considered satisfactory. "We should always try, even if it looks hard and we think we can't do it." "When in trouble try to get out of it yourself." "We've got to do things without help." "Not to be lazy."

Half credit; score 1. This is most often given for the response which contains the correct idea, but states it in terms of the concrete situation, e.g.: "The man ought to have tried himself first." "Hercules wanted to teach the man to help himself." "The driver was too much inclined to depend on others." "The man was too lazy. He should not have called for help until he had tried to get out by himself." "To get out and try instead of watching."

Unsatisfactory; score 0. Failures are mainly of five varieties: (1) generalized interpretations which entirely miss the point; (2) crude interpretations which not only miss the point, but are also stated in terms of the concrete situation; (3) irrelevant or incoherent remarks; (4) efforts to repeat the story; and (5) inability to respond.

Sample failures of type (1), entirely incorrect generalizations: "Teaches us to look where we are going." "Not to ask for anything when there is no one to help." "To help those who are in trouble." "Teaches us to be polite." "How to help others." "Not to be cruel to horses." "Always to do what people tell you" (or "obey orders," etc.). "Not to be foolish" (or stupid, etc.). "If you would have a thing well done, do it yourself."

Failures of type (2), crude interpretations stated in concrete terms: "How to get out of the mud." "Not to get stuck in the mud." "To carry a stick along to pry yourself out if you get into a mud-hole." "To help any one who is stuck in the mud." "Taught Hercules to help the horses along and not whip them too hard." "Not to be mean like Hercules."

Failures of type (3), irrelevant responses: "It was foolish not to thank him." "He should have helped the driver." "Hercules was mean." "If any one helps himself the horses will try." "The driver should have done what Hercules told him." "He wanted the man to help the oxen."

Type (4): Efforts to repeat the story.

Type (5): Inability to respond.

(b) The Maid and the Eggs

Full credit; score 2. "Teaches us not to build air-castles." "Don't count your chickens before they are hatched." "Not to plan too far ahead." Slightly inferior, but still acceptable: "Never make too many plans." "Don't count on the second thing till you have done the first."

Half credit; score 1. "It teaches us not to have our minds on the future when we carry milk on the head." "She was building air-castles and so lost her milk." "She was planning too far ahead."

The responses just given are examples of fairly correct interpretations in non-generalized terms. The following are examples of generalized interpretations which fall below the accuracy required for full credit: "Never make plans." "Not to be too proud." "To keep our mind on what we are doing." "Don't cross a bridge till you come to it." "Don't count your *eggs* before they are hatched." "Not to be wanting things; learn to wait." "Not to imagine; go ahead and do it."

Unsatisfactory; score 0. Type (1), entirely incorrect generalization: "That money does not buy everything." "Not to be greedy." "Not to be selfish." "Not to waste things." "Not to take risks like that." "Not to think about clothes." "Count your chickens before they are hatched."

Type (2), very crude interpretations stated in concrete terms: "Not to carry milk on the head." "Teaches her to watch and not throw down her head." "To carry her head straight." "Not to spill milk." "To keep your chickens and you will make more money."

Type (3), irrelevant responses: "She wanted the money." "Teaches us to read and write" (18-year-old of 8-year intelligence). "About a girl who was selling some milk."

Type (4), effort to repeat the story.

Type (5), inability to respond.

(c) The Fox and the Crow

Full credit; score 2. "Teaches us not to listen to flattery." "Don't let yourself be flattered." "It is not safe to believe people who flatter us." "We had better look out for people who brag on us."

Half credit; score 1. Correct idea in concrete terms: "The crow was so proud of herself that she lost all she had." "The crow listened to flattery and got left." "Not to be proud and let people think you can sing when you can't." "If anybody brags on you don't sing or do what he tells you."

Pertinent but somewhat inferior generalizations: "Not to be too proud." "Pride goes before a fall." "To be on our guard against people who are our enemies." "Not to do everything people tell you." "Don't trust every slick fellow you meet."

Unsatisfactory; score 0. Type (1), incorrect generalization: "Not to go with people you don't know." "Not to be selfish." "To share your food." "Look before you leap." "Not to listen to evil." "Not to steal." "Teaches honesty." "Not to covet." "Think for yourself." "Teaches wisdom." "Never listen to advice." "Never let any one get ahead of you." "To figure out what they are going to do." "Never try to do two things at once." "How to get what you want."

Type (2), very crude interpretation stated in terms of the concrete situation: "Not to sing before you eat." "Not to hold a thing in your mouth; eat it." "To eat a thing before you think of your beauty." "To swallow it before you sing." "To be on your watch when you have food in your mouth."

Type (3), irrelevant responses: "The fox was greedy." "The fox was slicker than what the crow was." "The crow ought not to have opened her mouth." "The crow should just have shaken her head." "It served the crow right for stealing the meat." "The fox wanted the meat and just told the crow that to get it." "Foolishness." "Guess that's where the old fox got his name—'Old Foxy'—Don't teach us anything."

Type (4), efforts to repeat the story.

Type (5), inability to respond.

(d) The Farmer and the Stork

Full credit; score 2. "You are judged by the company you keep." "Teaches us to keep out of bad company." "Birds of a feather flock together." "If you go with bad people you are counted like them." "We should choose our friends carefully." "Don't go with bad people." "Teaches us to avoid the appearance of evil."

Half credit; score 1. "The stork should not have been with the cranes." "Teaches him not to go with robbers." "Don't go with people who are not of your nation." "Not to follow others."

Unsatisfactory; score 0. Type (1), incorrect generalization: "Not to steal." "Not to tell lies." "Not to give excuses." "A poor excuse is better than none." "Not to trust what people say." "Not to listen to excuses." "Not to harm animals that do no harm." "To have pity on others." "Not to be cruel." "To be kind to birds." "Not to blame people for what they don't do." "Teaches that those who do good often suffer for those who do evil." "To tend to your own business." "Not to meddle with other people's things." "Not to trespass on people's property." "Not to think you are so nice." "To keep out of mischief."

Type (2), very crude interpretations in concrete terms: "Taught the stork to look where it stepped and not walk into a trap." "Taught the stork to keep out of the man's field." "Not to take the seeds."

Type (3), irrelevant responses: "The farmer was right; storks do eat grain." "Served the stork right, he was stealing too." "He should try to help the stork out of the field."

Type (4), efforts to repeat the story.

Type (5), inability to reply.

(e) The Miller, His Son, and the Donkey

Full credit; score 2. "When you try to please everybody you please nobody." "Don't listen to everybody; you can't please them all." "Don't take every one's advice." "Don't try to do what everybody tells you." "Use your own judgment." "Have a mind of your own." "Make up your mind and stick to it." "Don't be wishy-washy." "Have confidence in your own opinions."

Half credit; score 1. Interpretations which are generalized but somewhat inferior: "Never take any one's advice" (too sweeping a conclusion). "Don't take foolish advice." "Take your own advice." "It teaches us that people don't always agree."

Correct idea but not generalized: "They were fools to listen to everybody." "They should have walked or rode just as they thought best, without listening to other people."

Unsatisfactory; score 0. Type (1), incorrect generalization: "To do right." "To do what people tell you." "To be kind to old people." "To be polite." "To serve others." "Not to be cruel to animals." "To have sympathy for beasts of burden." "To be good-natured." "Not to load things on animals that are small." "That it is always better to leave things as they are." "That men were not made for beasts of burden."

Type (2), very crude interpretations stated in concrete terms: "Not to try to carry the donkey." "That walking is better than riding." "The people should have been more polite to the old man." "That the father should be allowed to ride."

Type (3), irrelevant responses: "The men were too heavy for the donkey." "They ought to have stayed on and they would not have fallen into the stream." "It teaches about a man and he lost his donkey."

Type (4), efforts to repeat the story.

Type (5), inability to respond.

Remarks. The fable test, or the "test of generalization," as it may aptly be named, was used by the writer in a study of the intellectual processes of bright and dull boys in 1905,[71] and was further standardized by the writer and Mr. Childs in 1911.[72] It has proved its worth in a number of investigations. It has been necessary, however, to simplify the rather elaborate method of scoring which was proposed in 1911, not because of any logical fault of the method, but because of the difficulty in teaching examiners to use the system correctly. The method explained above is somewhat coarser, but it has the advantage of being much easier to learn.

The generalization test presents for interpretation situations which are closely paralleled in the everyday social experience of human beings. It tests the subject's ability to understand motives underlying acts or attitudes. It gives a clue to the status of the social consciousness. This is highly important in the diagnosis of the upper range of mental defectiveness. The criterion of the subnormal's fitness for life outside an institution is his ability to understand social relations and to adjust himself to them. Failure of a subnormal to meet this criterion may lead him to break common conventions, and to appear disrespectful, sulky, stubborn, or in some other way queer and exceptional. He is likely to be misunderstood, because he so easily misunderstands others. The skein of human motives is too complex for his limited intelligence to untangle.

Ethnological studies have shown in an interesting way the social origin of the moral judgment. The rectitude of the moral life, therefore, depends on the accuracy of the social judgment. It would be interesting to know what proportion of offenders have transgressed moral codes because of continued failure to grasp the essential lessons presented by human situations.

For the intelligent child even the common incidents of life carry an endless succession of lessons in right conduct. On the average school playground not an hour passes without some happening which is fraught with a moral hint to those who have intelligence enough to generalize the situation. A boy plays unfairly and is barred from the game. One bullies his weaker companion and arouses the anger and scorn of all his fellows. Another vents his braggadocio and feels at once the withering scorn of those who listen. Laziness, selfishness, meanness, dishonesty, ingratitude, inconstancy, inordinate pride, and the countless other faults all have their social penalties. The child of normal intelligence sees the point, draws the appropriate lesson and (provided emotions and will are also normal) applies it more or less effectively as a guide to his own conduct. To the feeble-minded child, all but lacking in the power of abstraction and generalization, the situation conveys no such lesson. It is but a muddle of concrete events without general significance; or even if its meaning is vaguely apprehended, the powers of inhibition are insufficient to guarantee that right action will follow.

It is for this reason that the generalization test is so valuable in the mental examinations of delinquents. It presents a moral situation, imagined, to be sure, but none the less real to the individual of normal comprehension.

It tells us quickly whether the subject tested is able to see beyond the incidents of the given situation and to grasp their wider relations—whether he is able to generalize the concrete.

The following responses made by feeble-minded delinquents from 16 to 21 years of age demonstrate sufficiently their inability to comprehend the moral situation:—

Hercules and the Wagoner. "Teaches you to look where you are going." "Not to help any one who is stuck in the mud." "Not to whip oxen." "Teaches that Hercules was mean." "Teaches us to carry a stick along to pry the wheels out."

The Fox and the Crow. "Not to sing when eating." "To keep away from strangers." "To swallow it before you sing." "Not to be stingy." "Not to listen to evil." "The fox was wiser than the crow." "Not to be selfish with food." "Not to do two things at once." "To hang on to what you've got."

The Farmer and the Stork. "Teaches the stork to look where he steps." "Not to be cruel like the farmer." "Not to tell lies." "Not to butt into other people's things." "To be kind to birds." "Teaches us how to get rid of troublesome people." "Never go with anything else."

The following are the responses of an 18-year-old delinquent (intelligence level 10 years) to the five fables:—

Maid and Eggs. "She was thinking about getting the dress and spilled the milk. Teaches selfishness."

Hercules and the Wagoner. "He wanted to help the oxen out."

Fox and Crow. "Guess that's where the fox got his name—'Old Foxy.' Don't teach us anything."

Farmer and Stork. "Try and help the stork out of the field."

Miller, Son, and Donkey. "They was all big fools and mean to the donkey."

One does not require very profound psychological insight to see that a person of this degree of comprehension is not promising material for moral education. His weakness in the ability to generalize a moral situation is not due to lack of instruction, but is inherent in the nature of his mental processes, all of which have the infantile quality of average 9- or 10-year intelligence. Well-instructed normal children of 10 years ordinarily succeed no better. The ability to draw the correct lesson from a social situation is little developed below the mental level of 12 or 13 years.

The test is also valuable because it throws light on the subject's ability to appreciate the finer shades of meaning. The mentally retarded often show marked inferiority in this respect. They sense, perhaps, in a general way the trend of the story, but they fail to comprehend much that to us seems clearly expressed. They do not get what is left for the reader to infer, because they are insensible to the thought fringes. It is these which give meaning to the fable. The dull subject may be able to image the objects and activities described, but taken in the rough such imagery gets him nowhere.

Finally, the test is almost free from the danger of coaching. The subject who has been given a number of fables along with twenty-five or thirty other tests can as a rule give only hazy and inaccurate testimony as to what he has been put through. Moreover, we have found that, even if a subject has previously heard a fable, that fact does not materially increase his chances of giving a correct interpretation. If the situation depicted in the fable is beyond the subject's power of comprehension even explicit instruction has little effect upon the quality of the response.

Incidentally, this observation raises the question whether the use of proverbs, mottoes, fables, poetry, etc., in the moral instruction of children may not often be futile because the material is not fitted to the child's power of comprehension. Much of the school's instruction in history and literature has a moral purpose, but there is reason to suspect that in this field schools often make precocious attempts in "generalizing" exercises.

XII, 6. Repeating five digits reversed

The series are 3–1–8–7–9; 6–9–4–8–2; 5–2–9–6–1.
Procedure and **Scoring**. Exactly as in years <u>VII</u> and <u>IX</u>.[73]

XII, 7. Interpretation of pictures

Procedure. Use the same pictures as in <u>III, 1</u>, and <u>VII, 2</u>, and the additional picture *d*. Present in the same order. The formula to begin with is identical with that in <u>VII, 2</u>: *"Tell me what this picture is about. What is this a picture of?"* This formula is chosen because it does not suggest specifically either description or interpretation, and is therefore adapted to show the child's spontaneous or natural mode of apperception. However, in case, this formula fails to bring spontaneous interpretation for three of the four pictures, we then return to those pictures on which the subject has failed and give a second trial with the formula: *"Explain this picture."* A good many subjects who failed to interpret the pictures spontaneously do so without difficulty when the more specific formula is used.

If the response is so brief as to be difficult to classify, the subject should be urged to amplify by some such injunction as *"Go ahead,"* or *"Explain what you mean."*

One more caution. It is necessary to refrain from voicing a single word of commendation or approval until all the pictures have been responded to. A moment's thought will reveal the absolute necessity of adhering to this rule. Often a subject will begin by giving an inferior type of response (description, say) to the first picture, but with the second picture adjusts better to the task and responds satisfactorily. If in such a case the first (unsatisfactory) response were greeted with an approving "That's fine, you are doing splendidly," the likelihood of any improvement taking place as the test proceeds would be greatly lessened.

Scoring. *Three pictures out of four* must be satisfactorily interpreted. "Satisfactorily" means that the interpretation given should be reasonably plausible; not necessarily the exact one the artist had in mind, yet not absurd. The following classified responses will serve as a fairly secure guide for scoring:—

(a) Dutch Home

Satisfactory. "Child has spilled something and is getting a scolding." "The baby has hurt herself and the mother is comforting her." "The baby is crying because she is hungry and the mother has nothing to give her." "The little girl has been naughty and is about to be punished." "The baby is crying because she does not like her dinner." "There's bread on the table and the mother won't let the little girl have it and so she is crying." "The baby is begging for something and is crying because her mamma won't give it to her." "It's a poor family. The father is dead and they don't have enough to eat."

Unsatisfactory. "The baby is crying and the mother is looking at her" (description). "It's in Holland, and there's a little girl crying, and a mamma, and there's a dish on the table" (mainly description). "The mother is teaching the child to walk" (absurd interpretation).

(b) River Scene

Satisfactory. "Man and lady eloping to get married and an Indian to row for them." "I think it represents a honeymoon trip." "In frontier days and a man and his wife have been captured by the Indians." "It's a perilous journey and they have engaged the Indian to row for them."

Unsatisfactory. "They are shooting the rapids." "An Indian rowing a man and his wife down the river" (mainly description). "A storm at sea" (absurd interpretation). "Indians have rescued a couple from a shipwreck." "They have been up the river and are riding down the rapids."

The following responses are somewhat doubtful, but should probably be scored *minus*: "People going out hunting and have Indian for a guide." "The man has rescued the woman from the Indians." "It's a camping trip."

(c) Post-Office

Satisfactory. "It's a lot of old farmers. They have come to the post-office to get the paper, which only comes once a week, and they are all happy." "There's something funny in the paper about one of the men and they are all laughing about it." "They are reading about the price of eggs, and they look very happy so I guess the price has gone up." "It's a bunch of country politicians reading the election news."

Unsatisfactory. "A man has just come out of the post-office and is reading to his friends." "It's a little country town and they are looking at the paper." "A man is reading the paper and the others are looking on and laughing." "Some men are reading a paper and laughing, and the other man has brought some eggs to market, and it's in a little country town." (All the above are mainly description.)

Responses like the following are somewhat better, but hardly satisfactory: "They are reading something funny in the paper." "They are reading the ads." "They are laughing about something in the newspaper," etc.

(d) Colonial Home

Satisfactory. "They are lovers and have quarreled." "The man has to go away for a long time, maybe to war, and she is afraid he won't return." "He has proposed and she has rejected him, and she is crying because she hated to disappoint him." "The woman is crying because her husband is angry and leaving her." "The man is a messenger and has brought the woman bad news."

Unsatisfactory. "The husband is leaving and the dog is looking at the lady." "It's a picture to show how people dressed in colonial times." "The lady is crying and the man is trying to comfort her." "The man is going away. The woman is angry because he is going. The dog has a ball in its mouth and looks happy, and the man looks sad."

Such responses as the following are doubtful, but rather *minus* than *plus*: "A picture of George Washington's home." "They have lost their money and they are sad" (gratuitous interpretation). "The man has struck the woman."

Doubt sometimes arises as to the proper scoring of imaginative or gratuitous interpretations. The following are samples of such: (*a*) "The little girl is crying because she wants a new dress and the mother is telling her she can have one when Christmas comes if she will be good." (*b*) "The man and woman have gone up the river to visit some friends and an Indian guide is bringing them home." (*c*) "Some old Rubes are reading about a circus that's going to come." (*d*) "Napoleon leaving his wife."

Sometimes these imaginative responses are given by very bright subjects, under the impression that they are asked to "make up" a story based on the picture. We may score them *plus*, provided they are not too much out of harmony with the situation and actions represented in the picture. Interpretations so gratuitous as to have little or no bearing upon the scene depicted should be scored *minus*.

Remarks. The test of picture interpretation has been variously located from 12 to 15 years. It cannot be too strongly emphasized that everything depends on the nature of the pictures used, the form in which the question is put, and the standard for scoring. The Jingleman-Jack pictures used by Kuhlmann are as easy to interpret at 10 years as the Stanford pictures at 12. Spontaneous interpretation ("What is this a picture of?" or "What do you see in this picture?") comes no more readily at 14 years than provoked interpretation ("Explain this picture") at 12. The standard of scoring is no less important. If with the Stanford pictures we require three satisfactory responses out of four, the test belongs at the 12-year level, but the standard of two correct out of four can be met a year or two earlier.

Even after we have agreed upon a given series of pictures, the formula for giving the test, and upon the requisite number of passes, there remains still the question as to the proper degree of liberality in deciding what constitutes interpretation. There is no single point in mental development where the "ability to interpret pictures" sweeps in with a rush. Like the development of most other abilities, it comes by slow degrees, beginning even as early as 6 years.

The question is, therefore, to decide whether a given response contains as much and as good interpretation as we have a right to expect at the age level where the test has been placed. It is imperative for any one who would use the scale correctly to acquaint himself thoroughly with the procedure and standards described above.

XII, 8. Giving similarities, three things

Procedure. The procedure is the same as in VIII, 4, but with the following words:—

    a. Snake, cow, sparrow.
    b. Book, teacher, newspaper.
    c. Wool, cotton, leather.
    d. Knife-blade, penny, piece of wire.
    e. Rose, potato, tree.

As before, a little tactful urging is occasionally necessary in order to secure a response.

Scoring. *Three satisfactory responses out of five* are necessary for success. Any real similarity is acceptable, whether fundamental or superficial, although the giving of fundamental likenesses is especially symptomatic of good intelligence.

Failures may be classified under four heads: (1) Leaving one of the words out of consideration; (2) giving a difference instead of a similarity; (3) giving a similarity that is not real or that is too bizarre or far-fetched; and (4) inability to respond. Types (1), (3), and (4) are almost equally numerous, while type (2) is not often encountered at this level of intelligence.

This test provokes doubtful responses somewhat oftener than the earlier test of giving similarities. Those giving greatest difficulty are the indefinite statements like "All are useful," "All are made of the same material," etc. Fortunately, in most of these cases an additional question is sufficient to determine whether the subject has in mind a real similarity. Questions suitable for this purpose are: "Explain what you mean," "In what respect are they all useful?" "What material do you mean?" etc. Of course it is only permissible to make use of supplementary questions of this kind when they are necessary in order to clarify a response which has already been made.

While the amateur examiner is likely to have more or less trouble in deciding upon scores, this difficulty rapidly disappears with experience. The following samples of satisfactory and unsatisfactory responses will serve as a fairly adequate guide in dealing with doubtful cases:—

(a) Snake, cow, sparrow

Satisfactory. "All are animals" (or creatures, etc.). "All live on the land." "All have blood" (or flesh, bones, eyes, skin, etc.). "All move about." "All breathe air." "All are useful" (*plus* only if subject can give a use which they have in common). "All have a little intelligence" (or sense, instinct, etc.).

Unsatisfactory. "All have legs." "All are dangerous." "All feed on grain" (or grass, etc.). "All are much afraid of man." "All frighten you." "All are warm-blooded." "All get about the same way." "All walk on the ground." "All can bite." "All holler." "All drink water." "A snake crawls, a cow walks, and a sparrow flies" (or some other difference). "They are not alike."

(b) Book, teacher, newspaper

Satisfactory. "All teach." "You learn from all." "All give you information." "All help you get an education." "All are your good friends" (*plus* if subject can explain how). "All are useful" (*plus* if subject can explain how).

Unsatisfactory. "All tell you the news." "A teacher writes, and a book and newspaper have writing." "They are not alike." "All read." "All use the alphabet."

(c) Wool, cotton, leather

Satisfactory. "All used for clothing." "We wear them all." "All grow" (*plus* if subject can explain). "All have to be sent to the factory to be made into things." "All are useful" (*plus* if subject can give a use which all have in common). "All are valuable" (*plus* if explained).

Unsatisfactory. "All come from plants." "All grow on animals." "All came off the top of something." "All are things." "They are pretty." "All spell alike." "All are furry" (or soft, hard, etc.).

(d) Knife-blade, penny, piece of wire

Satisfactory. "All are made from minerals" (or metals). "All come from mines." "All are hard material."

Unsatisfactory. "All are made of steel" (or copper, iron, etc.). "All are made of the same metal." "All cut." "All bend easily." "All are used in building a house." "All are worthless." "All are useful in fixing things." "All have an end." "They are small." "All weigh the same." "Can get them all at a hardware store." "You can buy things with all of them." "You buy them with money." "One is sharp, one is round, and one is long" (or some other difference).

Such answers as "All are found in a boy's pocket," or "Boys like them," are not altogether bad, but hardly deserve to be called satisfactory. "All are useful" is *minus* unless the subject can give a use which they have in common, which in this case he is not likely to do. Bizarre uses are also *minus*; as, "All are good for a watch fob," "Can use all for paper weights," etc.

(e) Rose, potato, tree

Satisfactory. "All are plants." "All grow from the ground." "All have leaves" (or roots, etc.). "All have to be planted." "All are parts of nature." "All have colors."

Unsatisfactory. "All are pretty." "All bear fruit." "All have pretty flowers." "All grow on bushes." "All are valuable" (or useful). "They grow close to a house." "All are ornamental." "All are shrubbery."

Remarks. The words of each series lend themselves readily to classification into a next higher class. This is the best type of response, but with most of the series it accounts for less than two thirds of the successes among subjects of 12-year intelligence. The proportion is less than one third for subjects of 10-year intelligence and nearly three fourths at the 14-year level. It would be possible and very desirable to devise and standardize an additional test of this kind, but requiring the giving of an essential resemblance or classificatory similarity.

For discussion of the psychological factors involved in the similarities test, see VII, 5.

FOOTNOTES:

[68] See VIII, 6.

[69] See also p. 298 *ff.*

[70] See scoring card.

[71] "Genius and Stupidity," in *Pedagogical Seminary*, vol. xiii, pp. 307–73.

[72] "A Tentative Revision and Extension of the Binet-Simon Measuring Scale of Intelligence," *Journal of Educational Psychology* (1912).

[73] See discussion, p. 207 *ff.*

CHAPTER XVIII
INSTRUCTIONS FOR YEAR XIV.

XIV, 1. Vocabulary (fifty definitions, 9000 words)

Procedure and **Scoring**, as in <u>VIII</u>, <u>X</u>, and <u>XII</u>. At year XIV fifty words must be correctly defined.

XIV, 2. Induction test: finding a rule

Procedure. Provide six sheets of thin blank paper, say 8½ × 11 inches. Take the first sheet, and telling the subject to watch what you do, fold it once, and in the middle of the folded edge tear out or cut out a small notch; then ask the subject to tell you *how many holes there will be in the paper when it is unfolded.* The correct answer, *one,* is nearly always given without hesitation. But whatever the answer, unfold the paper and hold it up broadside for the subject's inspection. Next, take another sheet, fold it once as before and say: *"Now, when we folded it this way and tore out a piece, you remember it made one hole in the paper. This time we will give the paper another fold and see how many holes we shall have."* Then proceed to fold the paper again, this time in the other direction, and tear out a piece from the folded side and ask how many holes there will be when the paper is unfolded. After recording the answer, unfold the paper, hold it up before the subject so as to let him see the result. The answer is often incorrect and the unfolded sheet is greeted with an exclamation of surprise. The governing principle is seldom made out at this stage of the experiment. But regardless of the correctness or incorrectness of the first and second answers, proceed with the third sheet. Fold it once and say: *"When we folded it this way there was one hole."* Then fold it again and say: *"And when we folded it this way there were two holes."* At this point fold the paper a third time and say: *"Now, I am folding it again. How many holes* *will it have this time when I unfold it?*" Record the answer and again unfold the paper while the subject looks on.

Continue in the same manner with sheets four, five, and six, adding one fold each time. In folding each sheet recapitulate the results with the previous sheets, saying (with the sixth, for example): "*When we folded it this way there was one hole, when we folded it again there were two, when we folded it again there were four, when we folded it again there were eight, when we folded it again there were sixteen; now, tell me how many holes there will be if we fold it once more.*" In the recapitulation avoid the expression "*When we folded it once, twice, three times,*" etc., as this often leads the subject to double the numeral heard instead of doubling the number of holes in the previously folded sheet. After the answer is given, do not fail to unfold the paper and let the subject view the result.

Scoring. The test is passed *if the rule is grasped by the time the sixth sheet is reached*; that is, the subject may pass after five incorrect responses, provided the sixth is correct and the governing rule can then be given. It is not permissible to ask for the rule until all six parts of the experiment have been given. Nothing must be said which could even suggest the operation of a rule. Often, however, the subject grasps the principle after two or three steps and gives it spontaneously. In this case it is unnecessary to proceed with the remaining steps.

Remarks. This test was first used by the writer in a comparative study of the intellectual processes of bright and dull boys in 1905, but it was not standardized until 1914. Rather extensive data indicate that it is a genuine test of intelligence. Of 14-year-old school children testing between 96 and 105 I Q, 59 per cent passed this test; of 14-year-olds testing below 96 I Q, 41 per cent passed; of those testing above 105, 71 per cent passed. That is, the test agrees well with the results obtained by the scale as a whole. Of "average adults" only 10 per cent fail; and of "superior adults," fewer than 5 per cent. As a rule, the higher the grade of intelligence, the fewer the steps necessary for grasping the rule. Of the superior adults, only 35 per cent fail to get the rule as early as the end of the fourth step.

The test is little affected by schooling, and apart from differences in intelligence it is little influenced by age. Other advantages of the test are the keen interest it always arouses and its independence of language ability. It has been used successfully with immigrant subjects who had been in this country but a few months.

We have named the experiment an "induction test." It might be supposed that the solution would ordinarily be arrived at by deduction, or by an *a-priori* logical analysis of the principle involved. This, however, is rarely the case. Not one average adult out of ten reasons out the situation in this purely logical manner. It is ordinarily only after one or more mistakes have been made and have been exposed by the examiner holding up the unfolded paper to view that the correct principle is grasped. In the absence of deductive reasoning the subject must note that each unfolded sheet contains twice as many holes as the previous one, and must infer that folding the paper again will again double the number. The ability tested is the ability to generalize from particulars where the common element of the particulars can be discerned only by the selective action of attention, in this case attention to the fact that each number is the double of its predecessor.

XIV, 3. Giving differences between a president and a king

Procedure. Say: *"There are three main differences between a president and a king; what are they?"* If the subject stops after one difference is given, we urge him on, if possible, until three are given.

Scoring. The three differences relate to power, tenure, and manner of accession. Only these differences are considered correct, and the successful response must include at least two of the three. We disregard crudities of expression and note merely whether the subject has the essential idea. As regards power, for example, any of the following responses are satisfactory: "The king is absolute and the president is not." "The king rules by himself, but the president rules with the help of the people." "Kings can have things their own way more than presidents can," etc.

It may be objected that the reverse of this is sometimes true, that the king of to-day often has less power than the average president. Sometimes subjects mention this fact, and when they do we credit them with this part of the test. As a matter of fact, however, this answer is seldom given.

Sometimes the subject does not stop until he has given a half-dozen or more differences, and in such cases the first three differences may be trivial and some of the later ones essential. The question then arises whether we should disregard the errors and pass the subject on his later correct responses. The rule in such cases is to ask the subject to pick out the "three main differences."

Sometimes accession and tenure are given in the form of a single contrast, as: "The president is elected, but the king inherits his throne and rules for life." This answer entitles the subject to credit for both accession and tenure, the contrast as regards tenure being plainly implied.

Unsatisfactory contrasts are of many kinds and are often amusing. Some of the most common are the following:—

"A king wears a crown." "A king has jewels." "A king sits on a throne." ("A king sets on a thorn" as one feeble-minded boy put it!) "A king lives in a palace." "A king has courtiers." "A king is very dignified." "A king dresses up more." "A president has less pomp and ceremony." "A president is more ready to receive the people." "A king sits on a chair all the time and a president does not." "No differences; it's just names." "A president does not give titles." "A king has a larger salary." "A king has royal blood." "A king is in more danger." "They have a different title." "A king is more cruel." "Kings have people beheaded." "A king rules in a monarchy and a president in a republic." "A king rules in a foreign country." "A president is elected and a king fights for his office." "A president appoints governors and a king does not." "A president lets the lawyers make the laws." "Everybody works for a king."

It is surprising to see how often trivial differences like the above are given. About thirty "average adults" out of a hundred, including high-school students, give at least one unsatisfactory contrast.

The test has been criticized as depending too much on schooling. The criticism is to a certain extent valid when the test is used with young subjects, say of 10 or 12 years. It is not valid, however, if the use of the test is confined to older subjects. With the latter, it is not a test of knowledge, but of the discriminative capacity to deal with knowledge already in the possession of the subject. It would be difficult to find an adult, not actually feeble-minded, who is ignorant of the facts called for: That the king inherits his throne, while the president is elected; that the tenure of the king is for life, and that of the president for a term of years; that kings ordinarily have, or are supposed to have, more power. Even the relatively stupid adult knows this; but he also knows that kings are different from presidents in having crowns, thrones, palaces, robes, courtiers, larger pay, etc., and he makes no discrimination as regards the relative importance of these differences.

The test is psychologically related to that of giving differences in year VII and to the two tests of finding similarities; but it differs from these in requiring a comparison based on fundamental rather than accidental distinctions. The idea is good and should be worked out in additional tests of the same type.

The test first appeared in the Binet revised scale of 1911. Kuhlmann omits it, and besides our own there are few statistics bearing on it. Our results show that if two essential differences are required, the test belongs where we have placed it, but that if only one essential difference is required, the test is easy enough for year XII.

XIV, 4. Problem questions

Procedure. Say to the subject: *"Listen, and see if you can understand what I read."* Then read the following three problems, rather slowly and with expression, pausing after each long enough for the subject to find an answer:—

a. *"A man who was walking in the woods near a city stopped suddenly, very much frightened, and then ran to the nearest policeman, saying that he had just seen hanging from the limb of a tree a … a what?"*

b. *"My neighbor has been having queer visitors. First a doctor came to his house, then a lawyer, then a minister (preacher or priest). What do you think happened there?"*

c. *"An Indian who had come to town for the first time in his life saw a white man riding along the street. As the white man rode by, the Indian said—'The white man is lazy; he walks sitting down.' What was the white man riding on that caused the Indian to say, 'He walks sitting down'?"*

Do not ask questions calculated to draw out the correct response, but wait in silence for the subject's spontaneous answer. It is permissible, however, to re-read the passage if the subject requests it.

Scoring. *Two responses out of three must be satisfactory.* The following explanations and examples will make clear the requirements of the test:—

(a) What the man saw hanging

Satisfactory. The only correct answer for the first is "A man who had hung himself" (or who had committed suicide, been hanged, etc.). We may also pass the following answer: "Dead branches that looked like a man hanging."

A good many subjects answer simply, "A man." This answer cannot be scored because of the impossibility of knowing what is in the subject's mind, and in such cases it is always necessary to say: *"Explain what you mean."* The answer to this interrogation always enables us to score the response.

Unsatisfactory. There is an endless variety of failures: "A snake," "A monkey," "A robber," or "A tramp" being the most common. Others include such answers as "A bear," "A tiger," "A wild cat," "A cat," "A bird," "An eagle," "A bird's nest," "A hornet's nest," "A leaf," "A swing," "A boy in a swing," "A basket of flowers," "An egg," "A ghost," "A white sheet," "Clothes," "A purse," etc.

(b) My neighbor

Satisfactory. The expected answer is "A death," "Some one has died," etc. We must always check up this response, however, by asking what the lawyer came for, and this must also be answered correctly.

While it is expected that the subject will understand that the doctor came to attend a sick person, the lawyer to make his will, and the minister to preach the funeral, there are a few other ingenious interpretations which pass as satisfactory. For example, "A man got hurt in an accident; the doctor came to make him well, the lawyer to see about damages, and then he died and the preacher came for the funeral." Or, "A man died, the lawyer came to help the widow settle the estate and the preacher came for the funeral." We can hardly expect the 14-year-old child to know that it is not the custom to settle an estate until after the funeral.

The following excellent response was given by an enlightened young eugenist: "A marriage; the doctor came to examine them and see if they were fit to marry, the lawyer to arrange the marriage settlement, and the minister to marry them." The following logical responses occurred once each: "A murder. The doctor came to examine the body, the lawyer to get evidence, and the preacher to preach the funeral." "An unmarried girl has given birth to a child. The lawyer was employed to get the man to marry her and then the preacher came to perform the wedding ceremony." Perhaps some will consider this interpretation too far-fetched to pass. But it is perfectly logical and, unfortunately, represents an occurrence which is not so very rare.

If an incorrect answer is first given and then corrected, the correction is accepted.

Unsatisfactory. The failures again are quite varied, but are most frequently due to failure to understand the lawyer's mission. Of 66 tabulated failures, 26 are accounted for in this way, while only 6 are due to inability to state the part played by the minister. The most common incorrect responses are: "A baby born" (accounting for 5 out of 66 failures); "A divorce" (very common with the children tested by Dr. Ordahl, at Reno, Nevada!); "A marriage"; "A divorce and a remarriage"; "A dinner"; "An entertainment"; "Some friends came to chat," etc. In 20 failures out of 66, marriage was incorrectly connected with a will, a divorce, the death of a child, etc.

The following are not bad, but hardly deserve to pass: "Sickness and trouble; the lawyer and minister came to help him out of trouble." Or, "Somebody was sick; the lawyer wanted his money and the minister came to see how he was." A few present a still more logical interpretation, but so far-fetched that it is doubtful whether they should count as passes; for example: "A man and his wife had a fight. One got hurt and had to have the doctor, then they had a lawyer to get them divorced, then the minister came to marry one of them." Again, "Some one is dying and is getting married and making his will before he dies."

(c) What the man was riding on

The only correct response is "Bicycle." The most common error is *horse* (or *donkey*), accounting for 48 out of 71 tabulated failures. Vehicles, like *wagon, buggy, automobile*, or *street car*, were mentioned in 14 out of 71 failures. Bizarre replies are: "A cripple in a wheel chair"; "A person riding on some one's back," etc.

Remarks. The experiment is a form of the completion test. Elements of a situation are given, out of which the entire situation is to be constructed. This phase of intelligence has already been discussed.[74]

While it is generally admitted that the underlying idea of this test is good, some have criticized Binet's selection of problems. Meumann thinks the lawyer element of the second is so unfamiliar to children as to render that part of the test unfair. Several "armchair" critics have mentioned the danger of nervous shock from the first problem. Bobertag throws out the test entirely and substitutes a completion test modeled after that of Ebbinghaus. Our own results are altogether favorable to the test. If it is used in year XIV, Meumann's objection hardly holds, for American children of that age do ordinarily know something about making wills. As for the danger of shock from the first problem, we have never once found the slightest evidence of this much-feared result. The subject always understands that the situation depicted is hypothetical, and so answers either in a matter-of-fact manner or with a laugh.

The bicycle problem is our own invention. Binet used the other two and required both to be answered correctly. The test was located in year XII of the 1908 scale, and in year XV of the 1911 revision. Goddard and Kuhlmann retain it in the original location. The Stanford results of 1911, 1912, 1914, and 1915 agree in showing the test too difficult for year XII, even when only two out of three correct responses are required. If the original form of the experiment is used, it is exceedingly difficult for year XV. As here given it fits well at year XIV.

XIV, 5. Arithmetical reasoning

Procedure. The following problems, printed in clear type, are shown one at a time to the subject, who reads each problem aloud and (with the printed problem still before him) finds the answer without the use of pencil or paper.

a. If a man's salary is $20 a week and he spends $14 a week, how long will it take him to save $300?
b. If 2 pencils cost 5 cents, how many pencils can you buy for 50 cents?
c. At 15 cents a yard, how much will 7 feet of cloth cost?

Only one minute is allowed for each problem, but nothing is said about hurrying. While one problem is being solved, the others should be hidden from view. It is not permissible, if the subject gives an incorrect answer, to ask him to solve the problem again. The following exception, however, is made to this rule: If the answer given to the third problem indicates that the word *yard* has been read as *feet*, the subject is asked to read the problem through again carefully (aloud) and to tell how he solved it. No further help of any kind may be given.

Scoring. *Two of the three* problems must be solved correctly within the minute allotted to each. No credit is allowed for correct method if the answer is wrong.

Remarks. We have selected these problems from the list used by Bonser in his *Study of the Reasoning Ability of Children in the Fourth, Fifth, and Sixth School Grades.*[75]

Our tests of 279 "at age" children between 12 and 15 years reveal the surprising fact that the test as here used and scored is not passed by much over half of the children of any age in the grades below the high-school age. Of the high-school pupils 19 per cent failed to pass, 21 per cent of ordinarily successful business men (!), and 27 per cent of Knollin's unemployed men testing up to the "average adult" level. To find average intelligence cutting such a sorry figure raises the question whether the ancient definition of man as "the rational animal" is justified by the facts. The truth is, *average* intelligence does not do a great deal of abstract, logical reasoning, and the little it does is done usually under the whip of necessity.

At first thought these problems will doubtless appear to the reader to be mere tests of schooling. It is true, of course, that in solving them the subject makes use of knowledge which is ordinarily obtained in school; but this knowledge (that is, knowledge of reading and of addition, subtraction, multiplication, and division) is possessed by practically all adults who are not feeble-minded, and by many who are. Success, therefore, depends upon the ability to apply this knowledge readily and accurately to the problems given—precisely the kind of ability in which a deficiency cannot be made good by school training. We can teach even morons how to read problems and how to add, subtract, multiply, and divide with a fair degree of accuracy; the trouble comes when they try to decide which of these processes the problem calls for. This may require intelligence of high or low order, according to the difficulty of the problem. As for the present test, we have shown that almost totally unschooled men of "average adult" intelligence pass this test as frequently as high-school seniors of the same mental level.

XIV, 6. Reversing hands of clock

Procedure. Say to the subject: "*Suppose it is six twenty-two o'clock, that is, twenty-two minutes after six; can you see in your mind where the large hand would be, and where the small hand would be?*" Subjects of 12-

to 14-year intelligence practically always answer this in the affirmative. Then continue: *"Now, suppose the two hands of the clock were to trade places, so that the large hand takes the place where the small hand was, and the small hand takes the place where the large hand was. What time would it then be?"*

Repeat the test with the hands at 8.10 (10 minutes after 8), and again with the hands at 2.46 (14 minutes before 3).

The subject is not allowed to look at a clock or watch, or to aid himself by drawing, but must work out the problem mentally. As a rule the answer is given within a few seconds or not at all. If an answer is not forthcoming within two minutes the score is failure.

Scoring. The test is passed if *two of the three* problems are solved within the following range of accuracy: the first solution is considered correct if the answer falls between 4.30 and 4.35, inclusive; the second if the answer falls between 1.40 and 1.45, and the third if the answer falls between 9.10 and 9.15.

Remarks. It appears that success in the test chiefly depends upon voluntary control over constructive visual imagery. Weakness of visual imagery may account for the failure of a considerable percentage of adults to pass the test. Visual imagery, however, is not absolutely necessary to success. One 8-year-old prodigy, who had 12-year intelligence, arrived in forty seconds at a strictly mathematical solution for the second problem, as follows: "If it is 2.46, and the hands trade places, then the little hand has gone about one fourth of the distance from 9 o'clock to 10 o'clock. One fourth of 60 minutes is 15 minutes, and so the time would be 15 minutes after 9 o'clock." Such a solution is certainly possible by the use of verbal imagery of any type.

The test shows a high correlation with mental age, but more than most others it is subject to the influence of cribbing. For this reason, other positions of the clock hands should be tried out for the purpose of finding substitute experiments of equal difficulty. Until such experiments have been made, it will be necessary to confine the experiment to the three positions here presented.

Schooling seems to have no influence whatever on the percentage of passes.

This test was first used by Binet in 1905, but was not included in either the 1908 or 1911 series. Goddard and Kuhlmann both include the test in their revisions, placing it in year XV. They give only two problems (our *a* and *c*) and require that both be answered correctly. Neither Goddard nor Kuhlmann, however, indicates the degree of error permitted.

Something depends upon original position of the hands. Binet used 6.20 and 2.46. For some reason the 2.46 arrangement is much more difficult than either 8.10 or 6.22, yielding almost twice as many failures as either of the other positions.

XIV, Alternative tests: repeating seven digits

This time, as in year X, only two series are given, one of which must be repeated without error. The two series are: 2–1–8–3–4–3–9 and 9–7–2–8–4–7–5. Note that in none of the tests of repeating digits is it permissible to warn the subject of the number to be given.

Remarks. Binet originally placed this test in year XII, giving three trials, but later moved it to year XV. Goddard and Kuhlmann retain it in year XII. Our data show that when three trials are given the test is too easy for year XIV, but that it fits this age when only two trials are allowed; that after the age of 12 or 14 years memory for relatively meaningless material, like digits or nonsense syllables, improves but little; and that above this level it does not correlate very closely with intelligence.

FOOTNOTES:

[74] See IX, 5, and XII, 4.

[75] Columbia University Contributions to Education, no. 37, 1910.

CHAPTER XIX
INSTRUCTIONS FOR "AVERAGE ADULT"

Average adult, 1: vocabulary (sixty-five definitions, 11,700 words)

Procedure and **Scoring**, as in previous vocabulary tests.[76] At the average adult level sixty-five words should be correctly defined.

Average adult, 2: interpretation of fables (score 8)

Procedure. As in year XII, test 6. Use the same fables.

Scoring. The method of scoring is the same as for XII, but the total score must be 8 points to satisfy the requirements at this level.

Remarks. For discussion of test, see XII, 5.

Average adult, 3: differences between abstract terms

Procedure. Say: *What is the difference between:—*

a. *Laziness and idleness?*
b. *Evolution and revolution?*
c. *Poverty and misery?*
d. *Character and reputation?*

Scoring. *Three correct contrasting definitions out of four* are necessary for a pass. It is not sufficient merely to give a correct meaning for each word of a pair; the subject must point out a difference between the two words so as to make a real contrast. For example, if the subject defines *evolution* as a "growth" or "gradual change," and *revolution* as the turning of a wheel on its axis, the experimenter should say: *"Yes, but I want you to tell me the difference between evolution and revolution."* If the contrast is not then forthcoming the response is marked *minus*.

The following are sample definitions which may be considered acceptable:—

(a) Laziness and idleness. "It is laziness if you won't work, and idleness if you are willing to work but haven't any job." "Lots of men are idle who are not lazy and would like to work if they had something to do." "Laziness means you don't want to work; idleness means you are not doing anything just now." "Idle people may be lazy, or they may just happen to be out of a job." "It is laziness when you don't like to work, and idleness when you are not working." "An idle person might be willing to work; a lazy man won't work." "Laziness comes from within; idleness may be forced upon one." "Laziness is aversion to activity; idleness is simply the state of inactivity." "Laziness is idleness from choice or preference; idleness means doing nothing."

The essential contrast, accordingly, is that *laziness refers to unwillingness to work; idleness to the mere fact of inactivity.* This contrast must be expressed, however clumsily.

(b) Evolution and revolution. "Evolution is a gradual change; revolution is a sudden change." "Evolution is natural development; revolution is sudden upheaval." "Evolution means an unfolding or development; revolution means a complete upsetting of everything." "Evolution is the gradual development of a country or government; revolution is a quick change of government." "Evolution takes place by natural force; a revolution is caused by an outside force." "Evolution is growth; revolution is a quick change from existing conditions." "Evolution is a natural change; revolution is a violent change." "Evolution is growth step by step; revolution is more sudden and radical in its action." "Evolution is a change brought about by peaceful development, while revolution is brought about by an uprising."

The essential distinction, accordingly, is that *evolution means a gradual, natural, or slow change, while revolution means a sudden, forced, or violent change.* Non-contrasting definitions, even when the individual terms are defined correctly, are not satisfactory.

(c) Poverty and misery. "Poverty is when you are poor; misery means suffering." "Only the poor are in poverty, but everybody can be miserable." "Poverty is the lowest stage of poorness; misery means pain." "The poor are not always miserable, and the rich are miserable sometimes." "Poverty means to be in want; misery comes from any kind of suffering or anguish." "The poor are in poverty; the sick are in misery." "Poverty is the condition of being very poor financially; misery is a feeling which any class of people can have." "One who is poor is in poverty; one who is wretched or doesn't enjoy life is in misery." "Poverty comes from lack of money; misery, from lack of happiness or comfort." "Misery means distress. It can come from poverty or many other things."

(d) Character and reputation. "Character is what you are; reputation is what people say about you." "You have character if you are honest; but you might be honest and still have a bad reputation among people who misjudge you." "Character is your real self; reputation is the opinion people have about you." "Your character depends upon yourself; reputation depends on what others think of you." "Character means your real morals; reputation is the way you are known in the world." "A man has a good character if he would not do evil; but a man may have a good reputation and still have a bad character."

A little practice and a good deal of discrimination are necessary for the correct grading of responses to this test. Subjects are often so clumsy in expression that their responses are anything but clear. It is then necessary to ask them to explain what they mean. Further questioning, however, is not permissible. For uniformity in scoring it is necessary to bear in mind that the definitions given must, in order to be satisfactory, express the essential distinction between the two words.

Remarks. What we have said regarding the psychological significance of test 2, year XII, applies equally well here. The test on the whole is a valuable one. Our statistics show that it is not, as some critics have thought, mainly a test of schooling.

The main criticism to be made is that it imposes a somewhat difficult task upon the power of language expression. For this reason it is necessary in scoring to disregard clumsiness of expression and to look only to the essential correctness or incorrectness of the thought.

This test first appeared in year XIII of Binet's 1908 scale. The terms used were "happiness and honor"; "evolution and revolution"; "event and advent"; "poverty and misery"; "pride and pretension." In the 1911 revision, "happiness and honor" and "pride and pretension" were dropped, and the other three pairs were moved up to the adult group, two out of three successes being required for a pass. Kuhlmann places it in year XV, using "happiness and honor" instead of our "character and reputation," and requires three successes out of five.

Average adult, 4: problem of the enclosed boxes

Procedure. Show the subject a cardboard box about one inch on a side. Say: *"You see this box; it has two smaller boxes inside of it, and each one of the smaller boxes contains a little tiny box. How many boxes are there altogether, counting the big one?"* To be sure that the subject understands repeat the statement of the problem: *"First the large box, then two smaller ones, and each of the smaller ones contains a little tiny box."*

Record the response, and, showing another box, say: *"This box has two smaller boxes inside, and each of the smaller boxes contains two tiny boxes. How many altogether? Remember, first the large box, then two smaller ones, and each smaller one contains two tiny boxes."*

The third problem, which is given in the same way, states that there are *three* smaller boxes, each of which contains *three* tiny boxes.

In the fourth problem there are *four* smaller boxes, each containing *four* tiny boxes.

The problem must be given orally, and the solution must be found without the aid of pencil or paper. Only one half-minute is allowed for each problem. Note that each problem is stated twice.

A correction is permitted, provided it is offered spontaneously and does not seem to be the result of guessing. Guessing can be checked up by asking the subject to explain the solution.

Scoring. *Three of the four* problems must be solved correctly within the half-minute allotted to each.

Remarks. Success depends, in the first place, upon ability to comprehend the statement of the problem and to hold its conditions in mind. Subjects much below the 12-year level of intelligence are often unable to do this.

Granting that the problem has been comprehended, success seems to depend chiefly upon the facility with which the constructive imagination manipulates concrete visual imagery. In this respect it resembles the problem of reversing the hands of a clock. With some subjects, however, verbal imagery alone is operative. Tactual imagery would, of course, serve the purpose as well.

This is as good a place as any to emphasize the fact that the introspective study of mental imagery has little to contribute to the measurement of intelligence. Intelligence tests are concerned with the total result of a thought process, rather than with the imagery supports of that process. Thought may be carried on almost equally well by various kinds of imagery. As Galton showed, a person can be taught to carry on arithmetical processes by the use of smell imagery. The kind of imagery employed is the product of slight, innate preferences complicated by the more or less accidental effects of habit.

We may say that imagery is to thinking what scaffolding is to architecture. The important thing is the completed building rather than the nature of the scaffolding employed in erecting it. No one thinks of blaming the ill construction of a building upon the kind of scaffolding used, for if the architect and builder are competent satisfactory scaffolding will be found. Just as little are deficiencies or peculiarities of imagery the real cause of low-order intelligence. We cannot increase intelligence by formal drill in the use of supposedly important kinds of mental imagery, any more than we can transform a plain carpenter into a Michael Angelo by instructing him in the use of scaffolding materials such as were employed in the construction of St. Peter's Cathedral.

This test is of our own invention and has been brought to its present form only after a good deal of preliminary experimentation. It correlates fairly well with mental age as determined by the scale as a whole. It was passed by 55 per cent of high-school pupils and by 65 per cent of unschooled business men. Success in it is thus seen not to depend upon schooling.

Average adult, 5: repeating six digits reversed

The series used are: 4–7–1–9–5–2; 5–8–3–2–9–4; and 7–5–2–6–3–8.
Procedure and **Scoring**, as in year VII, alternative 2.
Remarks. The test is passed by approximately half of "average adults" and by three fourths of "superior adults." It shows no effect of schooling, the uneducated business men even surpassing our high-school students.

For the higher levels of intelligence, especially, the test is superior to that of repeating digits in the direct order. It is less mechanical and makes heavier demands upon higher intelligence.

Average adult, 6: using a code

Procedure. Show the subject the code given on the accompanying form. Say: *"See these diagrams here. Look and you will see that they contain all the letters of the alphabet. Now, examine the arrangement of the letters. They go* (pointing) *a b c, d e f, g h i, j k l, m n o, p q r, s t u v, w x y z. You see the letters in the first two diagrams are arranged in the up-and-*

down order (pointing again), *and the letters in the other two diagrams run in just the opposite way from the hands of a clock* (pointing). *Look again and you will see that the second diagram is drawn just like the first, except that each letter has a dot with it, and that the last diagram is like the third except that here, also, each letter has a dot. Now, all of this represents a code; that is, a secret language. It is a real code, one that was used in the Civil War for sending secret messages. This is the way it works: we draw the lines which hold a letter, but leave out the letter. Here, for example, is the way we would write 'spy?'"* Then write the word *spy*, pointing out carefully where each letter comes from, and emphasizing the fact that the dot must be used in addition to the lines in writing any letter in the second or the fourth diagram. Illustrate also with *war*.

Then add: *"I am going to have you write something for me; remember now, how the letters go, first* (pointing, as before) *a b c, d e f, g h i, then j k l, m n o, p q r, then s t u v, then w x y z. And don't forget the dots for the letters in this diagram and this one"* (pointing). At this point, take away the diagrams and tell the subject to write the words *come quickly*. Say nothing about hurrying.

The subject is given a pencil, but is allowed to draw only the symbols for the words *come quickly*. He is not permitted to reproduce the entire code and then to copy the code letters from his reproduction.

Scoring. The test is passed if the words are written in *six minutes and without more than two errors*. Omission of a dot counts as only a half error.

Remarks. It is not easy to analyze the mental functions which contribute to success in the code test. Contrary to what might be supposed, success does not necessarily depend upon getting and retaining a visual picture of the diagrams. Kinæsthetic imagery will answer the purpose just as well, or the original visual impression may even be translated at once into auditory-verbal imagery and remembered as such. The significance of the test must be expressed in other terms than the kind of imagery it may happen to bring into play.

Healy and Fernald describe the task of writing a code sentence without copy as one which requires "close attention and steadiness of purpose."

They also emphasize the fact that the attention must be directed inward, since there is no object of interest before the senses and since no special stimulus to attention is offered by the experimenter. Observations we have made on subjects during the test confirm this view as to the factors involved.

That inability to remember the code as a whole is not a common cause of failure is shown by the fact that subjects above 12-year intelligence who have failed on the test are nearly always able to reproduce the diagrams and insert the letters in their proper places. To give the code form of a given letter without copy, however, makes a much heavier demand on attention. Nearly all subjects find it necessary to trace the code form, in imagination, from the beginning up to each letter whose code form is sought. Subjects of superior intelligence, however, sometimes hit upon the device of remembering the position of the individual key letters e.g. (the first letter of each figure) from which, as a base, any desired letter form may be quickly sought out.

The test correlates well with mental age, but for some reason not apparent it is passed by a larger percentage of high-school pupils than unschooled adults of the same mental level.

The code test was first described by Healy and Fernald in their "Tests for Practical Mental Classification."[77] The authors gave no data, however, which would indicate the mental level to which the test belongs. Dr. Goddard incorporated it in year XV of his revision of the Binet scale, but also fails to give statistics. The location given the test in the Stanford revision is based on tests of nearly 500 individuals ranging from a mental level of 12 years to that of "superior adult." It appears that the test is considerably more difficult than most had thought it to be.

Average adult, alternative test 1: repeating twenty-eight syllables

The sentences for this test are:—

a. *Walter likes very much to go on visits to his grandmother, because she always tells him many funny stories.*

b. Yesterday I saw a pretty little dog in the street. It had curly brown hair, short legs, and a long tail.

Procedure. Exactly as in VI, 6. Emphasize that the sentence must be repeated without a single change of any sort. Get attention before giving each sentence.

Scoring. Passed *if one sentence is repeated without a single error*. In VI and X we scored the response as satisfactory if one sentence was repeated without error, or if two were repeated with not more than one error each.

Remarks. The test of repeating sentences is not as satisfactory in the higher intelligence levels as in the lower. It is too mechanical to tax very heavily the higher thought processes. It does, however, have a certain correlation with intelligence. Contrary to what one would have expected, uneducated adults of "average adult" intelligence surpassed our high-school students of the same mental level.

Binet located this test in year XII of the 1908 series, but shifted it to year XV in 1911. The American versions of the Binet scale have usually retained it in year XII, though Goddard admits that the sentences are somewhat too difficult for that year. Kuhlmann puts the test in year XII, but reduces the sentences to twenty-four syllables and permits one re-reading. We give only two trials and our sentences are considerably more difficult. With the procedure and scoring we have used, the test is rather easy for the "average adult" group, but a little too hard for year XIV.

Average adult, alternative test 2: comprehension of physical relations

(a) Problem regarding the path of a cannon ball

Procedure. Draw on a piece of paper a horizontal line six or eight inches long. Above it, an inch or two, draw a short horizontal line about an inch long and parallel to the first. Tell the subject that the long line represents the perfectly level ground of a field, and that the short line represents a cannon. Explain that the cannon is *"pointed horizontally (on a level) and is fired across this perfectly level field."* After it is clear that these conditions of the problem are comprehended, we add: *"Now, suppose that this cannon is fired off and that the ball comes to the ground at this point here* (pointing to the farther end of the line which represents the field). *Take this pencil and draw a line which will show what path the cannon ball will take from the time it leaves the mouth of the cannon till it strikes the ground."*

Scoring. There are four types of response: (1) A straight diagonal line is drawn from the cannon's mouth to the point where the ball strikes. (2) A straight line is drawn from the cannon's mouth running horizontally until almost directly over the goal, at which point the line drops almost or quite vertically. (3) The path from the cannon's mouth first rises considerably from the horizontal, at an angle perhaps of between ten to forty-five degrees, and finally describes a gradual curve downward to the goal. (4) The line begins almost on a level and drops more rapidly toward the end of its course.

Only the last is satisfactory. Of course, nothing like a mathematically accurate solution of the problem is expected. It is sufficient if the response belongs to the fourth type above instead of being absurd, as the other types described are. Any one who has ever thrown stones should have the data for such an approximate solution. Not a day of schooling is necessary.

(b) Problem as to the weight of a fish in water

Procedure. Say to the subject: *"You know, of course, that water holds up a fish that is placed in it. Well, here is a problem. Suppose we have a bucket which is partly full of water. We place the bucket on the scales and find that with the water in it it weighs exactly 45 pounds. Then we put a 5-pound fish into the bucket of water. Now, what will the whole thing weigh?"*

Scoring. Many subjects even as low as 9- or 10-year intelligence will answer promptly, "Why, 45 pounds and 5 pounds makes 50 pounds, of course." But this is not sufficient. We proceed to ask, with serious demeanor: *"How can this be correct, since the water itself holds up the fish?"* The young subject who has answered so glibly now laughs sheepishly and apologizes for his error, saying that he answered without thinking, etc. This response is scored failure without further questioning.

Other subjects, mostly above the 14-year level, adhere to the answer "50 pounds," however strongly we urge the argument about the water holding up the fish. In response to our question, *"How can that be the case?"* it is sufficient if the subject replies that "The weight is there just the same; the scales have to hold up the bucket and the bucket has to hold up the water," or words to that effect. Only some such response as this is satisfactory. If the subject keeps changing his answer or says that he *thinks* the weight would be 50 pounds, but is not certain, the score is failure.

(c) Difficulty of hitting a distant mark

Procedure. Say to the subject: *"You know, do you not, what it means when they say a gun 'carries 100 yards'? It means that the bullet goes that far before it drops to amount to anything."* All boys and most girls more than a dozen years old understand this readily. If the subject does not understand, we explain again what it means for a gun "to carry" a given distance. When this part is clear, we proceed as follows: *"Now, suppose a man is shooting at a mark about the size of a quart can. His rifle carries perfectly more than 100 yards. With such a gun is it any harder to hit the mark at 100 yards than it is at 50 yards?"* After the response is given, we ask the subject to explain.

Scoring. Simply to say that it would be easier at 50 yards is not sufficient, nor can we pass the response which merely states that it is "easier to aim" at 50 yards. The correct principle must be given, one which shows the subject has appreciated the fact that a small deviation from the "bull's-eye" at 50 yards, due to incorrect aim, becomes a larger deviation at 100 yards. However, the subject is not required to know that the deviation at 100 yards is exactly twice as great as at 50 yards. A certain amount of questioning is often necessary before we can decide whether the subject has the correct principle in mind.

Scoring the entire test. *Two of the three problems* must be solved in such a way as to satisfy the requirements above set forth.

Remarks. These problems were devised by the writer. They yield interesting results, when properly given, but are not without their faults. Sometimes a very superior subject fails, while occasionally an inferior subject unexpectedly succeeds. On the whole, however the test correlates fairly well with mental age. At the 14-year level less than 50 per cent pass; of "average adults," from 60 to 75 per cent are successful. Few "superior adults" fail.

The test as here given is little influenced by the formal instruction given in the grades or the high school. In fact, 80 per cent of our uneducated business men, as contrasted with 65 per cent of high-school juniors and seniors, passed the test. Success probably depends in the main upon previous interest in physical relationships and upon the ability to understand phenomena of this kind which the subject has had opportunity to observe.

It would be interesting to standardize a longer series of problems designed to test a subject's comprehension of common physical relationships. In the first few months of life a normal child learns that objects unsupported fall to the ground. Later he learns that fire burns; that birds fly in the air; that fish do not sink in the water; that water does not run uphill; that it is easy to lift a leg or arm as one lies prone in the water; that mud is thrown from a rotating wheel (and always in the same direction); that a stone which is flying through the air swiftly is more dangerous than one which is moving slowly; that it is more dangerous to be run over by a train than by a buggy; that it is hard to run against a strong wind; that cyclones blow down trees and houses; that a rapidly moving train creates a stronger wind than a slower train; that a feather falls through the air with less speed than a stone; that a falling object gains momentum; that a heavy moving object is harder to stop than a light object moving at the same rate; that freezing water bursts pipes; that sounds sometimes give echoes; that rainbows cannot be approached; that a lamp seems dim by daylight; that by day the stars are not visible and the moon only barely visible; that the headlights of an approaching automobile or train are blinding; that if the room in which we are reading is badly lighted we must hold the book nearer to the eyes; that running makes the heart beat faster and increases the rate of breathing; that if we are cold we can get warm by running; that whirling rapidly makes us dizzy; that heat or exercise will cause perspiration, etc.

Although the causes of some of these phenomena are not understood even by intelligent adults without some instruction, the facts themselves are learned by the normal individual from his own experience. The higher the mental level and the greater the curiosity, the more observant one is about such matters and the more one learns. Many items of knowledge such as we have mentioned could and should be standardized for various mental levels. In devising tests of this kind we should, of course, have to look out for the influences of formal instruction.

FOOTNOTES:

[76] See VIII, 6.

[77] *Psychological Review Monographs* (1911), vol. XIII, no. 2, p. 51.

CHAPTER XX
INSTRUCTIONS FOR "SUPERIOR ADULT"

Superior adult, 1: vocabulary (seventy-five definitions, 13,500 words)

Procedure and **Scoring**, as in previous vocabulary tests. At the "superior adult" level seventy-five words should be known.

The test is passed by only one third of those at the "average adult" level, but by about 90 per cent of "superior adults." Ability to pass the test is relatively independent of the number of years the subject has attended school, our business men showing even a higher percentage of passes than high-school pupils.

Superior adult, 2: Binet's paper-cutting test

Procedure. Take a piece of paper about six inches square and say: "*Watch carefully what I do. See, I fold the paper this way* (folding it once over in the middle), *then I fold it this way* (folding it again in the middle, but at right angles to the first fold). *Now, I will cut out a notch right here*" (indicating). At this point take scissors and cut out a small notch from the middle of the side which presents but one edge. Throw the fragment which has been cut out into the waste-basket or under the table. Leave the folded paper exposed to view, but pressed flat against the table. Then give the subject a pencil and a second sheet of paper like the one already used and say: "*Take this piece of paper and make a drawing to show how the other sheet of paper would look if it were unfolded. Draw lines to show the creases in the paper and show what results from the cutting.*"

The subject is not permitted to fold the second sheet, but must solve the problem by the imagination unaided.

Note that we do not say, "*Draw the holes,*" as this would inform the subject that more than one hole is expected.

Scoring. The test is passed *if the creases in the paper are properly represented, if the holes are drawn in the correct number, and if they are located correctly*, that is, both on the same crease and each about halfway between the center of the paper and the side. The shape of the holes is disregarded.

Failure may be due to error as regards the creases or the number and location of the holes, or it may involve any combination of the above errors.

Remarks. Success seems to depend upon constructive visual imagination. The subject must first be able to construct in imagination the creases which result from the folding, and secondly, to picture the effects of the cutting as regards number of holes and their location. It appears that a solution is seldom arrived at, even in the case of college students, by logical mathematical thinking. Our unschooled subjects even succeeded somewhat better than high-school and college students of the same mental level.

Binet placed this test in year XIII of the 1908 scale, but shifted it to the adult group in the 1911 revision. Goddard retains it in the adult group, while Kuhlmann places it in year XV. There have also been certain variations in the procedure employed. As given in the Stanford revision the test is passed by hardly any subjects below the 14-year level, but by about one third of "average adults" and by the large majority of "superior adults."

Superior adult, 3: repeating eight digits

Procedure and **Scoring**, the same as in previous tests with digits reversed. The series used are: 7–2–5–3–4–8–9–6; 4–9–8–5–3–7–6–2; and 8–3–7–9–5–4–8–2.

Guard against rhythm and grouping in reading the digits and do not give warning as to the number to be given.

The test is passed by about one third of "average adults" and by over two thirds of "superior adults." The test shows no marked difference between educated and uneducated subjects of the same mental level.

Superior adult, 4: repeating thought of passage

Procedure. Say: *"I am going to read a little selection of about six or eight lines. When I am through I will ask you to repeat as much of it as you can. It doesn't make any difference whether you remember the exact words or not, but you must listen carefully so that you can tell me everything it says."* Then read the following selections, pausing after each for the subject's report, which should be recorded *verbatim*:—

a. *"Tests such as we are now making are of value both for the advancement of science and for the information of the person who is tested. It is important for science to learn how people differ and on what factors these differences depend. If we can separate the influence of heredity from the influence of environment, we may be able to apply our knowledge so as to guide human development. We may thus in some cases correct defects and develop abilities which we might otherwise neglect."*

b. *"Many opinions have been given on the value of life. Some call it good, others call it bad. It would be nearer correct to say that it is mediocre; for on the one hand, our happiness is never as great as we should like, and on the other hand, our misfortunes are never as great as our enemies would wish for us. It is this mediocrity of life which prevents it from being radically unjust."*

Sometimes the subject hesitates to begin, thinking, in spite of our wording of the instructions, that a perfect reproduction is expected. Others fall into the opposite misunderstanding and think that they are prohibited from using the words of the text and must give the thought entirely in their own language. In cases of hesitation we should urge the subject a little and remind him that he is to express the thought of the selection in whatever way he prefers; that the main thing is to tell what the selection says.

Scoring. The test is passed if the subject is able to repeat in reasonably consecutive order the main thoughts of at least one of the selections. Neither elegance of expression nor *verbatim* repetition is expected. We merely want to know whether the leading thoughts in the selection have been grasped and remembered.

All grades of accuracy are found, both in the comprehension of the selection and in the recall, and it is not always easy to draw the line between satisfactory and unsatisfactory responses. The following sample performances will serve as a guide:—

Selection (a)

Satisfactory. "The tests which we are making are given for the advancement of science and for the information of the person tested. By scientific means we will be able to separate characteristics derived from heredity and environment and to treat each class separately. By doing so we can more accurately correct defects."

"Tests like these are for two purposes. First to develop a science, and second to apply it to the person to help him. The tests are to find out how you differ from another and to measure the difference between your heredity and environment."

"These tests are given to see if we can separate heredity and environment and to see if we can find out how one person differs from another. We can then correct these differences and teach people more effectively."

"The tests that we are now making are valuable along both scientific and personal lines. By using them it can be found out where a person is weak and where he is strong. We can then strengthen his weak points and remedy some things that would otherwise be neglected. They are of great benefit to science and to the person concerned."

"Tests such as we are now making are of great importance because they aim to show in what respects we differ from others and why, and if they do this they will be able to guide us into the right channel and bring success instead of failure."

Unsatisfactory. "Tests such as we are now making are of value both for the advancement of science and for the information of the person interested. It is necessary to know this."

"Such tests as we are now making show about the human mind and show in what channels we are fitted. It is the testing of each individual between his effects of inheritancy and environment."

"It is very interesting for us to study science for two reasons; first, to test our mental ability, and second for the further development of science."

"Tests such as we are now making help in two ways; it helps the scientists and it gives information to the people."

"Tests are being given to pupils to-day to better them and to aid science for generations to come. If each person knows exactly his own beliefs and ideas and faults he can find out exactly what kind of work he is fitted for by heredity. The tests show that environment doesn't count, for if you are all right you will get along anyway." (Note invention.)

Selection (b)

Satisfactory. "There are different opinions about life. Some call it good and some bad. It would be more correct to say that it is middling, because we are never as happy as we would like to be and we are never as sad as our enemies want us to be."

"One hears many judgments about life. Some say it is good, while others say it is bad. But it is really neither of the extremes. Life is mediocre. We do not have as much good as we desire, nor do we have as much misfortune as others want us to have. Nevertheless, we have enough good to keep life from being unjust."

"Some people have different views of life from others. Some say it is bad, others say it is good. It is better to class life as mediocre, as it is never as good as we wish it, and on the other hand, it might be worse."

"Some people think differently of life. Some think it good, some bad, others mediocre, which is nearest correct. It brings unhappiness to us, but not as much as our enemies want us to have."

Unsatisfactory. "Some say life is good, some say it is mediocre. Even though some say it is mediocre they say it is right."

"There are two sides of life. Some say it is good while others say it is bad. To some, life is happy and they get all they can out of life. For others life is not happy and therefore they fail to get all there is in life."

"One hears many different judgments of life. Some call it good, some call it bad. It brings unhappiness and it does not have enough pleasure. It should be better distributed."

"There are different opinions of the value of life. Some say it is good and some say it is bad. Some say it is mediocrity. Some think it brings happiness while others do not."

"Nowadays there is much said about the value of life. Some say it is good, while others say it is bad. A person should not have an ill feeling toward the value of life, and he should not be unjust to any one. Honesty is the best policy. People who are unjust are more likely to be injured by their enemies." (Note invention.)

Remarks. Contrary to what the subject is led to expect, the test is less a test of memory than of ability to comprehend the drift of an abstract passage. A subject who fully grasps the meaning of the selection as it is read is not likely to fail because of poor memory. Mere verbal memory improves but little after the age of 14 or 15 years, as is shown by the fact that our adults do little better than eighth-grade children in repeating sentences of twenty-eight syllables. On the other hand, adult intelligence is vastly superior in the comprehension and retention of a logically presented group of abstract ideas.

There is nothing in which stupid persons cut a poorer figure than in grappling with the abstract. Their thinking clings tenaciously to the concrete; their concepts are vague or inaccurate; the interrelations among their concepts are scanty in the extreme; and such poor mental stores as they have are little available for ready use.

A few critics have objected to the use of tests demanding abstract thinking, on the ground that abstract thought is a very special aspect of intelligence and that facility in it depends almost entirely on occupational habits and the accidents of education. Some have even gone so far as to say that we are not justified, on the basis of any number of such tests, in pronouncing a subject backward or defective. It is supposed that a subject who has no capacity in the use of abstract ideas may nevertheless have excellent intelligence "along other lines." In such cases, it is said, we should not penalize the subject for his failures in handling abstractions, but substitute, instead, tests requiring motor coördination and the manipulation of things, tests in which the supposedly dull child often succeeds fairly well.

From the psychological point of view, such a proposal is naïvely unpsychological. It is in the very essence of the higher thought processes to be conceptual and abstract. What the above proposal amounts to is, that if the subject is not capable of the more complex and strictly human type of thinking, we should ignore this fact and estimate his intelligence entirely on the ability he displays to carry on mental operations of a more simple and primitive kind. This would be like asking the physician to ignore the diseased parts of his patient's body and to base his diagnosis on an examination of the organs which are sound!

The present test throws light in an interesting way on the integrity of the critical faculty. Some subjects are unwilling to extend the report in the least beyond what they know to be approximately correct, while others with defective powers of auto-criticism manufacture a report which draws heavily on the imagination, perhaps continuing in garrulous fashion as long as they can think of anything having the remotest connection with any thought in the selection. We have included, for each selection, one illustration of this type in the sample failures given above.

The worst fault of the test is its susceptibility to the influence of schooling. Our uneducated adults of even "superior adult" intelligence often fail, while about two thirds of high-school pupils succeed. The unschooled adults have a marked tendency either to give a summary which is inadequate because of its extreme brevity, or else to give a criticism of the thought which the passage contains.

This test first appeared in Binet's 1911 revision, in the adult group. Binet used only selection (*b*), and in a slightly more difficult form than we have given above. Goddard gives the test like Binet and retains it in the adult group. Kuhlmann locates it in year XV, using only selection (*a*). On the basis of over 300 tests of adults we find the test too difficult for the "average adult" level, even on the basis of only one success in two trials and when scored on the rather liberal standard above set forth.

Superior adult, 5: repeating seven digits reversed

Procedure and **Scoring**, the same as in previous tests of this kind. The series are: 4–1–6–2–5–9–3; 3–8–2–6–4–7–5; and 9–4–5–2–8–3–7.

We have collected fewer data on this test than on any of the others, as it was added later to the test series. As far as we have used it we have found few "average adults" who pass, while about half the "superior adults" do so.

Superior adult, 6: ingenuity test

Procedure. Problem *a* is stated as follows:—

A mother sent her boy to the river and told him to bring back exactly 7 pints of water. She gave him a 3-pint vessel and a 5-pint vessel. Show me how the boy can measure out exactly 7 pints of water, using nothing but these two vessels and not guessing at the amount. You should begin by filling the 5-pint vessel first. Remember, you have a 3-pint vessel and a 5-pint vessel and you must bring back exactly 7 pints.

The problem is given orally, but may be repeated if necessary.

The subject is not allowed pencil or paper and is requested to give his solution orally as he works it out. It is then possible to make a complete record of the method employed.

The subject is likely to resort to some such method as to "fill the 3-pint vessel two thirds full," or, "I would mark the inside of the 5-pint vessel so as to show where 4 pints come to," etc. We inform the subject that such a method is not allowable; that this would be guessing, since he could not be sure when the 3-pint vessel was two thirds full (or whether he had marked off his 5-pint vessel accurately). Tell him he must *measure* out the water without any guesswork. Explain also, that it is a fair problem, not a "catch."

Say nothing about pouring from one vessel to another, but if the subject asks whether this is permissible the answer is "yes."

The time limit for each problem is 5 minutes. If the subject fails on the first problem, we explain the solution in full and then proceed to the next.

The second problem is like the first, except that a 5-pint vessel and a 7-pint vessel are given, to get 8 pints, the subject being told to begin by filling the 5-pint vessel.

In the third problem 4 and 9 are given, to get 7, the instruction being to "begin by filling the 4-pint vessel."

Note that in each problem we instruct the subject how to begin. This is necessary in order to secure uniformity of conditions. It is possible to solve all of the problems by beginning with either of the two vessels, but the solution is made very much more difficult if we begin in the direction opposite from that recommended.

Give no further aid. It is necessary to refrain from comment of every kind.

Scoring. *Two of the three* problems must be solved correctly within the 5 minutes allotted to each.

Remarks. We have called this a test of ingenuity. The subject who is given the problem finds himself involved in a difficulty from which he must extricate himself. Means must be found to overcome an obstacle. This requires practical judgement and a certain amount of inventive ingenuity. Various possibilities must be explored and either accepted for trial or rejected. If the amount of invention called for seems to the reader inconsiderable, let it be remembered that the important inventions of history have not as a rule had a Minerva birth, but instead have developed by successive stages, each involving but a small step in advance.

It is unnecessary to emphasize at length the function of invention in the higher thought processes. In one form or another it is present in all intellectual activity; in the creation and use of language, in art, in social adjustments, in religion, and in philosophy, as truly as in the domains of science and practical affairs. Certainly this is true if we accept Mason's broad definition of invention as including "every change in human activity made designedly and systematically."[78] From the psychological point of view, perhaps, Mason is justified in looking upon the great inventor as "an epitome of the genius of the world." To develop a Krag-Joergensen from a bow and arrow, a "velvet-tipped" lucifer match from the primitive fire-stick, or a modern piano from the first crude, stringed, musical instrument has involved much the same intellectual processes as have been operative in transforming fetishism and magic into religion and philosophy, or scattered fragments of knowledge into science.

Psychologically, invention depends upon the constructive imagination; that is, upon the ability to abstract from what is immediately present to the senses and to picture new situations with their possibilities and consequences. Images are united in order to form new combinations.

As we have several times emphasized, the decisive intellectual differences among human beings are not greatly dependent upon mere sense discrimination or native retentiveness. Far more important than the raw mass of sense data is the correct shooting together of the sense elements in memory and imagination. This is but another name for invention. It is the synthetic, or apperceptive, activity of the mind that gives the "seven-league boots" to genius. It is, however, a kind of ability which is possessed by all minds to a greater or less degree. Any test has its value which gives a clue, as this test does, to the subject's ability in this direction.

The test was devised by the writer and used in 1905 in a study of the intellectual processes of bright and dull boys, but it was not at that time standardized. It has been found to belong at a much higher mental level than was at first supposed. Only an insignificant number pass the test below the mental age of 14 years, and about two thirds of "average adults" fail. Of our "superior adults" somewhat more than 75 per cent succeed. Formal education influences the test little or not at all, the unschooled business men making a somewhat better showing than the high-school students.